# Spurgeon

# Spurgeon

*The Prayer-Powered Pulpit of the Prince of Preachers*

Keeney Dickenson

*Forewords by*
Donald S. Whitney and Daniel Henderson

WIPF & STOCK · Eugene, Oregon

SPURGEON
The Prayer-Powered Pulpit of the Prince of Preachers

**Copyright © 2024 Keeney Dickenson. All rights reserved.** Except for brief quotations in critical publications or reviews, no part of this book may be reproduced in any manner without prior written permission from the publisher. Write: Permissions, Wipf and Stock Publishers, 199 W. 8th Ave., Suite 3, Eugene, OR 97401.

Wipf & Stock
An Imprint of Wipf and Stock Publishers
199 W. 8th Ave., Suite 3
Eugene, OR 97401

www.wipfandstock.com

PAPERBACK ISBN: 978-1-7252-9990-0
HARDCOVER ISBN: 978-1-7252-9991-7
EBOOK ISBN: 978-1-7252-9992-4

VERSION NUMBER 12/19/24

Scripture taken from the New King James Version®. Copyright © 1982 by Thomas Nelson. Used by permission. All rights reserved.

"Early in this book, Keeney Dickinson wrote that each preacher must 'make the assumption that you have an understanding and a weekly practice of homiletics that could benefit from an increased saturation with prayer.' Further along he wrote, 'Praying is a crucial aspect of every stage of your pulpit ministry. To pause from prayer at any point in the process is to sever your preaching from God's power.' Using the entire corpus of Spurgeon's sermon as vital and experienced spiritual instruction, this book relentlessly pursues the premise that the preacher must first and foremost be a man of God before he can be of any use to his people. He must be a God-saturated person in his personal life and must inject prayer into every phase of self-examination and sermon preparation if he is to be a vessel 'unto honor, sanctified, and meet for the master's use' (2 Tim 2:21). Placed alongside all the needed training in theology, exegesis, and homiletics, this book will consistently remind the reader that he is a 'minister of Christ' and a 'steward of the mysteries of God' (1 Cor 4:1)."

—**Tom J. Nettles**, senior professor of historical theology, The Southern Baptist Theological Seminary, Louisville, Kentucky

"Charles Spurgeon stands as one of the most prolific gospel ministers in the history of the Christian Church. Most any study of Spurgeon and his prolific ministry will prove fruitful. That is why I am particularly thankful for Keeney Dickinson and his helpful book *Spurgeon: The Prayer-Powered Pulpit of the Prince of Preachers*. Those who read this work and apply Spurgeon's habits of prayer and personal piety for their pulpit ministry, will be blessed, as will those to whom they preach."

—**Jason K. Allen**, president, Midwestern Baptist Theological Seminary, Kansas City, Missouri

"Here is the book on the prayer-powered preaching of Charles Spurgeon I wish I could have written. Keeney Dickenson has spent a lifetime reading Spurgeon and reading those who have written about Spurgeon. The fruit of his research is carefully laid out for us in this wonderful book. Learn how to firmly plant your life and ministry in the knee-prints of this great preacher, and more importantly in the knee-prints of Jesus himself. Spurgeon took Acts 6:4 seriously. Dickenson will show you how to do the same in your preaching ministry. Highly recommended!"

—**David L. Allen**, distinguished visiting professor of practical theology, Mid-America Baptist Theological Seminary, Cordova, Tennessee

"E. M. Bounds once wrote, 'This unction comes to the preacher not in the study but in the closet.' Nobody understood that assertion better or practiced it more diligently than Charles Spurgeon. And nobody has written more thoroughly, accurately and clearly about the Prince of Preacher's resolve to wed the two ministries of prayer and preaching than Keeney Dickenson. In The Prayer-Powered Pulpit, he will inspire you—but even more—challenge you to follow suit in tapping into the Holy Spirit's attendance to your preaching through sacrificial prayer."

—**Jim Shaddix**, W. A. Criswell Professor of Expository Preaching, Southeastern Baptist Theological Seminary, Wake Forest, North Carolina

"Kenney Dickenson's new book *Spurgeon: The Prayer-Powered Pulpit of the Prince of Preachers* is not written from a lofty perch towering above the masses, but it comes from the pen of a godly pastor who is a faithful practitioner of prayer. I will go a step further. When I think of pastors and prayer, Kenney Dickenson is first to my mind. Dickenson knows his subject on two fronts: he knows Spurgeon and he knows and practices prayer. Get this book, read this book, practice this book."

—**Ray Rhodes Jr.**, author of *Susie: The Life and Legacy of Susannah Spurgeon* and *Yours, till Heaven: The Untold Love Story of Charles and Susie Spurgeon*

This book is dedicated to pastors throughout the world who fearlessly and faithfully preach the Word of God "in season and out of season."

# Contents

*Foreword by Donald S. Whitney* | ix
*Foreword by Daniel Henderson* | xiii
*Preface: How to Use This Book* | xv
*Introduction: Personally Mentored by Charles Spurgeon* | xix

1  Shadowing Spurgeon | 1
2  Scrutinizing Your Schedule | 10
3  Spotlighting the Savior | 22
4  Studying the Scriptures | 34
5  Securing the Sermon-Text | 46
6  Shaping the Sermon | 57
7  Seeking the Spirit | 80
8  Stirring the Soil | 100
9  Sowing the Seed | 112
10 Silencing the Satanic | 128
11 Submitting in Suffering | 140
12 Self-Examining the Soul | 152

*Appendix A: Spurgeon's Sermons That Strongly Emphasize Prayer* | 169
*Appendix B: Spurgeon: Prayer Is . . .* | 172
*Appendix C: Spurgeon: Preaching Is . . .* | 177
*Appendix D: Spurgeon on Ministry and Preaching in*
       *The Sword and the Trowel* | 180
*Bibliography* | 187

# Foreword
*by Donald S. Whitney*

THIS IS A BOOK for pastors (and those preparing to be pastors), particularly those who have the privilege and responsibility of proclaiming the Word of God to their local church on a regular basis. But it is especially for those pastors who have a deep hunger to be godly men, to shepherd the flock of God faithfully, and to preach the Bible truthfully and in the power of the Holy Spirit.

I love the story you are about to read on the first page of the book. It's about a young man taken under the wing of Charles Haddon Spurgeon who had the incalculable advantage of being personally mentored by the Prince of Preachers for many years. Despite the impossible demands upon Spurgeon's legendary schedule, over time he spent hundreds of hours writing letters to and spending time with the young man. What preacher wouldn't have jumped at such an opportunity? This book may be as close as you'll ever get to that.

In *The Prayer-Powered Pulpit of the Prince of Preachers*, Keeney Dickenson has distilled decades of study into the life, ministry, and works of Spurgeon and presented them in a way designed to provide practical help for the piety, pastoral labors, and preaching of ministers today. Don't expect merely a topical collection of Spurgeon quotations and anecdotes. This book is far deeper than that. Rather, it is primarily a tapestry of reflections upon Spurgeon's wisdom and example, and the application of them to overworked pastors today who struggle to maintain the apostolic priorities of "prayer and the ministry of the Word" (Acts 6:4) above all other ministry responsibilities.

# Foreword

These reflections and exhortations were not penned by an academic with merely a scholarly interest in Spurgeon and with little practical experience in the work of the local church. Rather they were forged in the fire of a pastoral ministry already almost as long as Spurgeon's. They were written by a man who for decades has sought to live out what he has learned from Spurgeon and who now commends these lessons to you.

But neither were these words written apart from serious research. When a middle-aged Keeney Dickenson decided to do formal and guided study on Spurgeon, I had the privilege of being his doctoral supervisor. He went above and beyond the normal expectations in his investigation into the Spurgeon corpus. Besides days spent in the Spurgeon Library at Midwestern Baptist Theological Seminary in Kansas City, Missouri, he traveled to London and parts beyond, combing through materials at the Metropolitan Tabernacle (where Spurgeon pastored), interviewing people knowledgeable about Spurgeon, and even acquiring a copy of the daily meteorological records for the years of Spurgeon's life. Until Keeney's thesis, I had never read anything about Spurgeon that included details about the weather on significant days in his life. I am certain that very few have read as much about and by Charles Spurgeon than Keeney Dickenson.

There's so much of value in this book that it's impossible to absorb it in one reading. So I suggest reading it repeatedly, a short chapter or so at a time, at the beginning of each session of sermon preparation. Whenever I write, I like to read a few pages from a book on writing before I start putting pen to paper. I find that this helps "prime the pump" inspirationally or educationally before I actually begin to write. I think preachers would benefit in a similar way—sermon after sermon, year after year—if they would pore over a portion of this book each time they work on their next sermon.

By the way, the four appendices (along with the nearly 400 footnotes) will give you some idea of the breadth and depth of Dr. Dickenson's research. But I mention them so that anyone wanting to study (for pastoral or academic purposes) Spurgeon on prayer, pastoral ministry, or preaching can take advantage of them. They will save you literally days of work.

My office at Midwestern Seminary is one hundred feet from the Spurgeon Library. This library and museum houses nearly seven thousand volumes of the preacher's personal library and the largest collection of Spurgeon memorabilia in the world. There's also a large collection of books about CHS. A well-deserved place on one of those shelves for *The*

## Foreword

*Prayer-Powered Pulpit of the Prince of Preachers* awaits its publication. Pastor, make a place for it in your library too.

Donald S. Whitney
Professor of Biblical Spirituality
Director of the Center for Biblical Spirituality
John H. Powell Professor of Pastoral Ministry
Midwestern Baptist Theological Seminary, Kansas City, MO

# Foreword
*by Daniel Henderson*

My friend H. B. Charles has often reflected that when you're flying in a plane thirty-five thousand feet in the air and someone asks you which wing is more important, the right or the left, you'd better have both of them working perfectly, or you will go down. He concludes that "prayer and the ministry of the Word" are the two wings of Christian ministry.

Many evangelical pastors complete their formal education with an adequately developed "Word" wing but an underdeveloped prayer life. Most have little sustained conviction or capacity to lead a church to become an authentic house of prayer for all nations. But we must fly with more than one good wing. The power of prayer and the effectiveness of the pulpit are inseparable. The nineteenth-century theologian Charles Bridges declared, "Prayer is one half of our ministry, and it gives to the other half all of its power and success."[1]

The devil doesn't have to destroy a pastor; he only needs to distract him. Today's leadership culture often drives us to drum up new ideas for "effective" ministry, hoping God will bless our clever plans. Our highest calling is to set our hearts and order our priorities to resolutely pursue the things God has already promised to bless. We must remind ourselves in every season of ministry that the next new thing must always be the first old thing. If you doubt Spurgeon understood this, Keeney Dickenson's excellent book will convince you otherwise.

Despite countless demands, overwhelming expectations, and the pressures of an expansive ministry, Spurgeon earnestly sought to embrace

---

1. Bridges, *Christian Ministry*, 139.

# Foreword

the priorities of the early church leaders who devoted themselves to "prayer and the ministry of the word" (Acts 6:4). These are pursuits that invite supernatural favor. Keeney's excellent book is rooted in these realities and designed to inspire hope for a more incredible blessing in your life, preaching, and leadership in the gospel.

I learned many years ago that we can't wear someone else's ministry clothes because they never fit. When it comes to preaching, God doesn't need an echo. He needs a sincere, unique, Spirit-empowered voice. No man can imitate Spurgeon's preaching gifts, but we can authenticate our preaching when the pulpit is the overflow of our genuine love for Jesus, rooted in an Acts 6:4 balance. To quote Spurgeon, "Be earnest, and you need not be elegant."[2]

I have the privilege of leading the Acts 6:4 Fellowship, calling pastors from across the globe to a resolute and consistent commitment to the biblical balance of prayer and the ministry of the Word. I am encouraged to see church leaders returning to the biblical model that Spurgeon clearly understood. Vance Pitman, a fellow leader in the 6:4 Fellowship, has said it well: "I used to think I was called to ministry but realized I was actually called to intimacy. Ministry is the overflow of intimacy."

Knowing Keeney as a friend, and observing the model of his life, inspires me to drink deeply of the truths he has so clearly and passionately espoused. This book will re-clarify your calling with fresh but proven insight. The truths will deepen your roots of intimacy and inspire greater fruits in the power of your preaching. What more could the modern church need from its leaders? Let's keep growing our passion with the expectation of divine blessing and supernatural grace in our declaration of the living Word of God.

Daniel Henderson
Global Director of the 6:4 Fellowship
Author of *Old Paths, New Power:*
*Awakening Your Church through Prayer*
*and the Ministry of the Word.*

---

2. Spurgeon, *All-Round Ministry*, 348.

# Preface
## *How to Use This Book*

THERE WILL NEVER BE another Charles Haddon Spurgeon! That goes without being said. However, much can be gleaned from his legacy and insight. The goal of this book is not to encourage you to imitate or even emulate the *Prince of Preachers*. When you consider the magnitude of his published works, his weekly correspondence, personal interviews with prospective members, oversight of the Pastors' College, the launching of a church-planting movement, his role as editor of *The Sword and the Trowel*, and the founding of over sixty ministries birthed from the Metropolitan Tabernacle, you may be tempted to view him as almost superhuman. Although you cannot do everything suggested in these pages, there are some principles and practices which will enhance your life and ministry. Consider the following realities.

### Personality

Let me begin by saying that you are uniquely created in the image of God with a divinely designed ministry to which he has called you. You are created in God's image with his intention to express himself through your individuality. Remember the words of the apostle Paul:

> For you see your calling, brethren, that not many wise according to the flesh, not many mighty, not many noble, are called. But God has chosen the foolish things of the world to put to shame the wise, and God has chosen the weak things of the world to put to shame the things which are mighty; and the base things of the world and

the things which are despised God has chosen, and the things which are not, to bring to nothing the things that are.[1]

Be content as a divinely designed servant in your God-given calling.

God wants to communicate who he is through who you are. Spurgeon made a clear challenge for every preacher to submit to God's ability to do just that:

> All the ministers that ever lived cannot bring to Christ those souls whom God has ordained that I shall be the means of turning to Christ; and neither I nor my brethren, preach as we may, can bring to Christ the man whom God has ordained to save through yonder obscure village local preacher who is now standing on a log on the village green, or holding forth in a wooden shed in the backwoods of America. There is a place for every man, and the way for every man to find that out is to be himself and nobody else; as he used to be himself when he was a sinner, so let him be himself now he has become a saint, and follow out, under God's guidance, the movements of his own individualities, the singularities of his own nature.[2]

Being yourself in life and ministry is only possible "under God's guidance." God has called you, and he longs to use you for his glory.

## Prayer

Spurgeon's life of prayerfulness was developed through his distinct personality. This should give you direction in developing your life of prayer in keeping with your divinely designed personality. You may not be able to preach with the eloquence or spontaneity of Spurgeon, but you can develop a life of prayer that fuels your ministry just as he did. Consider a father who has two children. The father's love for both of his children is unquestionable. However, the way in which that father relates to each child is different due to their distinct personality traits. This difference is not considered unequal but rather unique.

The same is true of each believer's walk with our heavenly Father. Although each of us can have a whole-hearted love for the Father, this love will be uniquely expressed in the way he has created us to individually relate to him. This is equally true of the way in which each preacher prayerfully

---

1. 1 Cor 1:26–28
2. Spurgeon, *Metropolitan Tabernacle Pulpit*, 16:215.

## Preface

relates to the Father in his pulpit ministry. The principles may be identical, but each personality and practice will be unique. Thus, the primary objective of this book is not imitation of Spurgeon but rather intimacy with God.

## Preparation

The weaving together of prayerfulness and preparation looks different for each of God's messengers. Preachers can be short-sighted with a narrow focus on the Saturday night routine of Spurgeon as a frantic search for a text and sermon content. However, Spurgeon's weekly schedule was saturated with proactive prayerfulness and voracious reading. He was also capable of treating his mind like a well-organized filing cabinet. Spurgeon provided a glimpse into this practice when addressing his students concerning extemporaneous preaching:

> Work hard at every available moment. Store your minds very richly, and then, like merchants with crowded warehouses, you will have goods ready for your customers, and having arranged your good things upon the shelves of your mind, you will be able to hand them down at any time without the laborious process of going to market, sorting, folding, and preparing.[3]

This provides insight into Spurgeon's ability to preach from brief outlines with a handful of profound points. It was his mental storehouse from which the Holy Spirit recalled to him that which filled the white spaces within his notes. Perhaps some of Spurgeon's most memorable phrases resulted from the collision of thoughts which no one else had combined. Because of Spurgeon's unique personality and peculiar investment of time in preparation it would be most impractical to simply attempt to replicate his practice. But the principles behind his practices can stimulate your God-given personality.

## Proclamation

Finally, in your pulpit ministry you will proclaim the same gospel that Spurgeon did, but it will be delivered through your personality and gifting. You can be just as true to the one who created and called you as Spurgeon was in his ministry. So, remember, you will not be able to do everything that Spurgeon practiced or suggested. However, you will be able to apply

---

3. Spurgeon, *Lectures to My Students*, 145–46.

some things which will increase your usefulness as a servant of God, and this will enhance your effectiveness for him. Let me allow Spurgeon to address your personal proclamation of the gospel as you prepare to embark on this journey with him:

> Dear friends, do not imagine that God will bless one preacher only . . . He does bless some preachers more than others, for he is Sovereign; but he will bless you all in your work, for he is God. I shall never forget one day, when my dear old grandfather was alive, I was to preach a sermon. There was a great crowd of people, and I did not arrive, for the train was delayed; and therefore, the venerable man commenced to preach in my stead. He was far on in his sermon when I made my appearance at the door. Looking to me, he said: "You have all come to hear my dear grandson, and therefore I will stop that you may hear him. He may preach the gospel better than I can, but he cannot preach a better gospel. Can you, Charles?" My answer from the aisle was: "I cannot preach the gospel better; but if I could, it would not be a better gospel."[4]

So it is, brethren: others may break the bread to more people, but they cannot break better bread than the gospel which you teach, for that is bread from our Savior's own hand. Get to work each one of you with your bread-breaking, for this is Christ's way of feeding the multitude.

---

4. Spurgeon, *Metropolitan Tabernacle Pulpit*, 32:96.

# Introduction

*Personally Mentored by Charles Spurgeon*

CAN YOU IMAGINE HAVING Charles Spurgeon as your personal ministry-mentor? What would it be like to have his undivided attention for several hours every week over the course of two years? That was exactly the experience of the humble twenty-year-old rope-maker apprentice, Thomas William Medhurst (1835–1917). This providential relationship was established through Spurgeon's preaching and timely personal correspondence regarding Medhurst's spiritual uncertainty. As a result of this, God used Spurgeon to bring him to an unshakable assurance of his salvation.

The two of them met in-person for the first time in the vestry of the Metropolitan Tabernacle for Medhurst's prospective member interview:

> Of this interview, Mr. Spurgeon preserved the following record in the book containing his notes concerning applicants for baptism and church-membership: "Thomas William Medhurst. A very promising young man—his letters to me evince various degrees of progress in the pilgrim's road. He has been very anxious, but has now, I trust, found refuge in the Rock of ages."[1]

Following his baptism, Medhurst soon began preaching the gospel in the open air whenever and wherever God gave him opportunity. Urged by Spurgeon and others, Medhurst began to pursue God's call to ministry. He also became the rare recipient of the pastoral instruction and personal intercession of Spurgeon.[2] Once a week for several hours the two of them

---

1. Spurgeon, *Autobiography*, 2:144.

2. This ministerial mentoring was initiated through criticism brought to Spurgeon about Medhurst: "When Mr. Medhurst began to preach in the street, some of the very

# Introduction

would have in-depth conversations regarding theology, pastoral ministry, and preaching.

In a letter dated September 22, 1855, Spurgeon wrote to Medhurst, "In prayer to God I have sought every blessing upon you, for I love you very much. Oh, how I desire to see you a holy and successful minister of Jesus! I need not bid you work at your studies. I am sure you will; but be sure to live near to God, and hold very much [intimacy] with Jesus."[3] Later, in that same letter, Spurgeon referred to him as "my dearly-beloved Timothy."[4] Spurgeon officiated Medhurst's wedding on May 26, 1859.[5] Spurgeon continued to encourage and mentor his pastoral protégé until his death on January 31, 1892, in Mentone, France.

In a newspaper interview published three days after Charles Spurgeon's death, Medhurst related a special gift he received from his mentor:

> In 1879 I received from him a copy of his book, "The Treasury of David," on the flyleaf of which he had written: "To my always loving and ever faithful friend and brother and son, T. W. Medhurst, to whom I am most tenderly attached, in whose usefulness I heartily rejoice, and by whose loving acts I am often solaced in my afflictions. A small token of my love.—C. H. Spurgeon." I value that book and its inscription very highly.[6]

As a result of the consistent mentorship and personal coaching of Spurgeon, Medhurst continued in lifelong pastoral ministry. The influence of

---

precise friends, who were at that time members at New Park Street, were greatly shocked at his want of education, so they complained to me about it, and said that I ought to stop him; for, if I did not, disgrace would be brought upon the cause. Accordingly, I had a talk with the earnest young brother; and, while he did not deny that his English was imperfect, and that he might have made mistakes in other respects, yet he said, "I must preach, sir; and I shall preach unless you cut off my head." I went to our friends, and told them what he had said, and they took it in all seriousness. "Oh!" they exclaimed, "you can't cut off Mr. Medhurst's head, so you must let him go on preaching." I quite agreed with them, and I added, "As our young brother is evidently bent on serving the Lord with all his might, I must do what I can to get him an education that will fit him for the ministry." Spurgeon, *Autobiography*, 2:150–51.

3. Spurgeon, *Autobiography*, 2:146.

4. Spurgeon, *Autobiography*, 2:146.

5. "The earliest marriage service conducted by Mr. Spurgeon, of which the record has been preserved, was that of T. W. Medhurst and his first wife, Miss M. A. Cranfield." Spurgeon, *Autobiography*, 3:348.

6. "Mr. Spurgeon's First Student," 2.

## Introduction

Spurgeon is clearly seen in the following excerpt from an article by Medhurst entitled "What Is the Right Kind of Preaching?":

> The right kind of preaching is preaching that exalts Jesus Christ the Anointed Saviour. It is preaching that gives forth a "certain sound," concerning the work of Jesus on the Cross at Calvary. It is preaching Jesus Christ as God, one with the Father and the Holy Spirit. It is preaching Jesus Christ as man, made in all points like unto his people, yet without sin. It is preaching Jesus Christ crucified the just for the unjust; that by his death divine justice was fully satisfied and a complete atonement made for sin. The right kind of preaching is that which declares the sinner to be nothing at all, and Jesus Christ to be all in all. It. is preaching that never omits to proclaim man's total ruin in Adam, the necessity of regeneration by God the Holy Spirit, and accomplished redemption by the vicarious blood-shedding of the Son of God. The right kind of preaching is that which, without hesitancy, asserts the sovereignty of God and the responsibility of man.[7]

In the research and writing of this book, I have experienced a small taste of what Medhurst received from Spurgeon. This process has deepened my walk with the Father and strengthened my own pulpit ministry. It is my prayer that this book will provide you with consistent transformative appointments with God through the example of Charles Spurgeon. Thus, this book is not designed for the accumulation of more information. Rather, it is intended for assimilation and application.

---

7. Medhurst, "Important Questions," 238.

# 1

# Shadowing Spurgeon

THIS BOOK IS NOT intended to be an informational or inspirational biography. Neither is it another book on the art and science of preaching. The objective of this work is to follow the example of Charles Spurgeon in permeating sermon preparation and delivery with a spirit of prayer. He told his students that a preacher "is not to be content with being equal to the rank and file of Christians, he must be a mature believer."[1] He continued by giving them a unique view of their calling and identity: "For the ministry of Christ has been truly called 'the choicest of His choice, the elect of His election, a church picked out of the church.'"[2] Maturity as a minister requires a shift in your self-perceived identity.

## Pursue an All-Consuming Love for Jesus

> Love is the chief endowment for a pastor. You must love Christ if you mean
> to serve Him in the capacity of pastors . . . You will fulfill that office well

---

1. Spurgeon, *Lectures to My Students*, 7–8.
2. Spurgeon, *Lectures to My Students*, 7–8. Here, Spurgeon quotes Jeremy Taylor (1613–67) from a sermon entitled "The Minister's Duty in Life and Doctrine."

if you love Jesus—your love will keep you in your Lord's company, it will hold you under His immediate supervision and will secure you His help.[3]

Spurgeon's love for Jesus was richly reflected in his preaching. Virtually every page of the sixty-three-volume *Metropolitan Tabernacle Pulpit* refers to Christ.[4] Spurgeon embraced the testimony of the apostle Paul—"For me to live is Christ . . ." (Phil 1:21)—by maintaining a lifelong pursuit of him. Spurgeon states, "If we get a burning love for Jesus Christ . . . How shall we do it? First, by desiring to be near Him."[5] A telling aspect of genuine love is a desire to be with the one upon whom we have set our affectionate allegiance. Failing to daily draw near to Christ is not a failure of your schedule; it is a failure of the heart. This heart issue must be resolved to be faithful to Christ in life and ministry. The longevity of your ministry is dependent upon your love for Jesus. Spurgeon emphasizes this: "When a man gets fully possessed with an enthusiastic love for Jesus, and there is no other love worth a moment's care, difficulties to him become only things to be surmounted, dangers become honors, sacrifices pleasures, sufferings delights, weariness rest. Life he looks upon but as a loan, and gives it back to Jesus Christ with interest."[6] There is a vast difference in spending your life in ministry and investing your life in a love relationship with Jesus. If you do not have this overflow from the master, you will fall victim to the undertow of ministry. Your ministry will become stale and lifeless without the overflow of an intimate love-relationship with Jesus.

In ministry, you experience every emotion from the highest to the lowest. An all-consuming love for Jesus is imperative for avoiding wreckage on this roller coaster ride filled with reward and rejection. The one constant in your life and ministry is the unconditional love of Christ for you regardless of your emotional state or ministry performance. Spurgeon understood this reality: "As the might of the north wind when it chaseth away the mist, such is the divine force of love for Jesus when it fills the heart; it chases away

---

3. Spurgeon, *Metropolitan Tabernacle Pulpit*, 56:399.

4. Within the 3,563 sermons of *The Metropolitan Tabernacle Pulpit*, the word "Jesus" appears 66,946 times, and the word "Christ" appears 100,223 times. *Spurgeon Sermon Collection*, Accordance Bible Software.

5. Spurgeon, *Metropolitan Tabernacle Pulpit*, 50:117.

6. Spurgeon, *Metropolitan Tabernacle Pulpit*, 9:416.

all lethargy and sin."[7] Whether the pressures are overwhelming or your joy is ecstatic, keep your eyes on Jesus and your affection burning toward him.

Spurgeon believed that Christ-centered passion produced Christlike piety:

> Love to Christ is that which makes us like Him. The eyes of love, like windows, let in the Savior's image, and the heart of love receives it as upon a sensitive plate, until the whole nature bears its impress. You are like that which you love, or you are growing like it. If Christ be loved you are growingly becoming like Him; but without love you will never bear the image of the heavenly. O Spirit of God, with wings of love brood over us, till Christ is formed in us."[8]

If your love for Christ compels you, then his power will transform you. In life and ministry, you must live on his love. It does not matter if you are just beginning in ministry or if you are a seasoned veteran—your love for people, pastoring, and preaching is not enough to sustain you. Spurgeon challenged his students with this solemn thought about Jesus' soul-searching words to Simon Peter: "He seems to say, 'You have read many men's books, do you still love Me? . . . Your people have treated some of you very badly, you have had to go from place to place, you have been slandered, reviled, maligned—do you still love Me? You have been sorely put to it to find sermons, I have sometimes left you, as you thought, to make you own your weakness, do you still love Me?'"[9] As a man of God, you will never outgrow your need for the love of Jesus. It is imperative that you never outlive your love for him. Spurgeon understood that the richest blessing in his life and ministry was experienced in the mutual love-relationship between him and the Lord Jesus.

## Embrace Your Identity as a Man of God

You will completely misunderstand Spurgeon if you explore his work for God apart from his walk with God. To explore the mechanics of Spurgeon's Saturday night sermon preparation divorced from his personal sanctification will leave you to question his preparedness to enter the pulpit. However,

---

7. Spurgeon, *Metropolitan Tabernacle Pulpit*, 19:707.
8. Spurgeon, *Metropolitan Tabernacle Pulpit*, 22:130.
9. Spurgeon, *Metropolitan Tabernacle Pulpit*, 56:401.

when these two realities are considered alongside each other, one begins to understand that Spurgeon was much more prepared than many a man who might spend hours upon hours secluded in his library poring over commentaries. Therefore, Spurgeon's walk with God should be the foundation of our consideration of his work for God. As you shadow Spurgeon in his walk and work, you will be challenged to embrace your identity as a man of God. You will constantly be reminded that the preacher's goal is faithfulness, not eloquence.

When you enter your study, you are not merely a public speaker searching for content to include in a public discourse. You are God's man opening God's Word to address God's people in the power of God's Spirit. Your message must be received from God before you can relay it for him. This was a lesson learned by Spurgeon in the trenches of pastoral ministry: "You can only gather what the Lord grants you. Before preaching, I was trying to find food for you all, and I began to pray for it, because I remembered that I could only gather for you what the Lord my God gave me."[10] You too should keep this at the forefront of your mind. If you are going to embrace your identity as a man of God who delivers messages from God, your life must center on prayer and the Word of God. This is not optional. It is indispensable!

You must become a *Psalm 1 Man*: "His delight *is* in the law of the Lord, and in His law he meditates day and night. He shall be like a tree planted by the rivers of water, that brings forth its fruit in its season, whose leaf also shall not wither; and whatever he does shall prosper" (Ps 1:1–3). True pastoral prosperity is only found by prayerfully planting your life in the pages of God's Word. It is ironic that Spurgeon, a man with a library of more than twelve thousand books, remained a man of one book. All the volumes in his library never drowned out the voice of God in Scripture. For instance, when Spurgeon and his wife were transitioning into their new residence at Westwood, his voluminous library had to be packed away for a season. He commented on the inaccessibility of his library in a sermon entitled "The Singing Pilgrim": "I am preaching to you tonight as a man without books. I cannot get at any of my books, for they are all packed away. But I have a library here in having this one volume, which is, in fact, a number of books bound together. This one Book is enough to last a man throughout the whole of his life, however diligently he may study it."[11] For Spurgeon, the

---

10. Spurgeon, *Metropolitan Tabernacle Pulpit*, 55:292.
11. Spurgeon, *Metropolitan Tabernacle Pulpit*, 28:190.

Bible was abundantly sufficient for life and learning. A man of God is a man of his Word.

## Become a Man After God's Own Heart

There are a variety of perspectives regarding the nature of sermon preparation and delivery. Some may view this process as little more than an intellectual exercise, while others might see it as the simple recitation of pre-written messages in the yearly lectionary. Both approaches manifest a disconnect between the act of preaching and the spirituality of the preacher. True preaching involves delivering messages that result from learning and living the truth of God's Word. It is virtually impossible to divorce preaching from piety, or the lack thereof. Spurgeon warned, "An unholy ministry would be the derision of the world, and a dishonor to God."[12] Contrasting an unholy ministry with the impact of a holy ministry, he continues, "But let a man once become really holy, even though he has but the slenderest possible ability, he will be a more fit instrument in God's hand than the man of gigantic acquirements, who is not obedient to the divine will, nor clean and pure in the sight of the Lord God Almighty."[13] Therefore, it is a tragic mistake to consider Spurgeon's homiletics apart from his heart. You cannot completely understand or appreciate Spurgeon as a herald of the gospel apart from his heart from God.

You can easily find a multitude of preachers with a mind for ministry methods but only a remnant of men who minister from a lifestyle of pursuing the heart of God. Contemporary pastors seem to value professional performance over personal piety. Spurgeon lamented this malady in his day: "Beware of trying to live before God as a minister. Brother minister, this is poor living: to live officially, to go to the closet or come into God's house merely as holding a certain profession, oh! this is starving work."[14] I have often found it necessary to bow before God and exclaim, "Father, I love you more than my ministry." You are much more than a pastoral professional. You are a man who belongs to Christ at the high price of his shed blood on your behalf. You have been called by him to humbly pursue his heart, as you call others to him. To accomplish this task, he does not need your ingenuity and innovation. But you desperately need intimacy

---

12. Spurgeon, *Soul Winner*, 47.
13. Spurgeon, *Soul Winner*, 47.
14. Spurgeon, *Metropolitan Tabernacle Pulpit*, 10:684.

with him. Never forget: "We love Him because He first loved us," and we serve him because he first served us.[15]

Relying on anything other than your call from God and your walk with him subtly degenerates into idolatry. Spurgeon warned that even those things that are designed to encourage and equip you in ministry can become idols:

> In the Christian church there is, I am afraid, at this moment too much exaltation of talent and dependence upon education, I mean especially in reference to ministers. I do not believe that a man of God who is called constantly to preach to the same people can be too thoroughly educated, neither do I believe that the highest degree of mental culture should be any injury to the Christian minister, but rather should be very helpful to him . . . O church of God, never set thou up human learning in the place of the Eternal Spirit, for "it is not by might nor by power, but by my Spirit, saith the Lord."[16]

When you are intimately engaged with the heart of God, you will be empowered by the hand of God.

## Cultivate a Desperate Dependence Upon God

> I do not see where the opportunity is given to the Spirit of God to help us in preaching, if every jot and tittle is settled beforehand . . . While you are preaching, believe that God the Holy Spirit can give you, in the selfsame hour what you shall speak; and can make you say what you had not previously thought of; yes, and make this newly-given utterance to be the very arrowhead of the discourse, which shall strike deeper into the heart than anything you had prepared.[17]

As you shadow Spurgeon, you will be challenged to cultivate a lifestyle of desperate dependence upon the power of God in your life and ministry. Spurgeon wholeheartedly believed the words of Jesus, "I am the vine, you *are* the branches. He who abides in Me, and I in him, bears much fruit; for without Me you can do nothing" (John 15:5). Spurgeon states, "When the

---

15. 1 John 4:19; Mark 10:45.
16. Spurgeon, *Metropolitan Tabernacle Pulpit*, 16:629.
17. Spurgeon, *All-Round Ministry*, 349–50.

preacher has achieved his usefulness, he knows that all his success comes through God. If a man shall suppose himself capable of stirring up a revival, or encouraging even one saint, or leading one sinner to repentance, he is a fool. As well might we attempt to move the stars, or shake the world, or grasp the lightning flash in the hollow of our hand, as think to save a soul, or even to quicken saints out of their lethargy. Spiritual work must be done by the Spirit."[18] As long as you have a delusion of providing anything for others apart from the enabling of Christ, your ministry will be a shallow caricature of what Christ could have done through you.

This should determine how you approach God in prayer. Despite the seemingly rapid developments of media and communication in Spurgeon's day, he remained completely immersed in a life of dependent prayer. Spurgeon pleaded, "When you preach, dear sir, do not preach as if you were only half awake; stir yourself up; fill your ministry to the brim . . . preach the gospel with all your might, and beg for power from on high."[19] Have you failed in this area? Dependence upon technology coupled with the neglect of personal prayerful immersion in God's Word is tragic. The question begs to be answered: Are your sermons marked more by commentaries of men than communion with God?

Following the example of Jesus, Spurgeon was driven to dependence upon the Holy Spirit through every personal challenge, spiritual attack, doctrinal duel, engagement with the enemy, and persistent periods of depression. He constantly pursued the filling, leading, and empowering of the Holy Spirit. Spurgeon observed, "A sermon is vain talk and dreary word-spinning unless the Holy Spirit enlivens it. He must give us both the preparation of the heart and the answer of the tongue, or we shall be as men who sow the wind."[20] In your life and ministry, there must be a genuine desperate dependence upon the Holy Spirit. When this becomes a reality, the preacher will be characterized by an urgent boldness in his preaching. Like Spurgeon, the preacher will view his hearers as being just as desperate to hear from God as he has been in receiving that word from him. The depth of your dependence upon God can easily be measured by the desperation with which you approach your preaching assignment. Hence, the preacher must weekly embrace the reality of 2 Cor 12:9–10: "And He said to me, 'My grace is sufficient for you, for My strength is made perfect in weakness.'

---

18. Spurgeon, *Metropolitan Tabernacle Pulpit*, 10:307.
19. Spurgeon, *Metropolitan Tabernacle Pulpit*, 26:502.
20. Spurgeon, *Metropolitan Tabernacle Pulpit*, 27:324.

Therefore, most gladly I will rather boast in my infirmities, that the power of Christ may rest upon me. Therefore I take pleasure in infirmities, in reproaches, in needs, in persecutions, in distresses, for Christ's sake. For when I am weak, then I am strong." Consider how Spurgeon learned a life of desperation and dependence upon God:

> Once, while preaching in Scotland, the Spirit of God was pleased to desert me, I could not speak as usually I have done. I was obliged to tell the people that the chariot wheels were taken off; and that the chariot dragged very heavily along. I have felt the benefit of that ever since. It humbled me bitterly, for I could have crept into a nut-shell, and I would have hidden myself in any obscure corner of the earth . . . Some may imagine that want of study brought me into that condition, but I can honestly affirm, that it was not so. I think that I am bound to give myself unto reading, and not tempt the Spirit by unthought-of effusions. Usually, I deem it a duty to seek a sermon of my Master and implore Him to impress it on my mind, but on that occasion, I think I had even prepared more carefully then than I ordinarily do, so that unpreparedness was not the reason. The simple fact was this—"The wind bloweth where it listeth;" and winds do not always blow hurricanes . . . Every minister will be made to feel his dependence upon the Spirit; and then will he, with emphasis, say, as Paul did, "If I preach the gospel, I have nothing to glorify of."[21]

When you leave the pulpit after a sermon, is your heart full of praise or pride? Because Spurgeon kept the praise of God on his lips, the power of God rested upon his life!

## Develop a Gospel-Saturated Pulpit Ministry

> The lifting up of Christ on the cross is the saving work of the gospel ministry, and in the cross of Jesus lies the hope of men. 'Look unto me and be ye saved, all the ends of the earth,' is God's gospel.[22]

Spurgeon preached the gospel of Jesus Christ in all its fullness. To read the *Metropolitan Tabernacle* is to appreciate the multifaceted beauty of the gospel. Many titles could be given to Spurgeon, but the one which he would

---

21. Spurgeon, *New Park Street Pulpit*, 1:266.
22. Spurgeon, *New Park Street Pulpit*, 1:263.

prize the most is that he was a gospel preacher. Many preachers look beyond the gospel itself and simply preach the benefits and blessings of the gospel. But Spurgeon preached the gospel:

> Am I asked what it is to preach the gospel? I answer to preach the gospel is to exalt Jesus Christ... Oh! to have a Christ-exalting ministry! Oh! to have preaching that magnifies Christ in his person, that extols his divinity, that loves his humanity; to have preaching that shows him as prophet, priest, and king to his people! to have preaching whereby the spirit manifests the Son of God unto his children... Calvary preaching, Calvary theology, Calvary books, Calvary sermons! These are the things we want, and in proportion as we have Calvary exalted and Christ magnified, the gospel is preached in our midst.[23]

Spurgeon's overwhelming love for Christ kept Christ at the heart of his life and central in his ministry. He strived to exalt Christ in every sermon that he preached, every book that he authored, and every organization he founded. The recurring theme of Christ resounded in all that he did.

Spurgeon gloried in the gospel. Nothing ever moved him away from the gospel which had transformed his life. He did not preach out of a love for oratory or performance. He preached for the glory of the gospel, Jesus Christ himself.

> The Gospel ministry is, in God's Word, compared to a fishery. God's ministers are the fishermen, they go to catch souls, as fishermen go to catch fish... Just preach a sermon that is full of Christ and throw it to your congregation, as you throw a net into the sea—you need not look where they are, nor try to fit your sermon to different cases. But throw it in and as sure as God's Word is what it is, it shall not return to Him void. It shall accomplish that which He pleases and prosper in the thing whereto He has sent it. The Gospel never was unsuccessful when it was preached with the demonstration of the Spirit and of power.[24]

Spurgeon knew that he had been called and commissioned by Jesus Christ to the gospel ministry. He lived, served, and preached in a gospel context. Spurgeon did so against the tide of theological trends and fads. Are you sold out to Jesus Christ and his gospel regardless of pressure to conform or compromise?

---

23. Spurgeon, *New Park Street Pulpit*, 1:263.
24. Spurgeon, *New Park Street Pulpit*, 3:262.

# 2

# Scrutinizing Your Schedule

> You count it a little thing to trespass on our minutes, but in so doing you may spoil our hours. Whether you think so or not, it is often distracting to us to be troubled with trivial things in the midst of our sacred engagements. We may be called from an absorbing study, we may be rudely interrupted when our knees are bent, and our heart is being lifted up to God in intercession, we may have our minds drawn from the weightiest matters to listen to the most frivolous observations . . . I wish it could be said of us, that we wasted neither an hour of our own time, nor an hour of other people's time.[1]

WHEN YOU SCRUTINIZE YOUR schedule, you get a clear glimpse of your soul. The priorities that you proclaim verbally may not be the same as those your schedule proclaims visibly. Consider the verbal and visible priorities of the apostles: "We will give ourselves continually to prayer and the ministry of the Word" (Acts 6:4). Does your schedule reflect these same priorities? It is easy for you to say that prayer is most important. However, your daily schedule can easily refute this claim. Do you reserve quality time every day for focused prayer? Does prayer occupy quantitative time throughout

---

1. Spurgeon, *Metropolitan Tabernacle Pulpit*, 49:592.

your daily life? Do you live in the atmosphere of prayer? To scrutinize your schedule is very helpful in examining your soul.

Your soul must be prepared to prepare the sermon. The sermon rises or falls in proportion to the sanctification of your soul. Therefore, personal sanctification is invaluable to the spiritual preparation of the sermon. Preparing sermons apart from personal sanctification quickly becomes shallow and superficial. But sermon preparation from the overflow of sanctification is spiritual and supernatural. This requires a daily surrender of your schedule to the Father. This sanctification of your soul will give birth to a God-given prophetic edge of your ministry.

## Repent of the Sin of Prayerlessness

> It would be a very singular jolting for us all if we were to keep a memorandum, and put down how long each day we were at prayer. My brethren, we should be startled to see what an immeasurably little time we spend on our knees! . . . I can bear my testimony, as a constant preacher of Christ's gospel, that it is prayer that makes me strong.[2]

Praying and preaching have been inseparably linked by God. What God has joined together let no preacher separate! To pray well is to preach well. Spurgeon states, "If we do not pray to God for a blessing, if the foundation of the pulpit be not laid in private prayer, our open ministry will not be a success."[3] Preaching is much more than an art or a science. It is a spiritual exercise that requires unceasing prayer. To truly live a life of prayerfulness may require a reorientation to the ways of God.

Genuine prayerfulness is a sure investment that brings incomparable dividends. Not every preacher will have the financial means to amass an impressive library. Even those who do so may not benefit greatly from the use of untold volumes. However, the preacher who declares war on prayerlessness and daily pursues the heart and mind of God is sure to nurture blessing upon his life and ministry. As Spurgeon says, "My brethren, let me beseech you to be men of prayer. Great talents you may never have, but you will do well enough without them if you abound in intercession."[4] Divine

---

2. Spurgeon, *Speeches at Home and Abroad*, 32.
3. Spurgeon, *Soul Winner*, 152.
4. Spurgeon, *Lectures to My Students*, 46–47.

blessing has been withheld from innumerable lifeless sermons of prayerless preachers.

It is imperative that prayer be scheduled and spontaneous. You will rarely hear an elderly minister say, "I wish I had bought more books." But they have repeatedly said, "I should have spent much more time alone with God in prayer!" Spurgeon lamented, "How much of blessing we may have missed through remissness in supplication we can scarcely guess, and none of us can know how poor we are in comparison with what we might have been if we had lived habitually nearer to God in prayer . . . We not only ought to pray more, but we *must*. The fact is, the secret of all ministerial success lies in prevalence at the mercy-seat."[5] You must avoid the trap of allowing matters of ministry to rob you of intimacy with the master.

Spurgeon implies that to be prayerless is to be careless:

> If we do that which is pleasing in God's sight the Lord will be with us in our work, but not else. Suppose a minister to have been living through the week a careless, prayerless life; he may preach his best, but as he is not a vessel fit for the Master's use, he may not reckon upon being used by the Lord . . . We must get rid of the things that displease God, if we are to be useful, and when that is done then shall we be able to say, "He that sent me is with me; the Father hath not left me alone."[6]

Hence, a prayerful ministry is favorable, and a prayerless ministry is dreadful. If you have been divinely called by God to commune with him and to communicate for him, to attempt to preach apart from time in his presence is not just a tragedy, it is a travesty.[7]

> Minister! preach on; you shall have no success unless you pray. If you do not know how to wrestle with God on your knees, you will find it hard work to wrestle with men on your feet in the pulpit. You may make efforts to do so, but you shall not be successful, unless you back up your efforts with prayer. You are not so likely to fail in your efforts as in your prayers . . . The more spiritual the duty, the more apt we are to tire of it. We could stand and preach all day, but we could not be in our closets all day one-half so easily.

5. Spurgeon, *Lectures to My Students*, 48–49.
6. Spurgeon, *Metropolitan Tabernacle Pulpit*, 20:191.
7. "Then He appointed twelve, that they might be with Him and that He might send them out to preach" (Mark 3:14). Notice the sequence in Christ's call of the apostles: (1) that they might be with him, and (2) that he might send them out to preach. This sequence is also true of you as a preacher.

> To spend a night with God in prayer would be far more difficult than to spend a night with men in preaching.[8]

The battle of ministry is won or lost in prayer. Prayerfulness and faithfulness are inseparable companions. Your goal should be intimacy with the Father and integrity in ministry.

## Commit Yourself to Be a Man of Prayer and Faith

> The effective, fervent prayer of a righteous man avails much. Elijah was a man with a nature like ours, and he prayed earnestly that it would not rain; and it did not rain on the land for three years and six months. And he prayed again, and the heaven gave rain, and the earth produced its fruit. (Jas 5:16b–18)

Prayer is the offspring of faith. To believe is to pray. "But without faith *it is* impossible to please *Him,* for he who comes to God must believe that He is, and *that* He is a rewarder of those who diligently seek Him" (Heb 11:6). Those who believe pray. Without faith, not only is it impossible to pray, but it is equally impossible to please God. Great men of prayer are ultimately great men of faith. Spurgeon acknowledges, "A man will succeed in prayer when his faith is strong; and this is the case with those who abide in Jesus. It is faith that prevails in prayer. The real eloquence of prayer is a believing desire. 'All things are possible to him that believeth.' A man abiding in Christ with Christ's words abiding in him, is eminently a believer, and consequently eminently successful in prayer."[9] To have a ministry which pleases God, you must pursue a life of faith-filled prayer. "Prayer and faith are sacred picklocks that can open secrets, and obtain great treasures."[10] It is this faith-filled prayer that will produce faithful powerful preaching.

Spurgeon recognized Christ's ultimate and intimate trust in the Father:

> Our blessed Lord lived in unbroken fellowship with the Father . . . Those nights of prayer, and days of perfect service must have brought their own calm to the tried heart of the Son of God . . . Christ Jesus was a man of faith—He was faith's highest exposition and example. He is "the author and the finisher of faith," in whom we see its life, walk, and triumph. Our Lord was

---

8. Spurgeon, *New Park Street Pulpit*, 3:47.
9. Spurgeon, *Metropolitan Tabernacle Pulpit*, 34:22.
10. Spurgeon, *New Park Street Pulpit*, 1:383.

the incarnation of perfect confidence in the Father—in His life all the histories of great believers are summed up."[11]

To endeavor to become a man of faith and prayer is to endeavor to exemplify Christlike priorities and values. Hence, you are allowing Jesus to be your ultimate mentor and ministry model.

To be faithful in the pulpit, you must exercise great faith in the study. You must place complete trust in the one who has entrusted you with his Word. Spurgeon challenged fellow ministers, "Brother ministers, let us take heed lest we be found qualified for our ministry in all respects except this one. You have learning, eloquence, industry, honesty, but do you so believe in God as to expect his word to act divinely on men's hearts. Do you preach believingly? Do you pray believingly?"[12] This should be your goal, not to preach intellectually or dynamically, but believingly! This begins with believing prayer.

## Live Each Day in the Spirit of Prayer by Immersing Yourself in Communion with God.

> You may not always be in the exercise but you may always be in the spirit of prayer. If there shall not always be iron in the furnace to melt, yet let there always be the fire to melt it, if not always shooting the arrow up to heaven, yet always keep the bow well stringed, so shall you always be archers, though not always shooting; so shall you always be men of prayer, though not always in the exercise of praying.[13]

The psalmist prayed, "Give ear to my words, O Lord, consider my meditation. Give heed to the voice of my cry, my King and my God, for to You I will pray. My voice You shall hear in the morning, O Lord; in the morning I will direct it to You, and I will look up" (Ps 5:1–3). Have these statements of the psalmist become a reality in your life? Does your day begin, proceed, and end with prayer? Is your life lived in the spirit of prayer? Are you daily immersed in communion with God?

---

11. Spurgeon, *Metropolitan Tabernacle Pulpit*, 26:674.
12. Spurgeon, *Metropolitan Tabernacle Pulpit*, 27:252.
13. Spurgeon, *Metropolitan Tabernacle Pulpit*, 7:51.

## Scrutinizing Your Schedule

At the 1889 annual conference for students and alumni of the Pastor's College, Spurgeon declared the importance of living in a spirit of prayer: "Above all, dear friends, if you want the blessing of God, keep up constant communion with God . . . When may a Christian safely be out of communion with God? Never."[14] In order to heed this instruction and immerse yourself in a spirit of prayer, you must begin to think of developing a life of prayer rather than maintaining a prayer life. Spurgeon addressed this distinction: "Praying is the end of preaching, and woe to the man who, prizing the means more than the end, allows any other form of service to push his prayers into a corner."[15] Prayers should envelop and transcend the preaching event.

Consider the differences between a prayer life and a life of prayer. A prayer life is usually viewed as an isolated segment of life, while a life of prayer is viewed as life itself. A prayer life is compartmentalized, but a life of prayer is all-consuming. A life of prayer is an ongoing, never-ending conversation with the Father, as opposed to the intermittent and inconsistent nature of isolated times of prayer. Consider Spurgeon's exhortation to his students, "Do not forsake the mercy-seat. Be in the frequent practice of prayer, and—what is better,—be in the spirit of prayer always."[16] Regardless of the circumstances, make it your goal to live in unbroken communion with the Father.

Prayer must become much more than an activity; it must become the very atmosphere of your life. Your life should grow into an open-ended conversation with the Father. Spurgeon provides a vivid description of what this looks like:

> Prayer to the preacher is like provender to the horse. It strengthens and cheers him to go forward. As the scribe halts to mend his pen, or the mower to wet his scythe, without loss of time, but rather with more facility to do his work; so you expedite instead of hindering your business by stopping in the middle of it to offer a word of prayer . . . It is a crying of his soul after divine teaching, divine direction, divine assistance; nor less, I believe, is it a yearning after divine fellowship. You know, beloved, we never walk aright unless we walk with God.[17]

---

14. Spurgeon, *All-Round Ministry*, 350.
15. Spurgeon, *Metropolitan Tabernacle Pulpit*, 20:508.
16. Spurgeon, *Metropolitan Tabernacle Pulpit*, 58:366.
17. Spurgeon, *Metropolitan Tabernacle Pulpit*, 21:234–35.

Ask God to give you an urgent desire for the purifying and empowering influence of the Holy Spirit.

The filling of the Holy Spirit is indispensable in pursuing a spirit of prayer. A heart which is filled with the Holy Spirit will produce a life that is filled with prayer because he is the Spirit of prayer. "And because you are sons, God has sent forth the Spirit of His Son into your hearts, crying out, 'Abba, Father!'" (Gal 4:6). The infilling presence of the Holy Spirit produces within you a life of prayer that brings forth a ministry of power. A ministry bathed in prayer will be birthed in power. Powerful messages flow from the life that you live much more than the library you own.

The depth of your devotion to Christ will determine the depth, direction, and delivery of your sermons. Are you truly living a Christ-centered life? Are your sermons from the overflow of your communication with Christ? Are you preaching Christ, or are you simply preaching *about* Christ? It is upon Christ that your people must feed to be edified and spiritual healthy. Hence, your goal as a pastor is not to be the lifeguard at the baby pool. Rather, it is to be used by God to move your people toward maturity in Christ and ministry in his name. Therefore, you must preach Christ in all his glory, majesty, and beauty. This is accomplished by preaching from a life immersed in communion with Son of God and saturated with the Word of God.

> Remember that stewards are servants under the more immediate command of the great Master. We should be as the steward who daily goes into his lord's private room to receive orders . . . How often ought you and I to say, "Lord, show me what Thou wouldst have me to do!" To cease to look up to God, so as to learn and practice His will, would be to quit our true position. A steward who never communicates with his master! Give him his wages, and let him go. He who does his own will, and not his master's, is of no value as a steward. Brethren, we must wait upon God continually. The habit of going for orders must be cultivated.[18]

Your life should become a call to communion and Christlikeness. It should be an invitation for your hearers to join you there. Spiritual maturity should make your passion for Christ courageous and contagious.

---

18. Spurgeon, *Metropolitan Tabernacle Pulpit*, 59:184.

## Build a Spiritual Bridge from the Prayer Closet to Your Study

> An experimental acquaintance with vital godliness is the first necessity for a useful worker for Jesus. That preacher is accursed who knows not Christ for himself. God may, in infinite sovereignty, make him the means of blessing to others, but every moment that he tarries in the pulpit he is an impostor, every time he preaches he is a mocker of God, and woe unto him when his Master calls him to his dread account . . . If a man voluntarily puts himself where it is taken for granted that he is godly, his next step will be to mimic godliness, and by-and-by he will flatter himself into the belief that he really possesses that which he so successfully imitates . . . Beware of a form of godliness which is not supported by the fervor of your heart and soul . . . Every one of us, before he shall seek to bring others to Christ, should deliberately ask himself, "Am I a follower of Christ myself? Am I washed in his blood? Am I renewed by his Spirit?" If not, my first business is not in the pulpit, but on my knees in prayer. . . in my closet, confessing my sin and seeking pardon through the atoning sacrifice.[19]

The ministry of prayer must undergird the ministry of preaching. If you are honest, there are times when looking from your prayer closet to the study, it would be appropriate to install a sign that reads, "Bridge Out!" Even Spurgeon confessed this failure:

> I have gone up to God's house to preach, without either fire or energy; I have read the Bible, and there has been no light upon it; I have tried to have communion with God, but all has been a failure. Shall I tell where that commenced! It commenced in my closet. I had ceased, in a measure, to pray. Here I stand, and do confess my faults; I do acknowledge that whenever I depart from God it is there it doth begin.[20]

The goal for rebuilding and/or reinforcing this bridge is to deliver messages that are initiated and orchestrated by the Holy Spirit. Your objective is to continue the communion of your prayer closet in your study. This open-ended conversation with the Father should become a permanent part of

---

19. Spurgeon, *Metropolitan Tabernacle Pulpit*, 15:87.
20. Spurgeon, *New Park Street Pulpit*, 1:122–23.

your sermon preparation. Spurgeon fostered this perspective and practice in his ministry: "Prayer should not be a matter of mornings and evenings alone, but all the day our spirit should commune with God. Father, thou art so near us, and yet how slow we are to speak to thee. Teach us, thy children, to be always talking with thee, so that while we walk on earth our conversation may be in heaven."[21] Spurgeon further observes, "If a forgotten-closet will make thee weep, a frequented-closet will make thee smile."[22] In reality, this is a spiritual bridge into the text of Scripture.

To prayerfully feed on the text is to prepare a feast from the text for your people. Practice laying down your pen, closing your books and/or computer to take *prayerful pauses* in your study. Inquire of him for wisdom in understanding the text. Seek the illumination of the Holy Spirit before you proceed further. Then, rejoice and commune with the Father over the insights that he gives you into his Word. Seek the Father for supporting Scriptures. Intercede from the God-given insights you have just discovered. Take a few moments to embrace your identity of an intercessor and relinquish the identity of an orator. Suspend your studying to worship in the Word! Capture those opportunities to cease wordsmithing and start worshiping. Both your preparation and preaching must become an act of worship, rather than just an exercise of intellect and an expression of eloquence.

Shift your focus from praying in the context of preparation to preparing in the context of prayer. Let that sink in. When you simply pray in the context of preparation, you are asking God to bless your efforts apart from communion with him in the text. However, when you prepare in the context of prayer, you are enveloped in an atmospheric awareness of God. To make this shift is for the Holy Spirit to be actively present and prominently preeminent in the preparation process. Is it not obvious why Satan longs to disconnect the study and pulpit from the prayer closet? He knows that if he can keep you prayerless, then he can render you powerless, and a powerless pulpit is a trophy that he treasures. Refuse to allow your prayer closet and study to become strangers to one another. But, when the prayer closet and study become best friends, there is a fresh outpouring of fullness in your ministry. Spurgeon recognized and experienced this reality:

> I would earnestly urge all Christian workers to be sure to get some time alone for the prayerful study of the Word. The more of such

21. Spurgeon, *Metropolitan Tabernacle Pulpit*, 22:415.
22. Spurgeon, *Metropolitan Tabernacle Pulpit*, 22:415.

## Scrutinizing Your Schedule

time that you can get, the better will it be both for yourself and for others. You know that it is impossible for a sower of seed to be always scattering, and never gathering—the seed-basket must be filled again and again, or the sowing must come to an end. You cannot keep on distributing bread and fish to the multitude, as the disciples did, unless every now and then, you go back to the Master, and say, "My Lord, I need more bread and more fish, for my supply is running short. Give me more that I may give out more." Make such occasions as often as you can.[23]

This consistent practice of prayerful transition from the prayer closet into the study will also give birth to extended seasons of supplication. These seasons will not be a detriment to your sermon preparation, but rather they are a vital necessity. You will be guided into higher heights and deeper depths of fellowship with God. Spurgeon described this as a transition from ordinary prayer to extraordinary prayer: "Ordinary closet prayer will only make ordinary Christians of us. It is in extraordinary seasons, when we are led by God to devote, say an hour, to earnest prayer—when we feel an impulse, we scarce know why, to cut off a portion of our time during the day to go alone. Then, beloved, we kneel down, and begin to pray in earnest."[24] Extraordinary persistent prayer will shift your focus on preaching as a performance to the Father's presence and power. You will no longer be concerned about your image. Instead, your heart's desire will be that the image of Christ is indelibly and visibly impressed on your life and ministry. If you build the bridge, God will bring his blessing! Spurgeon resolves:

> The knees may signify prayer. When a man becomes timid and desponding, his closet very soon becomes the chamber of woe. Our closets are either Bethels of Bochims,—the house of God or else the house of weeping... Herein lies the importance of having a strong hand that we may serve God, and of having a strong knee that we may wrestle with him in prayer, and get the blessing from him.[25]

To guard your personal piety is to frequent your prayer closet. And to frequent your prayer closet is to ignite your study and empower your pulpit.

---

23. Spurgeon, *Metropolitan Tabernacle Pulpit*, 46:219.
24. Spurgeon, *New Park Street Pulpit*, 2:23–24.
25. Spurgeon, *Metropolitan Tabernacle Pulpit*, 25:293.

# Spurgeon

## Anchor the Congregational Identity to Being a House of Prayer

> Then He went into the temple and began to drive out those who bought and sold in it, saying to them, "It is written, "*My house is a house of prayer*," but you have made it a "*den of thieves.*" (Luke 19:45–46)

What best describes the self-identity of your congregation? There seem to be many local churches suffering from an un-ebiblical identity crisis. The source of this crisis can be traced back to the pulpit. For a local church to become reoriented to its biblical identity as a house of prayer, the pastor must become reoriented to his biblical identity as a man of prayer. A house of prayer demands a pastor of prayer.

For Spurgeon, the primary congregational identity with which he referred to the Metropolitan Tabernacle and other local churches was *a house of prayer*.[26] Spurgeon declared, "The reason of our success under God in this house of prayer is, that we have always preached Christ as the atoning sacrifice, the sinner's substitute; and whosoever shall preach this boldly, clearly, and thoroughly, putting it as the crown of the gospel system, shall find God bless his word."[27] Hence, he viewed the context of preaching to be a house of prayer shaped by the apostolic objectives of "prayer and the ministry of the Word."[28] The coupling of these priorities positioned Spurgeon and his congregation for great blessing from God.

Spurgeon had a serious reverence in preparing to preach in a house of prayer. If you believe that the place of preaching is designated as a place of prayer, it is imperative that prayer become the foundation in your preparation of sermons. Spurgeon stressed, "The Word, is like the flour, but the sermon is the bread, for it is through the sermon that the Word is, as it were, prepared for human palates, and brought so that human souls may be able to receive it . . . Most Christians who have grown rich in grace, have been great frequenters of the house of prayer."[29] Those who frequent the

---

26. Within the sermons and expositions of *The Metropolitan Tabernacle Pulpit*, Spurgeon refers to the local church as a house of prayer over four hundred times. Two of the most prominent phrases Spurgeon uses are (1) this house of prayer, 162 times, and (2) the house of prayer, 139 times.

27. Spurgeon, *Metropolitan Tabernacle Pulpit*, 34:452.

28. Acts 6:4.

29. Spurgeon, *Metropolitan Tabernacle Pulpit*, 7:565.

## SCRUTINIZING YOUR SCHEDULE

house of prayer should be fed spiritually by men who have frequented the place of prayer. Spurgeon stated, "You cannot do your Lord's will except you live near to him. It is of no use trying to preach with power unless we get our message from our heavenly Father's own self . . . The word should come from the minister like bread hot from the oven, or better still, like a seed with life in it."[30] Your hearers are desperate for the timeless, life-giving seed of God's Word.

Spurgeon encouraged his hearers to speak to God about his speaking to them in the house of prayer. They were encouraged to see themselves as a people of prayer and the local church as a place of prayer. This nurtured an expectancy of receiving a message from God through his servant. Hence, Spurgeon admonished his hearers to connect their prayers with the reception of the Word preached to them: "As melted wax is fitted to receive the impress of the seal, so let us be ready to accept the Master's teaching . . . Here, in this house of prayer let us offer the petition, 'Speak, Lord; for thy servant heareth.'"[31] This prayerful perspective promoted a God-consciousness within the congregation. Spurgeon preached and the people listened to the Word of God as those accountable to the God of the Word.

---

30. Spurgeon, *Metropolitan Tabernacle Pulpit*, 25:429.
31. Spurgeon, *Metropolitan Tabernacle Pulpit*, 10:483.

# 3

# Spotlighting the Savior

> And I, brethren, when I came to you, did not come with excellence of speech or of wisdom declaring to you the testimony of God. For I determined not to know anything among you except Jesus Christ and Him crucified. I was with you in weakness, in fear, and in much trembling. And my speech and my preaching *were* not with persuasive words of human wisdom, but in demonstration of the Spirit and of power, that your faith should not be in the wisdom of men but in the power of God (1 Cor 2:1–5).

YOU HAVE BEEN CREATED, converted, and called to place the spotlight on Jesus![1] If you are not consistently cautious, you can subtly lose sight of this. Spurgeon specifies:

---

1. In the preface to *The New Park Street Pulpit*, Spurgeon proclaims, "We believe in Him—not merely in His words. He himself is Doctor and Doctrine, Revealer and Revelation, the Illuminator and the Light of Men. He is exalted in every word of truth, because He is its sum and substance. He sits above the gospel, like a prince on His own throne. Doctrine is most precious when we see it distilling from His lips and embodied in His person. Sermons are valuable in proportion as they speak of Him and point to Him. A Christless gospel is no gospel, and a Christless discourse is the cause of merriment to devils. The Holy Ghost who has ever been our sole instructor, will, we trust, teach us more of Jesus, until we comprehend with all saints, what are the heights and depths,

## Spotlighting the Savior

> The theme of a minister should be Christ Jesus in opposition to mere doctrine. Some of my good brethren are always preaching doctrine. Well, they are right in so doing, but I would not care myself to have as the characteristic of my preaching, doctrine only. I would rather have it said, "He dwelt much upon the person of Christ, and seemed best pleased when he began to tell about the atonement and the sacrifice. He was not ashamed of the doctrines, he was not afraid of threatening, but he seemed as if he preached the threatening with tears in his eyes, and the doctrine solemnly as God's own word; but when he preached of Jesus his tongue was loosed, and his heart was at liberty."[2]

Whether or not Jesus will be exalted in your sermon is determined in your study. When you read the Scripture, is Christ in the forefront of your mind, or do you read the Scripture from a self-centered perspective? As you read the Scripture, are you seeking the Savior, or are you searching for sermons? Remember, the Bible is much more than a sermon idea sourcebook. The Old Testament is a searchlight anticipating Christ, and the New Testament is a spotlight magnifying him. Can you even fathom the Scripture without the Savior? That question is almost offensive to a preacher. However, when we scrutinize sermons and discover a glaring absence of Christ, is it possible that we are giving our people a glimpse of Scripture apart from the Savior himself? Just as you cannot imagine the Scripture without the Savior, you should not be able to conceive of a sermon delivered apart from him!

Is the primary focus of your sermon preparation Christ-centered or congregation-centered? Your initial mindset in sermon preparation should not be "How does this passage apply to the congregation?" but rather "How does this passage magnify the Lord Jesus Christ and point people to Him?" This appears to have been the overarching objective in Spurgeon's ministry: "Christ is the minister's great theme, in opposition to a thousand other things which most men choose. I would prefer that the most prominent feature in my ministry should be the preaching of Christ Jesus."[3] A sermon that is Christless is a sermon in crisis. Divine blessing rests upon sermons that magnify Jesus Christ, who alone is the heart of Scripture.

---

and know the love of Christ which passeth knowledge. Jesus, Jesus, Jesus, only have we labored to extol: may the Lord Himself succeed our endeavors." Spurgeon, *New Park Street Pulpit*, 1:ii.

2. Spurgeon, *New Park Street Pulpit*, 3:260.
3. Spurgeon, *New Park Street Pulpit*, 3:259.

# Spurgeon

## Prayerfully Meditate Upon the Son of God in the Word of God

> To meditate much upon the Lamb of God, is to occupy your minds with the grandest subject of thought in the universe . . . He is the sum and substance of all truth, the essence of all creation, the soul of life; the light of light, the heaven of heavens, and yet He is greater far than all this, or all else that I could utter. There is no subject in the world so vast, so sublime, so pure, so elevating, so divine; give me to behold the Lord Jesus, and my eye seeth every precious thing. Brethren, no subject so well balances the soul as Jesus, the Lamb of God . . . Beloved, this indeed is the most needful subject of contemplation that can be brought before you . . . The crucified Savior is as needful for our meditation as the air is for our breathing.[4]

Seek to give Christ your undivided attention and affection. To fill your ministry with Christ, you must begin by occupying your mind with him. This is an activity which brings far-reaching effect and eternal blessing. Spurgeon argues:

> We shall do well to exercise our hearts in frequent acts of devotion to the Son of God. I do not mean offering prayers petitions, excellent as these are, but holy contemplation, meditation, admiration, thanksgiving, and worship of Jesus . . . When you have adored him in secret you should do the like in public by speaking well of him and extolling him before others, not so much for their good as, for Christ's glory.[5]

Without a healthy consistent spiritual diet of meditation upon Christ, your ministry will suffer spiritual starvation. It will be parched with unquenchable thirst, and struggle to keep from suffocating. A life-giving ministry demands steady meals of meditation upon one's message, Jesus himself.

Jesus proclaimed, "You search the Scriptures, for in them you think you have eternal life; and these are they which testify of Me" (John 5:39). To study the Scriptures is to encounter Jesus. To preach the Bible is to proclaim the person and work of Jesus Christ. He is to be your ultimate meditation and your constant message. As you meditate on the person and work of Jesus Christ, contemplate about his deity (John 1:1–2); stand in awe of

---

4. Spurgeon, *Metropolitan Tabernacle Pulpit*, 18:393.
5. Spurgeon, *Metropolitan Tabernacle Pulpit*, 20:669.

his uncreatedness (John 1:3); bow in humble reverence of his incarnation (John 1:14; Phil 2:6–8); contemplate his wholehearted dependence upon the Father (John 5:19); consider his unconditional surrender to the Father and his will (John 6:38; Matt 26:39); come under conviction as you study his holy perfection as your high priest (Heb 7:26–28); praise him for his sinless life and substitutionary sacrifice on your behalf (1 Pet 1:18–19; 1 John 4:10); worship him from the threshold of his empty tomb (Rom 6:9; Rev 1:17–18); rest in his intercession for you at the right hand of the Father (Eph 4:10; Heb 8:1); mull over his majesty (2 Pet 1:16); feast on his faithfulness (2 Tim 2:13; Rev 19:11); take lingering in at his love (John 15:13; Rom 8:35–39); rejoice over his righteousness (Isa 53:11; Rev 19:11); pause to ponder his power (Luke 22:69; Rev 5:11–12); consider the weight of his preeminence (Col 1:15–19); investigate his incomparability (Rom 9:5; Rev 5:1–14); place your trust in his immutability (Heb 13:8); allow his glory to cause you to gasp (Matt 17:1–8); anticipate with longing his second coming (Rev 19:11–16); look toward his eternal reign as King of kings and Lord of lords (Rev 21:22).

## Embrace Christlikeness as Your Daily Lifestyle

> He who says he abides in Him ought himself also
> to walk just as He walked (1 John 2:6).

Not only should your messages be consumed with Christ, but your very life should also be conformed to him. A personal desire for likeness to Christ must touch every facet of your ministry for him. Your most effective sermon illustration should be the Christlike lifestyle which you live before your people! Your personal Christlikeness in life and ministry will reinforce the Christ-centered messages that you preach. In a real sense, if your life is not centered on Christ, then most likely your messages will not be either. They will simply become a cheap caricature of the true Christ. Spurgeon once prayed publicly, "Bring back to us whatever of energy and holiness we once had, and somewhat more. Oh make us like Christ: we do pray Thee, make us like Christ. We would even accept His cross and the vinegar, if we might have His holiness . . . only let Christ be formed in us, the hope of glory."[6] A common temptation in the life of a pastor is seeking to become like another

---

6. Spurgeon, *Behold the Throne of Grace*, 85.

well-respected preacher. This can be a tragic mistake due to differences in personality and spiritual gifts.

You are most likely reading this book because of your admiration for Spurgeon. However, Spurgeon's example, as marvelous as it is, should not become a distraction from your unique calling and God-given gifts. Spurgeon himself warns against this: "The all-important matter is not that you should be like me, or that I should be like you, but that both of us should be like Christ . . . There may be a thousand minor diversities in the imitators of the one great Exemplar, and the individuality of every one of them shall be as definite as the identity of the whole of them as followers of Christ."[7] Ultimately, you should not look through the halls of history for an honorable homiletical example. Neither should you be looking around at pastoral peers. Rather you should be looking up to Christ as the ultimate mentor and model in ministry. You are to be an imitator of Christ in all areas of your life and ministry. Spurgeon observes, "I think we always associate with the name of Christ not simply humility, and service, and love, but devotion and prayerfulness. We know that when he had ceased to preach he began to pray . . . We can never be like the Master, till not only in public but in private we are God's own; never till we know the power of knee-work."[8] To live as Christ lived, is to preach as he would have you preach.

## Firmly Plant Your Life and Ministry in the Knee-prints of Jesus

He Himself *often* withdrew into the wilderness and prayed (Luke 5:16).

Now in the morning, having risen a long while before daylight, He went out and departed to a solitary place; and there He prayed (Mark 1:35).

Spurgeon devoted no less than forty-six entire sermons to Jesus' life of prayer.[9] He also repeatedly referenced the intercession of Christ on our behalf. Jesus Christ was his ultimate mentor in prayer and preaching. Thus, Christ was the distinguishing priority and passion of his life and ministry. He not only

---

7. Spurgeon, *Metropolitan Tabernacle Pulpit*, 55:619.
8. Spurgeon, *Metropolitan Tabernacle Pulpit*, 7:59.
9. Spurgeon also refers to the prayers and praying of Jesus no less than 527 times in 355 sermons out of the 3,563 sermons in *The Metropolitan Tabernacle Pulpit*.

preached Christ, but he also pursued Christ. For him, Christ was both his master and his model; his Lord and his life. He breathed Christ, thought Christ, and lived Christ. Thus, Spurgeon patterned his walk with the Father and his work for the Father after the earthly life and ministry of Jesus Christ. He welcomed fellow servants to join him in the pursuit of Jesus' earthly example: "His (Christ's) prayers always kept pace with His work. This is where most of us fail. When our Lord had a long day's work, we find Him taking a long night's prayer . . . God help you to be like His Son, who, though He was sent, and had the Father with Him, yet could not live without prayer."[10]

Many preachers pray in the context of life and ministry. However, Jesus lived and ministered in the context of prayer. For Jesus, prayer was not a religious activity to practice but rather a relational atmosphere in which to live. He and the Father were one, inseparable and indivisible. When Jesus preached, he was delivering a message from the Father's heart.

Jesus made prayer a priority in his preaching, and he modeled and mentored a life of prayer for the soon-to-be preachers of the gospel of his kingdom. It is obvious that the apostles were aware of the power generated in the life and ministry of Jesus through prayer. Consider the contagious impact the praying of Jesus had on them: "Now it came to pass, as He was praying in a certain place, when He ceased, *that* one of His disciples said to Him, 'Lord, teach us to pray, as John also taught his disciples.'"[11] Spurgeon remarks:

> He was the greatest of preachers, but His prayers made even a deeper impression on His disciples than His sermons, for they did not say, "Lord, teach us to preach," but they did exclaim, "Lord, teach us to pray." They felt that He was Master of that heavenly art, and at His feet they desired to sit, that they might learn how to move heaven and earth with sacred wrestling . . . You are to be conformed to the image of Christ—be conformed in this respect, that you be men of prayer. You desire to know the secret of His power with men—seek to obtain His power with God.[12]

Spurgeon, like the first disciples, made the connection between prayer and power in the earthly life and ministry of Jesus. Therefore, he lived with the perpetual desire, "Lord, teach me to pray." To seek power for your ministry from any other source is to fail in your pursuit.

10. Spurgeon, *Metropolitan Tabernacle Pulpit*, 36:274–75.
11. Luke 11:1.
12. Spurgeon, *Metropolitan Tabernacle Pulpit*, 14:131.

In response to the request of the apostles, Jesus taught them that a prayerful and powerful ministry seeks the kingdom of God and the will of God (Luke 11:2). Jesus' power from the Father resulted from his intimacy with the Father. Spurgeon points out, "In all that Jesus did He remained in constant fellowship with the Father." Spurgeon sought to follow this example of Jesus by preaching from the overflow of intimacy with the Father (John 5:19).

Jesus also prioritized intercession for others. Spurgeon extols the consistent intercession of Jesus:

> Our Lord Jesus prayed much for His people while He was here on earth. He made Peter the special subject of His intercession when He knew that he was in extraordinary danger. The midnight wrestling of the Son of man were for His people. In the sacred record, however, much more space is taken up by our Lord's intercessions as He nears the end of His labors. After the closing supper, His public preaching work being ended, and nothing remaining to be done but to die, He gave Himself wholly unto prayer. He was not again to instruct the multitude, nor to heal the sick, and in the interval which remained, before He should lay down His life, He girded Himself for special intercession. He poured out His soul in life before He poured it out unto death.[13]

Spurgeon was an avid student of both the praying and preaching of Jesus. As you join Spurgeon in studying this aspect of Christ's earthly life, you will discover that Jesus preached as he prayed and he prayed as he preached.

Because prayer was a lifestyle not a liturgy, Jesus preached in the atmosphere of prayer. It was the preeminent atmosphere of his life rather than a peripheral additive to his ministry. Jesus prayed before (Luke 6:12), after (John 17), and during (Luke 10:21–22; John 12:27–28) his preaching and teaching. Spurgeon did the same. He confidently asserts, "You cannot have power with man for God until first you have power with God for man. Solitary prayer was the equipment for the Prince of preachers when He came forth among the crowds; it is the best equipment for you also."[14] How much time do you spend in prayer solely focused on intimacy with the Father? Do you daily invest quality time interceding for those whom you are leading and to whom you are preaching?

---

13. Spurgeon, *Metropolitan Tabernacle Pulpit*, 32:145.
14. Spurgeon, *Metropolitan Tabernacle Pulpit*, 30:144.

Spurgeon further observed that not only is prayer to be your source of power but also a means by which you maintain a proper perspective: "Workers for God, I do entreat you to be abundant in supplication, that if success comes you may not be elevated unduly by it, that if nonsuccess comes you may not be depressed unduly by it."[15] Remaining persistent in prayer can help you avoid the cliff of conceit and the desert of depression.

The lasting impact and influence of Charles Spurgeon's ministry is not the result of what he did for God but rather what God did through him. God speaks most clearly through those who walk closest to him and who most resemble his Son. Your ultimate focus should shift from working for God to walking with God in Christlike humility and prayerfulness. The pattern that Jesus modeled was that of receiving and relaying; receiving a message from the Father and relaying it for the Father to his people. Thus, he delivered messages from the heart of God to the hearts of his hearers. Many a minister has failed by attempting to relay a message without investing the time, undivided attention, and intimate communion with the Father to receive before the relay. Avoid lazy shortcuts which offer empty promises.

## Prayerfully Meditate on Your Calling to Preach the Gospel of Jesus Christ

> You must have faith, brethren, about your call to the ministry; you must believe without question that you are really chosen of God to be ministers of the gospel of Christ. If you firmly believe that God has called you to preach the gospel, you will preach it with courage and confidence; and you will feel that you are going to your work because you have a right to do it. If you have an idea that possibly you are nothing but an interloper, you will do nothing of any account; you will be only a poor, limping, diffident, half-apologetic preacher, for whose message no one will care. You had better not begin to preach until you are quite sure that God has called you to the work.[16]

Contemplate your calling. Although the call of God is difficult to explain, it is undeniably experienced by those whom he has called. Remember the divinely bestowed cravings of your heart. As Spurgeon observes, "In order

---

15. Spurgeon, *Metropolitan Tabernacle Pulpit*, 30:144.
16. Spurgeon, *Soul Winner*, 56.

to a true call to the ministry there must be an irresistible, overwhelming craving and raging thirst for telling to others what God has done to our own souls."[17] It was out of humility that you longed to become a herald of the good news found in Jesus Christ. Your call is not the result of your own merit but of the mercy of God. It is not because of your goodness but because of God's graciousness. Meditate on Christ's ministry *to* you and *through* you. Reflect on his faithfulness to equip you and encourage you in ministry. The fulfillment of your call to ministry is sustained by the fulfillment of God's promises on your behalf.

Consider God's call of Jeremiah: "Before I formed you in the womb I knew you, and before you were born I consecrated you; I appointed you a prophet to the nations" (Jer 1:5). The apostle Paul declared, "I thank Christ Jesus our Lord who has enabled me, because He counted me faithful, putting *me* into the ministry" (1 Tim 1:12). God's call to preach is both personal and providential. Your call to preach is sure and certain in its focus. If you have been called, God has called you to preach the gospel of Jesus Christ. Hence, Christ is to be the mainstay of your life and the meat of your message. It is he and he alone who can save your hearers and sustain your ministry. Spurgeon boldly proclaims, "When the pulpit is without Christ the pews are soon without people . . . A sermon without Christ as its beginning, middle, and end is a mistake in conception and a crime in execution. However grand the language it will be merely much-ado-about-nothing if Christ be not there."[18] As the gospel is proclaimed, the power of God will rest upon both the messenger and his message.

God not only calls men to preach, but he confirms those whom he calls. Spurgeon avows, "No man has any right to address a congregation on things spiritual, unless he believes that God was given him a special calling to the work, and unless he has also in due time received certain seals which attest his ministry as being the ministry of God."[19] You are not called to preach what comes to mind or that which is appealing to your hearers. If you are genuinely called by God, you are called to preach the gospel of Jesus Christ. This good news never changes, and never needs an upgrade. The gospel has stood the test of time and eternity. It will never be shaken by those who chose to preach something new and novel to people who are eager to be entertained. When a person is drawn to an alteration

---

17. Spurgeon, *Lectures to My Students*, 26.
18. Spurgeon, *Metropolitan Tabernacle Pulpit*, 27:598.
19. Spurgeon, *New Park Street Pulpit*, 3:319.

of the gospel of Christ, that is not a reflection on the long-standing truth of God's Word. It is simply a statement about a person's spiritual immaturity at best—or his lostness at worst.

Our love for Jesus will create a longing for him and him alone, as revealed in the pages of Scripture. Spurgeon declares, "Faith cometh by hearing, and hearing by the Word of God. Christ himself is the essential Word, and the preaching of Jesus is the operative Word."[20] The Old Testament is a prophetic searchlight anticipating his coming. The New Testament is a spotlight celebrating his arrival. From Genesis to Revelation, the Scripture is centered on and saturated with Jesus Christ: his eternal existence, virgin birth, sinless life, atoning substitutionary sacrifice, undeniable resurrection, visible ascension, and anticipated return for his bride! For Spurgeon, to love the Lord Jesus Christ was to proclaim him in all his fullness without addition, alteration or adaptation:

> If you love Jesus, you wish for nothing new. Modern gospels are forthcoming on all sides . . . The preachers of them cannot have the delight in preaching their new gospels that I have in preaching the old one . . . When I get preaching up Christ, and his precious blood, and eternal love, and covenant securities, there I beat them all. With such a theme I can compete with the most renowned of the world's orators. When I speak on these themes, my lips drop pearls and diamonds. Brethren, when we declare unto you the Lord Jesus we sail upon a sea of sweetness. The novelties of "modern thought" are a Dead Sea, but our gospel is an ocean of firing water.[21]

You have been called to call others to Christ. You have also been called to call upon Christ on behalf of those whom you will call to him.

## Prepare to Preach the Gospel of Jesus Christ from the Overflow of Communion with Him

> When you come fresh from talking with God; the truth is vividly realized, an awe is upon you, holy zeal and sacred ardour inflame your breast . . . When the voice of Jesus' love is still ringing in your ears, then with a deep

---

20. Spurgeon, *Metropolitan Tabernacle Pulpit*, 11:640.
21. Spurgeon, *Metropolitan Tabernacle Pulpit*, 33:29.

awestruck solemnity your whole soul is poured forth at your mouth... The tongue must speak when the ear is tingling with the message of the Lord.[22]

Spurgeon was more focused on his Savior than his sermons. His sermons were saturated with Christ because they were prepared and shaped in communion with him. Hence, Christ was the source and substance of his sermons. Spurgeon sought to have the heart of Christ within him and the hand of Christ upon him each time he entered the pulpit: "A man may go to College, he may learn all about the letter of Scripture, but he is no minister of God if he has not sat at Jesus' feet, and learned of Him; and when he has learned of Him, and the truth has come home to his heart as his own personal possession given to him by Christ, then shall he speak with more than mortal power, but not till then."[23] It is sad how many sermons exclusively exegete commentaries at the expense of exalting Christ. Spurgeon scripturally asserts, "The most prominent agency in the church of God is the preaching of Christ—this is the trumpet of heaven and the battering-ram of hell!... O that preaching might once again be recognized to be God's power unto salvation, and used everywhere... for the voice of truth in the preaching of Jesus is the great power of God."[24] Spurgeon knew that a Christless sermon was a powerless sermon.

Christ must be enthroned, exalted, and emulated in both life and ministry. Concentration results in imitation. Spurgeon concludes, "They preach Christ best who see him best."[25] It is through extensive time with Christ that you will be shaped to represent him. Spurgeon queries, "Do you not love to listen to a brother who abides in fellowship with the Lord Jesus? Even a few minutes with such a man is refreshing, for, like his Master, his paths drop fatness."[26] When Christ is the preacher's primary companion, he will become the mold which shapes the heart and habits of the preacher. Spurgeon declares, "When I preach Christ and his salvation to you I do not preach what I learned in a college or was taught by men: I preach to you what I would die for; what is the chief joy of my soul; what I know and believe and have experienced."[27] Your molding model must be Jesus! He is

---

22. Spurgeon, *Metropolitan Tabernacle Pulpit*, 24:489.
23. Spurgeon, *Metropolitan Tabernacle Pulpit*, 46:218.
24. Spurgeon, *Metropolitan Tabernacle Pulpit*, 18:718.
25. Spurgeon, *Metropolitan Tabernacle Pulpit*, 18:386.
26. Spurgeon, *All-Round Ministry*, 125.
27. Spurgeon, *Metropolitan Tabernacle Pulpit*, 18:306.

## Spotlighting the Savior

to be the goal and guide of your preaching. This will enable Christ to draw people to himself through you. As you commune with Christ in sermon preparation, the following questions can be very helpful in determining the text and the tone of your sermon:

- How does your sermon-text point to Christ?
- What facet of Christ's character is implied and/or magnified in your text?
- Does your sermon-text present Christ as prophet, priest, and/or king?
- Does Christ speak to the theme of your sermon-text in the Gospels?
- Does your sermon-text embody a Christocentric doctrine?
- How does your sermon-text address the lordship of Christ?
- How does your sermon-text challenge hearers to a renewed submission to the lordship of Christ?
- How does your sermon-text exalt the name of Jesus?

You should make it your goal to preach every sermon from the overflow of your love for Jesus. No love in the soul means no life in the sermon. Every sermon should be an exaltation of the person and work of Jesus Christ. Spurgeon emphasizes that without Christ, we have nothing to proclaim:

> If you leave out Christ, you have left the sun out of the day, and the moon out of the night, you have left the waters out of the sea, and the floods out of the river, you have left the harvest out of the year, the soul out of the body, you have left joy out of heaven, you robbed all of it's all. There is no gospel worth thinking of, much less worth proclaiming, if Jesus be forgotten. We must have Jesus as Alpha and Omega in all our ministries.[28]

The true prayer-powered pulpit is home to a Christlike, Spirit-filled courier who delivers messages from the heart of Christ to his people. He spends extended time with the Lord, seeking his face and studying his Word. As the preacher is transformed by the very presence, he becomes an effective servant and spokesman on his behalf. The living Word of God is alive in him and issues forth in life to the hearers.

---

28. Spurgeon, *Metropolitan Tabernacle Pulpit*, 9:720.

# 4

# Studying the Scriptures

Open my eyes that I may see, wondrous things from Your law (Ps 119:18).

SCRIPTURE INTAKE IS AN important spiritual discipline. Set aside time to read the Bible with prayerful concentration and focus. This was a daily practice maintained by Spurgeon. However, he warns against valuing the quantity of Scripture that you read over the quality with which you read it. He states, "I think you make a great mistake when you go galloping through the whole Bible, reading half-a-dozen chapters every day; you do much better when you get a text and ruminate upon it, just as the cows chew the cud. Turn the Scripture over, and over, and get all the juice, sweetness, and nourishment out of it and you will do well."[1] Consequently, Spurgeon emphasized the consistent reading of Scripture accompanied by intense meditation in the life of a preacher. The Word of God must be absorbed into his heart and life, the Bible is the preacher's spiritual lifeline. Spurgeon knew this well: "When I take my Bible and want to feed on it for myself, I generally get thinking about preaching upon the text and what I should say to you from it. This will not do. I must get away from that and forget that there is a Tabernacle, that I may sit personally at Jesus' feet. And oh, there

---

1. Spurgeon, *Metropolitan Tabernacle Pulpit*, 30:573.

is an intense delight in being overshadowed by Him!"[2] Without consistent Scripture intake, the pastor becomes nothing more than the oddity of a malnourished, emaciated gourmet chef. If the preacher fails in daily immersing himself in the pages of God's Word, it is not only detrimental to him, but it will create a spiritual wasteland among his hearers.

Keep in mind that sermon preparation is no substitute for personal Bible reading and meditation. Neither is personal Bible reading and meditation a replacement for sermon preparation. However, your personal time in the Word of God will prove to be a stream of life for your sermons. In both settings, enter the pages of Scripture prayerfully. You are desperate for the enlightenment of the Holy Spirit when you open the Word of God in your study. It is imperative that you consecrate the study as a place of prayer. Spurgeon illustrates this consecration:

> There is more got out of the Bible by praying than by anything else. When a certain Puritan had a dispute upon matters of doctrine with another, he was observed to speak very fluently and with great power. While his opponent spoke, he was observed taking notes, and one desired to see his notes, and what think you were they? They were just those words, "More light, Lord! More light, Lord! More light, Lord!" That is the best way of taking notes, a cry for more light! On a sudden, that very text of Scripture, which seemed as hard as a flint, will fly open by a touch of the Holy Spirit's finger when you have said in prayer, "Help, Lord."[3]

Thus, the rumination over Scripture depends upon the illumination of the Holy Spirit. Acknowledgement of the presence of the Holy Spirit in your study is irreplaceable in your ministry. He is your intercessor and illuminator.[4]

According to Spurgeon, depth of thought must accompany the prayerful consideration of Scripture: "There are texts of Scripture which are made and constructed on purpose to make us think . . . We must meditate, brethren. These grapes will yield no wine till we tread upon them . . . The Word of God is always most precious to the man who most lives upon it."[5] He further states: "It is a grand thing to be driven to think, but it is a grander thing

---

2. Spurgeon, *Metropolitan Tabernacle Pulpit*, 57:221.
3. Spurgeon, *Metropolitan Tabernacle Pulpit*, 54:293–94.
4. Rom 8:26–27; John 14:26
5. Spurgeon, *Metropolitan Tabernacle Pulpit*, 25:629.

to be driven to pray through having been made to think."⁶ Thus, Spurgeon prescribed Scripture-prompted thoughtful prayer and prayerful thought as a means of quality Scripture intake.

## Confess, Lament, and Repent of Ministerialism

> Do you not know that those who run in a race all run, but one receives the prize? Run in such a way that you may obtain *it*. And everyone who competes *for the prize* is temperate in all things. Now they *do it* to obtain a perishable crown, but we *for* an imperishable *crown*. Therefore I run thus: not with uncertainty. Thus I fight: not as *one who* beats the air. But I discipline my body and bring *it* into subjection, lest, when I have preached to others, I myself should become disqualified (1 Cor 9:24–27).

*Ministerialism* is the practice of preaching as an occupational routine, depending upon human talent, research, and personality rather than the maintaining of a life-giving intimacy with God and dependence upon him. Is preaching your passion or your profession? If you are not guarded and cautious concerning personal Scripture intake, you will tragically find yourself opening the Bible and subconsciously asking, "To whom does this apply?" rather than "How can I apply this to my life?" Spurgeon referred to this as the never-ending battle against *ministerialism*:

> You must remember, too, that we have need of a very vigorous piety, because our danger is so much greater than that of others. Upon the whole, no place is so assailed with temptation as the ministry . . . of these the worst is the temptation to ministerialism—the tendency to read our Bibles as ministers, to pray as ministers, to get into doing the whole of our religion as not ourselves personally, but only relatively, concerned in it . . . How one kicks and struggles against officialism, and yet how easily it besets us, like a long garment which twists around the racer's feet and impedes his running! Beware dear brethren, of this and all other seductions of your calling; and if you have done so until now, continue still to watch till life's latest hour.⁷

---

6. Spurgeon, *Metropolitan Tabernacle Pulpit*, 25:629.
7. Spurgeon, *Lectures to My Students*, 15.

Spurgeon attempted to turn the tide of a manicured ministerialism which was catering to a carnal culture. This led him to be very transparent concerning this struggle: "I have had to confess, and have mentioned it at ministers' meetings often, and have heard others confess, that familiarity with sacred things is a temptation, very often, to lead us to read our Bibles for our congregations and not for ourselves, and to pray ex officio instead of praying with our whole hearts to God ourselves, as though we ourselves needed the blessing."[8] This personal reality led him to consistently and passionately plead with the next generation of pastors: "I pray you, moreover, measure your work in the light of God. Are you God's servant or not? Yours is not a trade, or a profession."[9] Because Spurgeon sought to preach messages which were Scripture-fed and Spirit-led, he paid a high price to overcome temptations to do otherwise. He passionately admonished his students, "Anything is better than mechanical sermonising, in which the direction of the Spirit is practically ignored . . . I say, therefore, watch the course of Providence; cast yourselves upon the Lord's guidance and help."[10] He clearly understood that theological education has the potential of shaping the condition of the pulpit for generations. Thus, he was relentless in faithfully mentoring young ministerial students.

Ministerialism is the offspring of pride. It values the finding of a text and the development of a sermon over the filling of the Spirit and the denial of self. Spurgeon expressed his concern for those preparing for vocational ministry:

> I fear that sometimes our preparatory studies for the ministry injure our earnestness. I saw in Melrose Abbey a stone, under which is said to lie the heart of Robert Bruce. I am afraid that it might be written on the floors of some of our universities, 'Here lies the heart of such-and-such a student.' That is a poor education which fills the head, but leaves the heart empty. Let us have learning by all means; you cannot have too much of it if it be of the right sort, but let the heart be also engaged.[11]

Spurgeon further warns that this temptation will pursue preachers the entirety of their ministry: "I am afraid that when reading the Bible in our studies we are often the victims of a temptation, for we read it officially as

---

8. Spurgeon, *Metropolitan Tabernacle Pulpit*, 55:462.
9. Spurgeon, *Lectures to My Students*, 319.
10. Spurgeon, *Lectures to My Students*, 92.
11. Spurgeon, *Speeches*, 58.

ministers, thinking of texts, and how to divide them."[12] He then confesses, "Before the Lord I have had to clothe my soul in sackcloth about that sin: but when I read the Bible, or come to the people as a poor sinner saved by grace like others, it is then that I feel true power. Oh, that dreadful getting into ministerialism, which is so much the mischief of us." Preachers should avoid this ministerial mischievousness at all costs.

Further, persistent ministerialism can create an unhealthy carnal focus on one's personal performance. Spurgeon described this very struggle: "I know how a minister can put his light under a bushel. He can be a mere official and perform service, being nothing more than a performer. The worst thing to do with the gospel is to parsonificate it. As soon as we preach as mere officials, we have lost all power: we must speak as men to men."[13] To do anything other than this is to enter a blurry area. You can tragically shift your focus onto yourself and the perception which others have of you. This can lead you to look to people for topics and subjects that impress and entertain, rather than looking to God and his Word for his sole direction and guidance. If you are not cautious in this matter, he can become intimidated and paralyzed by the desire to be viewed as intelligent, creative, and gifted. This leads to the inability to write sermons with pure motives, full of Scriptural content. Your view of the Bible can become blurred and skewed to the extent that you begin to see it merely as a sourcebook for sermons rather than a lifeline for spiritual survival.

Ministerialism is detrimental and dangerous because it can lead you to substitute the completion of the sermon for the cleansing of the heart. There is a vast difference in attempting to be mentally competent and being spiritually consecrated when you enter the pulpit. This carnal craving for confirmation from others can subtly morph into prophetic plagiarism, the preaching of sermons that are not your own. Second-hand sermons produce stale spiritual meals. It is imperative that Scripture first be applied and assimilated into your life. You should feed your people from the feast you have received alone in the presence of the Father.

---

12. Spurgeon, *Speeches*, 58.
13. Spurgeon, *Metropolitan Tabernacle Pulpit*, 27:224.

## Studying the Scriptures
## Prayerfully Humble Yourself Before God and His Word

> Thus says the Lord: "Heaven *is* My throne, and earth *is* My footstool. Where *is* the house that you will build Me? And where *is* the place of My rest? For all those *things* My hand has made, and all those *things* exist," says the Lord. "But on this *one* will I look: on *him who is* poor and of a contrite spirit, and who trembles at My word" (Isa 66:1–2).

The Word of God is a tangible expression of God, his ways, and his will. Spurgeon repeatedly emphasized this among his hearers: "If you wish to know God you must know His word; if you wish to perceive His power you must see how He worketh by His word."[14] The Bible is a means by which you explore and gain understanding of the very heart and mind of God. This is not just a mental exercise. You are beginning a spiritual conversation with the God of the universe. He has welcomed you into his presence as his child, and he desires to reveal his heart and mind to you through his Word. Therefore, opening the Word of God should never be taken lightly or be done routinely. Approach the Word of God with humble reverence for the God of the Word.

The way you approach, handle, and respond to the Word of God gives clear indication of the degree to which you reverence the Son of God. According to Spurgeon, irreverent interaction with the Word of God exposes arrogance, carnality, and callousness toward Christ himself: "How much that can be said of the Lord Jesus may also be said of the inspired volume! How closely are these two allied! How certainly do those who despise the one reject the other! How intimately are the Word made flesh, and the Word uttered by inspired men, joined together!"[15] God and his Word are inseparable. If you truly love God, you will love his Word. Consider how David spoke of the majestic holy nature of both God and his Word:

> The heavens declare the glory of God; and the firmament shows His handiwork. Day unto day utters speech, and night unto night reveals knowledge. *There is* no speech nor language *where* their voice is not heard. Their line has gone out through all the earth, and their words to the end of the world. In them He has set a tabernacle for the sun, which *is* like a bridegroom coming out of his chamber, *and* rejoices like a strong man to run its race. Its rising *is* from one

---

14. Spurgeon, *Metropolitan Tabernacle Pulpit*, 27:377.
15. Spurgeon, *Metropolitan Tabernacle Pulpit*, 34:109.

end of heaven, and its circuit to the other end; and there is nothing hidden from its heat. The law of the Lord *is* perfect, converting the soul; the testimony of the Lord *is* sure, making wise the simple; the statutes of the Lord *are* right, rejoicing the heart; the commandment of the Lord *is* pure, enlightening the eyes; the fear of the Lord *is* clean, enduring forever; the judgments of the Lord *are* true *and* righteous altogether. More to be desired *are they* than gold, yea, than much fine gold; sweeter also than honey and the honeycomb. Moreover by them Your servant is warned, *and* in keeping them *there is* great reward. Who can understand *his* errors? Cleanse me from secret *faults*. Keep back Your servant also from presumptuous *sins;* let them not have dominion over me. Then I shall be blameless, and I shall be innocent of great transgression. Let the words of my mouth and the meditation of my heart be acceptable in Your sight, O Lord, my strength and my Redeemer.[16]

Contrast the words of Ps 19 with the irreverent way many preachers handle God's Word in and out of the pulpit. Do you hold and handle the Bible reverently as the living active Word of a holy God?

## Prayerfully Meditate on the Nature of God's Word

God reigns sovereignly above all other gods, and his Word is infinitely above all other books![17] This reality should be a constant reminder to place your primary focus on Scripture, not the sermon. You must never view the Bible as anything less than the divinely inspired Word of God. Commentaries may be interesting and instructive, but only the Bible is inspired and infallible! The Bible is a personal treasure, not just a professional tool. It will be helpful for you to consistently meditate on the nature of God's Word: (1) God's Word is like a scalpel in the hand of a surgeon (Heb 4:12–13); (2) It is like a seed in the hand of a sower (Matt 13:1–23); (3) It is like a sword in the hand of a soldier (Eph 6:17). These three aspects of the nature of God's Word can be very helpful in preventing the mishandling of Scripture as you pursue balance between personal Scripture intake and sermon preparation.

First, God's Word is like a scalpel in the hand of a surgeon: "For the word of God *is* living and powerful, and sharper than any two-edged sword, piercing even to the division of soul and spirit, and of joints and marrow,

---

16. Ps 19.

17. Spurgeon preached no less than fifty-two sermons on the nature of the Word of God.

and is a discerner of the thoughts and intents of the heart. And there is no creature hidden from His sight, but all things *are* naked and open to the eyes of Him to whom we *must give* account" (Heb 4:12–13). When you open the Bible to receive spiritual nourishment, it is important to keep its razor-sharpness in mind. Spurgeon stated:

> The Word of God is so sharp a thing, so full of cutting power that you may be bleeding under its wounds before you have seriously suspected the possibility of such a thing. You cannot come near the gospel without its having a measure of influence over you, and, God blessing you, it may cut down and kill your sins when you have no idea that such a work is being done . . . I trust you and I may go on to know more and more of its edge till it has killed us outright, so far as the life of sin is concerned. Oh, to be sacrificed unto God, and His Word to be the sacrificial knife![18]

As a two-edged sword, it is initially to be turned on oneself, allowing the work of the Holy Spirit to be fulfilled in your own heart. This can be likened to the work of a surgeon. A scalpel in the hand of a surgeon is skillfully used to repair that which is severed, to replace that which is useless, and/or to remove that which is diseased and, at times, possibly life-threatening. It is important that you daily bring yourself under the searching and illuminating influence of the Spirit of God through the Word of God. The resulting healing and wholeness must constantly occur in the preacher's life to be pleasing and useful to God. When you consistently experience this aspect of the nature of the Word of God, you will become an effective instrument in God's hand.

Second, the Word of God is like a seed in the hand of a sower. Consider the explanation Jesus gives of his parable of the sower and the seed:

> Therefore, hear the parable of the sower: When anyone hears the word of the kingdom, and does not understand *it*, then the wicked *one* comes and snatches away what was sown in his heart. This is he who received seed by the wayside. But he who received the seed on stony places, this is he who hears the word and immediately receives it with joy; yet he has no root in himself, but endures only for a while. For when tribulation or persecution arises because of the word, immediately he stumbles. Now he who received seed among the thorns is he who hears the word, and the cares of this world and the deceitfulness of riches choke the word, and he becomes unfruitful. But he who received seed on the good ground is

---

18. Spurgeon, *Metropolitan Tabernacle Pulpit*, 34:115–16.

> he who hears the word and understands *it*, who indeed bears fruit and produces: some a hundredfold, some sixty, some thirty (Matt 13:18–23).

In reflecting on the meaning of this parable, Spurgeon emphasizes that the one who has seed in his hand to sow must first have that very seed sown into his heart. "The Gospel is seed for the sower, and bread for the eater, and every man, who really goes out to sow for God, must first have been an eater . . . If there be any who pretend to sow, but who have never themselves eaten, God have mercy upon them! What a desecration of the pulpit it is for a man to attempt to preach what he does not himself know!"[19] It is the preacher who has been transformed by the power of the seed of God's Word who has greatest confidence in the life-changing power of that same seed as it is proclaimed to others.

Third, the Word of God is like a sword in the hand of a soldier: "And take the helmet of salvation, and the sword of the Spirit, which is the word of God" (Eph 6:17). The preaching and hearing of the Word is indispensable in the spiritual battle in which you are involved. Hence, this imagery intimately weds the Word of God with the Spirit of God. Spurgeon expounds on this powerful reality:

> The ministers of the gospel may preach God's Word in all sincerity and purity, and yet, if the Spirit of God is not present, we might as well have preached mere moral essays, for no good can come of our testimony . . . The Spirit of God works in, by, and through, and with the Word, and if we keep to that Word, we may rest assured that the Holy Spirit will keep with us, and make our testimony to be a thing of power. Let us pray the blessed Spirit to put an edge on our preaching, lest we say much and accomplish little. Hear us in this thing, O blessed One![20]

As a result of humbly practicing prayerful Spirit-led application of God's Word, you will be equipped to handle the Word of God among the people of God.

## Prayerfully Saturate Your Mind with the Word of God

> Oh, how I love Your law! It *is* my meditation all the day (Ps 119:97).

---

19. Spurgeon, *Metropolitan Tabernacle Pulpit*, 49:364.
20. Spurgeon, *Metropolitan Tabernacle Pulpit*, 37:233.

## Studying the Scriptures

John Bunyan was one of the most influential author outside of the Bible in Spurgeon's life.[21] In describing the Bible-saturated mind of Bunyan, Spurgeon coined a new term, *Bibline*:

> He (Bunyan) had studied our Authorized Version ... He had read it till his very soul was saturated with Scripture; and, though his writings are charmingly full of poetry, yet he cannot give us his *Pilgrim's Progress*—that sweetest of all prose poems—without continually making us feel and say, "Why, this man is a living Bible!" Prick him anywhere; his blood is Bibline, the very essence of the Bible flows from him. He cannot speak without quoting a text, for his very soul is full of the Word of God. I commend his example to you, beloved, and, still more, the example of our Lord Jesus.[22]

This was also true of Spurgeon. He too had *Bibline* flowing through his veins due to his unfailing love for Scripture. He spent extensive and extended time with God and his Word. This practice transformed his perspective. It enabled him to think scripturally about the situations of his life and ministry.

Love for God and his Word requires extensive time and undivided attention. Loving God's Word with your time and mind is the fertile soil of scriptural expository sermons. A word *from* God must grow out of the Word *of* God. His Word is complete without your comment upon it. However, God has called you to proclaim his Word on his behalf. This demands that the Bible be above all other books in your affection and attention. A steady healthy diet of Scripture intake will immunize you from the poison of novel new ideas or twisted trends.

---

21. Spurgeon expressed his endearment for Bunyan on May 22, 1962, at Bunhill Fields for the dedication of Bunayn's restored tomb: "Spurgeon, after some introductory remarks, spoke at length on the three grounds on which Bunyan was to be commemorated—as a preacher, as an author, and as a sufferer. With regard to his qualities as a preacher, he dwelt on the simplicity of his language—plain and homely speech, which all loved, and by which all were attracted.... he was a diligent reader of the Bible in our good old English version. After adverting to the sufferings of Bunyan from imprisonment and bitter poverty, the rev. gentleman urged his hearers to raise monuments to Bunyan in their hearts, and to be his spiritual descendants, by imbibing and cherishing the truths which he taught, living in his faith, and so keeping his memory green ("Restoration of Bunyan's Tomb," 105). Also, Spurgeon wrote, "Next to the Bible, the book I value most is John Bunyan's *Pilgrim's Progress*. I believe I have read it at least a hundred times" (Spurgeon, *Pictures from Pilgrim's Progress*, 11). He quoted and/or alluded to Pilgrim's Progress in over six hundred of his sermons in *The Metropolitan Tabernacle Pulpit*.

22. Spurgeon, Metropolitan Tabernacle Pulpit, 45:495.

Mental saturation must be accompanied by daily application. This will bring priceless divine dividends to your life and ministry. God has given you his Word as a window through which to behold his heart. When you saturate your heart and mind with Scripture, you become more intimately acquainted with the works and ways of God. This enables you to connect the situation of your hearers with the revealed will of God. Your mind will become a fertile seedbed for expository insight and imagery. Preaching the Word of God from the overflow of a life immersed in the Word and ways of God is a blessed experience.

## Pursue an Acts 6:4 Mindset by Sanctifying the Study as a Place of Prayer

> Then the twelve summoned the multitude of the disciples and said, "It is not desirable that we should leave the word of God and serve tables. Therefore, brethren, seek out from among you seven men of *good* reputation, full of the Holy Spirit and wisdom, whom we may appoint over this business; but we will give ourselves continually to prayer and to the ministry of the word" (Acts 6:2–4).

Spurgeon's pursuit of piety was clearly practiced in the spiritual disciplines of prayer and Scripture intake. This is not surprising when one considers his devotion to the Word of God and his priority of prayer. He took very seriously these words of the apostles: "We will continually give ourselves to prayer and the ministry of the word." Spurgeon states, "Preparation for preaching and teaching is most important: God's work is not to be done carelessly as boys shoot arrows at random in their play. We must prepare both by reading and pleading: we must, like the apostles, give ourselves to the word of God and prayer."[23] There are basically two kinds of preachers, those who are men of prayer and those who are not. Many preachers pray in the context of sermon preparation, rather than preparing sermons in the context of prayer. Spurgeon stressed the combination of studying with praying: "A passage in Scripture will often open up when you pray over it, which will defy mere criticism or looking to expositors ... The text is God's letter, full of loving words, but prayer must break the seal. When reading goes with praying and praying goes with reading, then a man goes on both

---

23. Spurgeon, *Metropolitan Tabernacle Pulpit*, 29:153.

his feet, the bird flies with both his wings."[24] When prayer becomes the atmosphere in which you study and prepare messages, you will have a strong awareness that you are studying in the shadow of the Almighty.

Embrace your identity as a man of prayer and a man of God's Word. You are to *continually give yourself to prayer and the ministry of the Word.* Spurgeon repeatedly upheld these nonnegotiable priorities in the preacher's ministry:

> The minister of Christ is intended to execute two offices for the people of his charge. He is to speak for God to them, and for them to God. The pastor hath not fulfilled the whole of his sacred commission when he hath declared the whole counsel of God. He hath then done but half. The other part is that which is to be performed in secret, when he carrieth upon his breast, like the priest of old, the wants, the sins, the trials of his people, and pleads with God for them. The daily duty of the Christian pastor is as much to pray for his people, as to exhort, instruct, and console.[25]

Pray as you study, and study as you pray. This will help you to keep in mind that you are handling the holy Word of God and not just developing a sermon.

To faithfully deal with the Word of God, the Word of God must first deal with you. This must give birth to sermon preparation in the context of an open-ended conversation with God centering on his Word. Sermon preparation is both a spiritual experience and an academic exercise. However, your weekly journey through the Word of God should be enveloped in the presence of the God of the Word. Academics should be immersed in his presence. The privacy of your study should be conducive for repentance before God and his Word and the application of its truth initially and immediately in your personal life. Your study is not a hideaway for mental labor alone. It is to be a place where you abide under the shadow of the Almighty.

---

24. Spurgeon, *Metropolitan Tabernacle Pulpit*, 58:427.
25. Spurgeon, *New Park Street Pulpit*, 6:49.

# 5

# Securing the Sermon-Text

With regard to the sermon, we shall be most anxious, first of all, respecting the selection of the text . . . Among many gems we have to select the jewel most appropriate for the setting o the occasion. We dare not rush into the King's banquet hall with a confusion of provisions as though the entertainment were to be a vulgar scramble, but as well-mannered servitors we pause and ask the great Master of the feast, "Lord, what wouldst thou have us set upon thy table this day?"[1]

An intense investment of prayer should accompany every aspect and stage of sermon preparation. Absolute dependence upon the Holy Spirit must begin in the seemingly simple selection of the text upon which you will preach. The way you begin your journey of sermon preparation will set the focus for the way you will proceed. It will also determine the destination of the process. When you review this journey from week to week, may you clearly discern the guidance of the Holy Spirit. If you are preparing to represent God in the pulpit, it is imperative that you receive guidance from him in the study.

---

1. Spurgeon, *Lectures to My Students*, 82.

## Securing the Sermon-Text

A common question that the preacher will hear is "What are you preaching on this Sunday?" On the surface, this appears to be a simple question with an easy answer. However, those who enter the pulpit week after week recognize the overwhelming weight this question represents. Every aspect of sermon preparation hinges on the selection of the text. This begs a weightier question: "What text or passage will the Holy Spirit guide you to explore in your study that you may share your discoveries in the pulpit with His people?" The sermon-text is a precious gift from God, but it requires much discernment and decisiveness on the part of the preacher. Spurgeon states, "The Bible is, to me, like a long row of iron safes full of precious treasures; I try my key in a great many of them, and presently one opens at my touch, and there is my sermon. At another time, I am like a gold miner who finds the quartz in which the precious metal is imbedded, and my great concern is to get out all the gold, that it may be minted and used for my Master's service."[2] This text will become the topic of private conversation between you and the Father, as you prepare to address his people.

The process of securing your sermon-text requires flexible discernment and discerning flexibility: flexible discernment to see truth beyond your comfort-zone and discerning flexibility to receive the truth transparently and submissively. It must not be done lightly or legalistically. Guard yourself against the temptation of overthinking or under-praying this decision. You are seeking to get on the same page and in the same passage with the Father. The act of determining the location and length of your sermon-text should not be taken lightly or done without the investment of much prayer and thought. Spurgeon warns, "If we play at preaching, we have chosen an awful game. To shuffle texts like cards, and make literary essays out of themes which move all heaven and hell, is shameful work. We must be serious as death in this solemn work."[3] The sermon-text is a serious consideration and venture because it will become the arena in which you will develop thoughts regarding the things of God.

Not only will the sermon-text be your constant companion until it is preached. It will also be a weekly test of your devotion to the Father and your discernment of his voice in the text. This should become a weeklong immersion in intimacy with him. No intimacy, no insight! The text will be used by God to occupy your mind and open your eyes. It will be a recurring conversation piece between you and the Father. Because your sermon will

---

2. Crosby, *Spurgeon's Forgotten College Addresses*, 148.
3. Spurgeon, *Metropolitan Tabernacle Pulpit*, 59:189.

be the summation of this conversation, you must look intently into the text, learn deeply from the text, and listen attentively for the Father's voice in the text. This decision should not be made apart from the guidance of the Holy Spirit. To preach a text which is received as a Spirit-placed burden upon your heart is to preach with the assurance of Spirit-placed anointing upon your message.

## Prepare Sermons and Preach from the Overflow of Personal Piety

> Meditate on these things; give yourself entirely to them, that your progress may be evident to all. Take heed to yourself and to the doctrine. Continue in them, for in doing this you will save both yourself and those who hear you (1 Tim 15–16).

Even something as seemingly simple as the selection of your sermon-text must be the outgrowth of your personal piety and your walk with God. The purity of the message is dependent upon the piety of the messenger. Genuine preaching involves delivering messages that result from learning and living the truth of God's Word. It is virtually impossible to divorce your preaching from your piety. Spurgeon warned, "An unholy ministry would be the derision of the world, and a dishonor to God."[4] He also examines the inconsistency of an ungodly preacher:

> How shall a holy God send out unholy messengers? An unsanctified minister is an unsent minister . . . Only in proportion as you are sanctified unto God can you hope for the power of the Holy Spirit to rest on you, and to work with you, so as to bring others to the Savior's feet. How much may each of us have been hampered and hindered by want of holiness! God will not use unclean instruments; nay, he will not even have his holy vessels borne by unclean hands.[5]

From God's perspective, an un-sanctified minister is an unsent messenger. To be unsent is to be unaccompanied and un-annointed.

A preacher void of personal piety is to be pitied, because nothing in his ministry can adequately compensate for a failure in godliness and piety.

---

4. Spurgeon, *Soul Winner*, 4
5. Spurgeon, *Metropolitan Tabernacle Pulpit*, 32:151.

Godliness and piety are non-negotiable in a preacher's life. Any man who truly has a heart for God will pursue personal piety in every area of his life. This will position him to be greatly used by God. Consider Spurgeon's contrast between the impact of a holy ministry and the emptiness of an unholy ministry: "But let a man once become really holy, even though he has but the slenderest possible ability, he will be a more fit instrument in God's hand than the man of gigantic acquirements, who is not obedient to the divine will, nor clean and pure in the sight of the Lord God Almighty."[6] Buttressing your message begins with applying the truth you will preach.

The preacher's goal is to preach from the overflow of personal piety. If your piety is weak or nonexistent you will experience the undertow produced by your carnality and disobedience. Spurgeon expressed a strong Godward desire concerning this: "God grant that we may never stretch the arm of our testimony beyond the sleeve of our experience! It shall be well for any minister if it may be written upon his tombstone, 'He never preached what he did not practice.'"[7] It is your experiential piety that provides providential protection in your life. To neglect piety is to jeopardize your well-being and to rob yourself of God's blessing.

The sad reality in the church today is that there are untold pulpits inhabited by lost men preaching sermons to overwhelmingly lost congregations. Spurgeon addresses this malady of lostness in the pulpit: "Without true religion in his heart, he is an impostor; he has taken upon himself an errand upon which the Master never sent him; a responsibility which shall crush his soul lower than the lowest hell. Lord, have mercy upon those ministers who dare to preach what they have not felt themselves."[8] An unregenerate minister is almost unimaginable. God blesses in his work that which he stresses in his Word. Scripture stresses that God expects holy obedience from those who represent him:

> God's solid foundation stands firm, sealed with this inscription: "The Lord knows those who are his," and, "Everyone who confesses the name of the Lord must turn away from wickedness." In a large house there are articles not only of gold and silver, but also of wood and clay; some are for noble purposes and some for ignoble. If a man cleanses himself from the latter, he will be an instrument

---

6. Spurgeon, *Soul Winner*, 47.
7. Spurgeon, *Metropolitan Tabernacle Pulpit*, 32:419.
8. Spurgeon, *Metropolitan Tabernacle Pulpit*, 61:355.

for noble purposes, made holy, useful to the Master and prepared to do any good work (2 Tim 2:19–22).

Personal holiness precedes powerful usefulness. Two unmistakable characteristics of God's preparation of a man are purging him of sin and purifying his heart. Spurgeon admonishes fellow servants to cry out to God for this preparatory work: "Pray, then, this prayer, 'Let not any iniquity have dominion over me' . . . I say this especially to myself and to all ministers, for there are so many ways in which ministers may deceive themselves; we may preach to others, and yet be ourselves castaways . . . Take heed to yourselves, and every one of you breathe this prayer, 'Let not any iniquity have dominion over me.'"[9] To be purged and purified is to be prepared to proclaim God's Word. From the selection of the sermon-text to the conclusion of preaching the sermon, God is gracious to work in the heart and mind of his servant.

## Prayerfully Select the Text of Your Sermon

Although Spurgeon did not consistently practice preaching sermon series, the principles with which he searched for texts every week can be very valuable to preachers who do. Even when you are preaching through a specific book in the Bible, there is the weekly necessity of determining the length of the passage upon which you will preach. Spurgeon provides helpful principles for this process. The sermon and its preparation should begin and end with God's will and his Word rather than your will and your words. Spurgeon emphasizes the vast difference between the words of a man, and mighty Word of God: "If you need as a minister, or a worker, anything that will cut your hearers to the heart, go to this Book for it . . . There is nothing so cutting as the Word of God. Keep to that . . . The Word of God has a very keen edge about it, and all the cutting words you want you had better borrow therefrom."[10] Remember that even the text from which you will preach is ultimately God's choice, not yours. Therefore, you should not attempt to select your sermon-text independent from the illumination of the Holy Spirit. Spurgeon sternly warns, "Our work is the most important under heaven, or else it is sheer imposture. If you are not earnest in carrying out His instructions, your Lord will give His vineyard to another; for

---

9. Spurgeon, *Metropolitan Tabernacle Pulpit*, 42:500.
10. Spurgeon, *Metropolitan Tabernacle Pulpit*, 34:119.

He will not put up with those who turn His service into trifling."[11] The topic of conversation between God and his people in your message will be the overflow of your weeklong conversation with him. Allow the Father should initiate and facilitate that conversation from the very outset in the selection of the text.

Spurgeon did not view this text-selection as a mysterious mystical experience. Rather, he viewed it as a decision to be made in the context of focused intense prayer. He encouraged his students: "If anyone inquire of me, 'How shall I obtain the most proper text?' I should answer, 'Cry to God for it . . . When your text comes in answer to prayer, it will be all the dearer to you; it will come with divine savour and unction altogether unknown to the formal orator to whom one theme is as another."[12] Viewing your sermon-text as a God-given treasure is to invite the Holy Spirit to be involved throughout the discovery of the text and the delivery of the sermon.

## Prayerfully Read and Reread Your Sermon-Text on Your Knees

Kneeling before the Word of God and the God of the Word is a physical posture that brings spiritual profit. Bending the knee is conducive to bowing the heart. Kneeling before the Word of the Lord is an appropriate expression of submitting to the God of the Word. It is to be an outward expression of inward submission. Reading the Bible on bended knees is an act of consecration and concentration. Calloused knees will prevent a calloused heart. Spurgeon testifies, "Remember that the quickest way into a text is praying in the Holy Ghost. Pray the chapter over. I do not hesitate to say that, if a chapter is read upon one's knees, looking up at every word to him that gave it, the meaning will come to you with infinitely more light than by any other method of studying it."[13] When reading and rereading the sermon-text on your knees, keep in mind that the text alone will be used by the Holy Spirit as the source, structure, substance, and strength of your message. Shallow sermons are preached by men who mentally hover on the surface of a text and become strangers to the depth of the text. However, once you have sought and experienced the Spirit-illumination of the text, it

---

11. Spurgeon, *Metropolitan Tabernacle Pulpit*, 59:190.
12. Spurgeon, *Lectures to My Students*, 86.
13. Spurgeon, *Metropolitan Tabernacle Pulpit*, 37:377–78.

will be deeply imprinted on your heart and mind. This results in an honest and humble handling of the Word of God before the people of God.

This repetitious reading of Scripture on bended knee is a simple yet submissive act of humility before the Word of God and the God of the Word. Genuine humility, or its absence, is clearly perceived by those to whom the preacher speaks. If the preacher reads the sermon-text on his knees in his study, he is even more likely to read the text humbly, reverently, and meaningfully in the pulpit. What a tragedy it is for a preacher to stumble and stammer through the reading of the sermon-text, leaving the hearers to wonder if he too is reading that text for the first time that week. Kneeling before the Word of God should be an outward expression of your genuine desire to hear from God through the text, so that your hearers will hear from God through the text as well.

To kneel before God and his Word is also a personalized expression of Acts 6:4.[14] This initial focus on prayer and the Word of God should prevent you from entering the study focused on your performance in the pulpit. Remember, the spiritual posture with which you approach the Word of God privately will be expressed publicly. Your spiritual posture in the pulpit will never exceed your spiritual posture in the study. These two are inseparable.

## Prayeraphrase Your Sermon-Text into Your Mind, Heart, and Life

> Above all things, if you would hold fast the truth, pray yourselves right into it . . . He that prays himself into God's truth will never be gotten out of it by the very devil, himself, though he were to put on the garb of an angel of light! Pray yourselves into the truth.[15]

The preparation of sermons should be viewed as a life experience instead of a mental exercise. An initial way for the sermon-text to move from your head to your heart is *prayeraphrasing* it. Prayeraphrasing the sermon-text is simply restating it as a prayer to the Father. Doing this has the potential of moving your prayers from typical praying to biblical praying. This will center your praying on the Father and anchor it to his Word. When you use the vocabulary and viewpoint of Scripture to shape your praying, you are

---

14. "We will continually give ourselves to prayer and the ministry of the Word."
15. Spurgeon, *New Park Street Pulpit*, 2:207.

more likely to avoid vain repetitions which are nothing more than prayerless prayers.

Prayeraphrasing is simply taking what God has said to you in his Word and praying it back to him. As you prayeraphrase Scripture back to the Father, it will sensitize you to the Father's heart and mind within the passage. There are two steps to this process: (1) meditate on the passage, and (2) restate the passage to the Father. This simple practice has the potential of preventing your prayers during sermon preparation from becoming shallow and superficial, detached from God's Word. The practice of prayeraphrasing can prevent your prayers from being disconnected from the Father's heart. Praying in line with the purpose and priority of the Father enables him to honor your praying and preaching with his presence and power. Prayeraphrasing also positions you to have the truths of that passage burned into your heart by the Holy Spirit! In a sense, you are practicing "prayeregesis" in preparation for exegesis. Until you have prayed through a passage of Scripture, you are not sufficiently prepared to preach from it. Prayeraphrasing a passage of Scripture attunes the preacher's mind and heart to the themes emphasized and magnified within the passage.

Prayeraphrasing can be done in a variety of prayer focuses: (1) your prayeraphrase can praise and thank God for what he has revealed about himself in the passage; (2) your prayeraphrase can be a prayer of confession of what the passage has revealed about yourself, or (3) your prayeraphrase can take the form of intercession on behalf of your hearers. It can also be helpful to pray "me/my" personal prayers of supplication through the text, followed by "we/us" prayers of intercession.

Some passages of Scripture will be conducive for phrase-by-phrase prayeraphrasing. If it is a lengthy passage, you can pray summary phrases or simply prayeraphrase the heart or thematic thrust of the text. Regardless of how you apply prayeraphrasing, it can easily become a springboard for your pastoral prayer and/or your prayer before or after the sermon. Prayeraphrasing the passage publicly can model biblical praying for your congregation. It can also be effective to use your prayeraphrase as a suggestive prayer focus for the congregation in preparation for hearing the message or for prayerfully applying it afterwards.

# Spurgeon

## Spend Extended Time in Prayerful Meditation on Your Sermon-Text

> Readers of it I believe you are, but are you searchers? The promise is not to those who merely read, but to those who delight in the law of the Lord, and meditate therein both day and night. Are you sitting at the feet of Jesus, with His word as your schoolbook? If not, remember, though you may be saved, you lack very much of the blessing which otherwise you might enjoy.[16]

Prayer and meditation mutually enhance one another. Their vital relationship can be described as prayerful meditation or meditative prayer. However, in using the terms *meditative prayer,* one must be clear that this is not to be done apart from God's Word but is to be concentrated on it. "An old divine says, 'I have lost many things I learned in the house of God, but I never lost anything I ever learned in the closet.' That which a man learns on his knees, with his Bible open, he will never forget. Well, have you ever bowed your knees and said, 'Open You my eyes, that I may behold wondrous things out of Your law'? If you have seen that wondrous thing, you will never forget it."[17] You are accountable to God to make yourself accountable to the text of his Word. The sermon-text should become your constant companion and daily counselor. Therefore, it must become indelible on your mind and undeniable in your life. Applying the text to your life, can overflow in application to your hearers.

Meet with the Father in the context of your sermon-text. Allow the sermon-text to guide you into conversation with the Father. Before you speak to the people about the text, you should spend hours vocally and mentally conversing about the text with the Father. When you leave your study, your text should never leave your heart and mind. You should spend more time thinking about and meditating on your text than you spend reading about it. Spurgeon rehearses the blessedness of meditating on the sermon-text:

> I always find that I can preach best when I can manage to lie a-soak in my text. I like to get a text, and find out its meaning and bearings, and so on; and then, after I have bathed in it, I delight to lie down in it, and let it soak into me . . . Dwell in the truth, and

---

16. Spurgeon, *Metropolitan Tabernacle Pulpit,* 17:592.
17. Spurgeon, *New Park Street Pulpit,* 2:207.

> let the truth dwell in you. Be baptized into its spirit and influence, that you may impart thereof to others . . . Do not preach it until you have taken it up into yourself as the wick takes up the oil. So only can you be a burning and a shining light.[18]

Your sermon-text demands your undivided attention and constant meditation. The text must be deeply digested before it can be dynamically delivered. Spurgeon exhorts, "Read, mark, learn, and inwardly digest the word of God . . . If ever your mind is more clear and active at one time than at another, then sow the principal wheat of godly contemplation and gracious devotion."[19] Rather than your text and sermon being an afterthought, it should be given much forethought and deliberate development.

This intense level of meditation should also be applied to the reading of commentaries. Because a commentary is not infallible like the Scripture upon which it is commenting, there is a great need to mentally remove any dross lest it corrupt the purity of Scripture within your sermon. Give heed to Spurgeon's instruction:

> Meditation is the machine in which the raw material of knowledge is converted to the best uses. Let me compare it to a winepress. By reading, and research and study, we gather the grapes; but it is by meditation that we press out the juice of those grapes, and obtain the wine. How is it that many men who read very much know very little? . . . They extract none of the sweet juice of wisdom from the precious fruits of the vine . . . Animals, after they have eaten, lie down and ruminate; they first crop the grass, and afterwards digest it. So, meditation is the rumination of the soul; thereby we get that nutriment which feeds and supports the mind.[20]

Meditation keeps the truths of God's Word fresh in one's mind and heart. It is tragic when the truth loses its freshness somewhere between the study and the pulpit. Consider the insightful remedy which Spurgeon prescribes for this dilemma: "When thou hast gathered flowers in the field or garden, arrange them in proper order, and bind them together with the string of memory; but take heed that thou dost put them into the water of meditation, else they will soon fade, and be fit only for the dunghill . . . We need meditation to make use of what we have discovered."[21] It is through medita-

---

18. Spurgeon, *All-Round Ministry*, 124–25.
19. Spurgeon, *Metropolitan Tabernacle Pulpit*, 27:611.
20. Spurgeon, *Metropolitan Tabernacle Pulpit*, 46:411–12.
21. Spurgeon, *Metropolitan Tabernacle Pulpit*, 46:413.

tion that your Scripture-prompted thoughts will begin to align themselves with each other. This will be an effective process of allowing the sermon to be shaped by the structure of the sermon-text rather than allowing the sermon to impose a structure upon the text.

# 6

# Shaping the Sermon

> A sermon should be like a meal; it should in every instance feed the
> soul with heavenly meat. Mere words, however well arranged, can
> never do this; there must be sound exposition, and solid doctrine,
> or the hungry will look up despairingly, and depart sorrowing.[1]

THE WAY IN WHICH you enter the study influences the way in which you will enter the pulpit. How you begin your preparation to preach is an accurate indicator of what you believe about the nature of the sermon and your call to preach. You should approach sermon preparation with a desire to be immersed in the presence of God, illumined by the Spirit of God, and inspired by the Son of God, with a message from the Word of God for the people of God. Hence, you should enter your study more focused on praying than preaching. The sermon should never overshadow the Savior in your study. Your goal is to encounter the Savior, not just to exposit a sermon. Christ is to be both the source and substance of the sermon in that order. There is a vast difference between the man who is acquainted with Christ and the man who is intimately and atmospherically aware of him.

---

1. Spurgeon, "Less Gilding and More Carving," 449.

It is in this atmospheric awareness of Christ is conducive for the fine-tuned of your focus and the purifying of your motives. Spurgeon emphasized the necessary perspective of the preacher who is divinely called and commissioned by Christ: "The true minister of Christ knows that the true value of a sermon must lie, not in its fashion and manner, but in the truth which it contains. Nothing can compensate for the absence of teaching; all the rhetoric in the world is but as chaff to the wheat in contrast to the gospel of our salvation."[2] From the selection of the sermon-text to the conclusion of the message, the centrality of Christ must remain preeminent. Christ constantly be consulted and exalted at every stage. The message is to center upon the inspired Word of God, not upon your imagination and innovation. It is not God's desire for you to write and preach a sermon off the top of your head. Rather, it is his desire for you to prayerfully position yourself before him in order that he may shape the message and deliver it through you.

Remember, you are not the creator of the sermon. You are simply the conduit through which it passes. Your message is to be anchored to Scripture as an avenue of access to divine truth. Spurgeon pictures this: "Whatever else may be present, the absence of edifying, instructive truth, like the absence of flour from bread, will be fatal."[3] This does not imply that you are to put your mind in neutral and foolishly wait for God to bypass your intellect to mystically use you. What it does imply is that you are to prayerfully, humbly, and sincerely seek God with all your heart and mind. As you open Scripture to read and meditate, the Holy Spirit will guide you to formulate the message God would have you preach. When a message comes together in this manner, the result is a sermon that bears the indelible mark of a God-given text and a Scripture-born structure anchored to biblical truth.

## Pray About Your Sermon Preparation and Repent of Prophetic Plagiarism

When was the last time you took time to spend focused prayer regarding your sermon preparation? This should be a matter of perpetual prayer. Make it your constant prayer that your head will not outgrow your heart. Satan would love for your head to outgrow our heart. He does not fear academic preaching, but he does fear anointed preaching. Your mind should be greatly exercised in your study but never to the neglect of your heart.

2. Spurgeon, *Lectures to My Students*, 70.
3. Spurgeon, *Lectures to My Students*, 71.

God blesses the healthy balance between preparation of the heart and the head. This is accomplished with unceasing prayer throughout your sermon preparation. Spurgeon elaborates on the requirement and reward of intense studiousness: "The preacher should think it out, get it well masticated and digested; and having first fed upon the word himself should then prepare the like nutriment for others. Our sermons should be our mental lifeblood—the out-flow of our intellectual and spiritual vigour."[4] Any shortcut in this process will be very detrimental.

Access to the sermons of others has escalated. This has been an enticing possibility for lazy and carnal preachers from the prophet Jeremiah's day until now. "Is not My word like a fire?" says the Lord, "and like a hammer *that* breaks the rock in pieces? Therefore behold, I *am* against the prophets," says the Lord, "who steal My words every one from his neighbor" (Jer 23:29–30). Preaching a secondhand sermon is as reckless as it would have been for David to wear the armor of Saul into battle against Goliath (1 Sam 17:32–39). Over time, this practice is spiritually deadening for the preacher and increasingly deadly for the hearer. Spurgeon contends:

> What a dreadful thing it must be for a man to set up to be a teacher of others if he does not know the things of God experimentally himself. It can be done, you know, and done very cheaply. You can buy sermons ready lithographed and guaranteed not to have been preached within so many miles . . . But there will be a heavy account at the last for the man who does that sort of thing . . . Go down on your knees and cry, "Make me to understand the way of thy precepts, so shall I talk of thy wondrous works." Dear brethren, especially you who are to be ministers of the gospel and have begun to preach, seek a deeper understanding of divine things, or else your ministry will be lean and poverty-stricken.[5]

Consider how many intimate seasons with the Father are lost to the man who chooses a carnal shortcut over personal prayerful interaction with God and his Word.[6] Spurgeon lamented this widespread practice:

---

4. Spurgeon, *Lectures to My Students*, 141.

5. Spurgeon, *Metropolitan Tabernacle Pulpit*, 23:167.

6. There is a carnal shortcut that is just as detrimental as preaching the sermons of others. It is the temptation for a seasoned preacher to reproach one of his own sermons with little thought and even less prayer. Spurgeon gives this warning: "It will not please God for us to offer Him that which costs us nothing. Others have a stock of sermons, and I have heard that, just before the time of entering the pulpit, they turn over their precious manuscripts, pick out a likely one, and without further preparation read it as

> We have heard of ministers preaching other men's sermons, and we have even been informed of the existence of mills in which the olives of doctrine are bruised wholesale, and the extract is sent forth bottled up for immediate use . . . Those who purchase and habitually use such substitutes for personal study hardly deserve the name of ministers of Christ . . . We are persuaded that sermons which are borrowed, which cost their reader no thought, no emotion, no prayerful agony, are not at all the offerings which the Lord requires at the hands his true ministers.[7]

A borrowed sermon in hand is no substitute for a burning message in the heart.[8] Your goal is to preach messages delivered from the heart of God in the Word of God to the people of God. This demands more than an acquaintance with the minds of men on a particular topic or text. Hermeneutics and homiletics must be seen as a holy laborious process in which you ultimately look beyond human sources and look up to heaven! Allow your message to be fashioned by and filled with the Word of God and not just the words of men. Give ear to Spurgeon's advice:

---

God's message to the people. The Lord deliver us from a state of mind in which we dare to put on the table of shewbread the first loaf which come to hand!" Spurgeon, *All-Round Ministry*, 156.

7. Crosby, *Spurgeon's Forgotten College Addresses*, 166.

8. Although Spurgeon discouraged the verbatim preaching of sermon's written by other preachers, he did not object to making use of helpful resources. He even provided help of this nature, entitled "My Sermon Notes." In the preface to this volume Spurgeon writes, "It's not always easy to select themes for sermons. Even those who are able to give all their time to reading and study are sometimes glad of a suggestion by which they are directed to a topic; how much more is this the case when a man is all the week engaged in commercial pursuits and then had to preach twice on the Lord's day! These are called lay-brethren by those who believe in a special priesthood; I can only say that whatever they are called they are among the right-honorables of the pulpit. Frequently have brethren assured me of the difficulty they have found in choosing a text when they could only get a brief interval at a time when they were well-nigh worn out . . . I have prepared these frameworks not to encourage indolence, but to help the bewildered industry; and I hope that I have not written so much as to enable any man to preach without thought, nor so little as to leave a weary mind without help . . . As we pour a little water down a pump to help it draw up a stream from below, so may 'My Sermon-Notes' refresh many a jaded mind, and then set it working so as to develop its own resources. May the Holy Spirit use these outlines for the help of his busy servants. To him shall be all the praise, and to His Church the profit" (Spurgeon, *My Sermon Notes*, 1:5–7). It is also important to hear Spurgeon's clarification regarding these notes: "So far as I remember, none of these outlines have been in the printer's hands before. They are notes of sermons which have not been included in the Metropolitan Tabernacle Pulpit." Spurgeon, *My Sermon Notes*, 1:7. It is important to note that these were not full sermons made available for complete duplication.

> Before we venture on the high and honorable service of instructing the Lord's people, let us go to the Lord himself for a supply of his grace, and when he has directed our minds to the chosen subject, let us further ask his aid that we may, in devout meditation, extract from the Word its fatness and unction; and then let us spare no effort, but cast our whole strength into the endeavor to prepare that which we hope to present to the people of God.[9]

According to Spurgeon, this requires thoughtful persistent prayer throughout the entire sermon preparation process:

> Because of our absolute need of the Holy Spirit, we must give ourselves to prayer before our work and after our work. A man who believes that, do what he may, no soul will be quickened apart from the work of the Spirit of God, a man who has a longing desire that he may save souls, will not venture to his pulpit without prayer. He will not deliver his message without a thousand groans and cries to God for help in every sentence that he utters. And when the sermon is done, his work will not be done; it will have scarcely begun. His sermons will be but a text for long-continued prayer. He will be crying to God continually to anoint him with the heavenly oil.[10]

You should be characterized by integrity and honesty at every stage of the pulpit ministry with which God has entrusted you. Are you truthful and trustworthy in the solitude of your study? If not, that will eventually become clear to all who hear you in the pulpit.

## Practice Spirit-Led Exegesis of the Sermon-Text in the Atmosphere of Prayer

> Be diligent to present yourself approved to God, a worker who does not need to be ashamed, rightly dividing the word of truth (2 Tim 2:15).

As you study Scripture for a sermon, your primary focus should be on what God is saying *to* you, and secondly, on what God will say *through* you. This requires a sanctified searching of Scripture with both head and heart.

> You will find that the best preparation for preaching is much praying. I have always found that the meaning of a text can be better

---

9. Crosby, *Spurgeon's Forgotten College Addresses*, 166.
10. Spurgeon, *Metropolitan Tabernacle Pulpit*, 38:112.

> learned by prayer than in any other way. Of course, we must consult lexicons and commentaries to see the literal meaning of the words, and their relation to one another; but when we have done all that, we shall still find that our greatest help will come from prayer... Our Savior's example teaches us that, for seasons of special service, we need not only prayers of a brief character, excellent as they are for ordinary occasions, but special protracted wrestling with God like that of Jacob at the brook Jabbok.[11]

Many powerful preachers throughout church history have spent hours upon hours of protracted prayer. This nurtured a powerful connection between their walk with God and their work for God. There is a distinct difference between mere mental exegesis and that which is a proper combination of the prayerful and mental exegesis of a text of Scripture. There is no evidence that the Holy Spirit completely bypasses the mental faculty of a preacher in the preparation of sermons. However, there is an obvious need in the preacher's life for a sanctified mind and a prayerful heart in the development of the message.

Pray yourself into and through the text. Ask the Holy Spirit to guide you through the terrain of the truth within the text. The biblical prophets, from Samuel to John the Baptist, did not preach from the overflow of commentaries or classrooms but from the overflow of communion with God. Personal exegesis of the text should be intertwined with conversation with the Father. In the context of your interaction with the Father, remember that the best commentary on Scripture is Scripture itself. As you converse with the Father, explore parallel passages and similar statements in other parts of the Bible. Do as much with the text as possible before turning to the minds of men for assistance. These are secondary sources and must be kept in a proper perspective. Spurgeon was not opposed to books; however, as voracious as he was in his reading, he attempted to keep them secondary to the Scripture.

When moving from the text to commentaries, proceed with caution and continued communion with God. Before opening the first commentary, you must consult the Father about which commentaries should be consulted. The goal of sermon preparation should be to maintain a focus on the Father and his Word rather than shifting your focus to compiling content and meeting a deadline. Remember: intimacy produces illumination, insight, and instruction from the Holy Spirit. To miss this is to preach from the minds of men to the minds of men, rather than preaching from the

---

11. Spurgeon, *Metropolitan Tabernacle Pulpit*, 56:5.

heart of God to the heart of the hearer. Commentaries must be kept in the complementarian role of secondary resources, not as sanctified substitutes for Spirit-led exegesis and exposition.

Although Spurgeon would not fit many of the current models of expository preaching, he was most definitely a textual preacher in his approach. Even when preaching on one or two verses, he practiced good principles of exegesis and exposition. Consider how Spurgeon expressed his conscientious love for the proper handling of the Word of God to his students: "We need more expository preaching; and for that, we need more diligent and intelligent study of the Scriptures . . . Let your aim and object be, to bring God's mind *out of the text* rather than to put your own mind *into it* . . . So mind that you get the true teaching of your text, then expound it to your congregation."[12] If prayer is truly the key to powerful preaching, then why do so many preachers fail to maintain prayer in its proper place of priority? The goal is to prayerfully fill your mind as well as your message with the Word of God. Your message should come through your praying life, not just your preaching lips. Remember, applied truth will be anointed truth. It is imperative that public proclamation be anchored to personal application. Spurgeon lamented the failure of preachers to do this: "I am fearful that even preaching against sin may have an injurious effect upon the preacher. I frankly confess, my brethren, that there is a tendency with those of us who have to speak upon these themes, to treat them professionally, rather than to make application of them to ourselves; and thus we lose our dread of evil in some degree"[13] Casually dealing with biblical truth as a mere professional quickly causes the heart to become calloused and complacent. This must be avoided at all costs. It is the calloused and complacent preacher that becomes a spiritual casualty! Consulting commentaries prematurely as a substitute for communion with Christ is a symptom of the shift of the heart.

Spurgeon's library was filled with the best of commentaries. He even published an annotated catalog entitled *Commenting and Commentaries*. He could be referred to as a *commentary connoisseur par excellence*. His caution and critique regarding their use is well-taken:

> We turn the text round and round and cannot make anything out of it. We look at the commentators . . . But when we have no commentator or minister, we have still the Holy Spirit; and let me tell you a little secret: whenever you cannot understand a text, open

12. Crosby, *Spurgeon's Forgotten College Addresses*, 149.
13. Spurgeon, *Metropolitan Tabernacle Pulpit*, 11:159.

> your Bible, bend your knee, and pray over that text . . . Prayer is the key that openeth the cabinets of mystery. Prayer and faith are sacred picklocks that can open secrets, and obtain great treasures. There is no college for holy education like that of the blessed Spirit, for He is an ever-present tutor, to whom we have only to bend the knee, and He is at our side, the great expositor of truth . . . Now, man can guide us to a truth, but it is only the Holy Spirit who can "guide us into a truth."[14]

As you peruse the pages of a commentary, you must do so with Spirit-given discernment and discretion. Spurgeon further clarifies his concern with excessive use of some commentaries: "There is no being much more unnatural than a cold-blooded commentator, who bites at every letter, and nibbles at the grammatical meaning of every syllable, translating with his lexicon, but never exercising common sense, or allowing even the least play to his heart."[15] In this regard, you must proceed with cautious discernment.

Commentaries are very helpful secondary tools, but they are sorry substitutes for a lack of communion with Christ himself as you explore the text. Therefore, be careful that you do not rush prematurely to consult a commentator before you have fully consulted Christ. In your study, surrounded by your library, it is easy to overestimate the consultation of commentaries and to underestimate communion with Christ. Even the consulting of commentaries should be done in the context of communing with Christ. Spurgeon prayerfully emphasized the necessity of being immersed in communion with Christ throughout the process of studying Scripture:

> O living Christ, make this a living Word to me. Your Word is life, but not without the Holy Spirit . . . Lord, be present here . . . He is here with me in this chamber of mine—I must not trifle. He leans over me. He puts His finger along the lines. I can see His pierced hand. I will read it as in His Presence. I will read it knowing that He is the substance of it, that He is the proof of this book as well as the writer of it—the sum of this Scripture as well as the author of it. That is the way for true students to become wise! You will get at the soul of Scripture when you can keep Jesus with you while you are reading.[16]

---

14. Spurgeon, *New Park Street Pulpit*, 1:383.
15. Spurgeon, *Metropolitan Tabernacle Pulpit*, 22:591.
16. Spurgeon, *Metropolitan Tabernacle Pulpit*, 25:634.

To be spiritually competent as a preacher requires an undistracted focus on Christ in the study. This means actively recognizing his presence and engaging in communion with him.

The Holy Spirit longs to guide you in your sermon preparation by illuminating the text of Scripture. Intense prayerfulness is the link between your mind and the Spirit's active illumination of the text. Spurgeon uses rich imagery to make this point:

> You will frequently find fresh streams of thought leaping up from the passage before you . . . new veins of precious ore will be revealed to your astonished gaze as you quarry God's Word and use diligently the hammer of prayer . . . Use prayer as a boring rod, and wells of living water will leap up from the bowels of the Word.[17]

Simply ask the Holy Spirit to illuminate that which he has inspired. Spurgeon states, "If you cannot understand a book, do you know the best way to reach its meaning? Write to the author and ask him what he meant. If you have a book to read, and you have got that author always accessible, you need not complain that you do not understand it. The Holy Spirit is come to abide with us for ever. Search the Scriptures, but cry for the Spirit's light, and live under His influence."[18] When you consult secondary sources, such as commentaries, do so with a prayer in your heart for discernment and discretion from the Holy Spirit.

There is a vast difference between prayerful Spirit-led exegesis and professional dissecting of a text. In exegeting the sermon-text, your goal should be to prayerfully allow the Holy Spirit to illuminate that which he has placed in the text, nothing more and nothing less. This is not a mystical revelation of something new, hidden, or spectacular. It is simply God-given insight and discernment in your exploration of the text. Spurgeon explains, "My dear hearers, if you would understand the Word of God in its knotty points, if you would comprehend the mystery of the gospel of Christ, remember, Christ's scholars must study upon their knees. Depend upon it, that the best commentator upon the Word of God is its author, the Holy Ghost, and if you would know the meaning, you must go to Him in prayer."[19] Your goal is for the Holy Spirit to illuminate your thoughts as to the intended meaning of the text, rather than imposing your thoughts upon it.

---

17. Spurgeon, *Lectures to My Students*, 44.
18. Spurgeon, *Metropolitan Tabernacle Pulpit*, 20:708.
19. Spurgeon, *New Park Street Pulpit*, 6:20.

Spurgeon admonished his students, "We have urgent need to study, for the teacher of others must himself be instructed. Habitually to come into the pulpit unprepared is unpardonable presumption: nothing can more effectually lower ourselves and our office."[20] He then initiated a deeper probing with penetrating questions: "If we are not instructed, how can we instruct? If we have not thought, how shall we lead others to think? It is in our study-work, in that blessed labour when we are alone with the Book before us, that we need the help of the Holy Spirit. He holds the key of the heavenly treasury, and can enrich us beyond conception."[21] Your active relationship with God should guide and govern your research and interaction with the sermon-text. Hence, it should be viewed more as a life text for you, rather than just a sermon-text for others.

## Prayerfully Determine the Original Meaning of the Text

> All our libraries and studies are mere emptiness compared with our closets. We grow, we wax mighty, we prevail in private prayer.[22]

The prayerful selection of the sermon-text must be followed by careful exploration of the context and prayerful exegesis of the passage. It is at this level of preparation that the preacher will wrestle with the text in sanctified thought and prayer. Whether or not you have the academic credentials and a library of original language resources or not, you never move beyond the desperate need to rely on the Holy Spirit in your work with the text. Neither should one view the lack of education and resources as an unconquerable handicap. Spurgeon lacked advanced theological academic achievement; however, he did amass an impressive host of resources to assist him in his exegesis. However, he seemed to keep this in perspective and never viewed these volumes as a replacement for walking with God. Regardless of academic attainment, or the lack thereof, prayerful dependence upon the leadership of the Holy Spirit must be constant as you move through the exegetical process.

It is in this area of sermon preparation that a preacher will face the testing of his integrity regarding his intellectual capacity. First, if the preacher

---

20. Spurgeon, *Lectures to My Students*, 188.
21. Spurgeon, *Lectures to My Students*, 188.
22. Spurgeon, *Lectures to My Students*, 41.

is skilled in translating and parsing the original languages, it is important that he not become self-reliant in his knowledge and ability. There is a rich blessing when the preacher discovers insight from his work in Greek or Hebrew. But this can quickly breed a desire to display one's knowledge at the expense of simply unfolding the meaning of the text before the people. Bridled intellect is expressed through discretionary meekness.

Second, if the preacher has lexicons, volumes of word studies, and/or academic commentaries within his library, he too faces the subtle temptation of shifting his dependence upon the minds of scholars rather than the ministry of the Spirit. For preachers in this situation, balance is of the essence. A third temptation that may hound the preacher is the creation of an illusion concerning his knowledge and comprehension of the original languages. This can occur by subtly relishing in unwarranted compliments regarding your personal ability. To exaggerate one's level of ability by using lexicons and commentaries can create a prideful persona, when the preacher is simply echoing the education of others. Your God-given responsibility is not to impress your hearers but to instruct them in the truths of God's Word. Honesty and humility must constantly be practiced in the study and in the pulpit.

Humble prayerfulness heightens your sensitivity to the leadership of the Holy Spirit. It deepens your expectancy to encounter God himself within the pages of Scripture. Spurgeon graphically visualizes this process:

> A stonebreaker was one day on his knees breaking flints, when a minister came by and said, "I see you are doing what I often do, breaking up hard things." "Yes, sir," was the answer, and I am doing it in the way in which you must do it, on my knees." A passage in Scripture will often open up when you pray over it, which will defy mere criticism or looking to expositors ... We may hammer away at a text sometimes in meditation and strike it again and again, and yet it may not yield to us, but we cry to God, and straightway the text opens, and we see concealed in it wondrous treasure of wisdom and of grace. But the prayer should not be merely that we may understand the text. I think we should pray over every passage in order that we may be enabled to get out of it what God would impart to us.[23]

The focus of exegesis is not simply to explore the minds of men and determine the meaning of words but rather to pursue the heart of God within

---

23. Spurgeon, *Metropolitan Tabernacle Pulpit*, 58:427.

the passage. You should prayerfully allow the Holy Spirit to be vitally involved as you consult lexical aids and commentaries. Spurgeon further emphasized, "The commentators are good instructors, but the author himself is far better, and prayer makes a direct appeal to Him and enlists Him in our cause. It is a great thing to pray one's self into the spirit and marrow of a text."[24] The goal is not just for you to get into the text but for the text to get into you. It is imperative that the Holy Spirit speak *to* you in order that he may speak *through* you. The Father is faithful to answer your prayers for help to understand the interpretation and application of a passage of Scripture in your life, and then the lives of your hearers.

## Prayerfully Select the Text-Based Topic and/or Title for Your Sermon

> As a further assistance to a poor stranded preacher, who cannot launch his mind for want of a wave or two of thought, I recommend him in such a case, to turn again and again to the Word of God itself, and read a chapter, and ponder over its verses one by one; or let him select a single verse, and get his mind fully exercised upon it. It may be that he will not find his text in the verse or chapter which he reads, but the right word will come to him through his mind being actively engaged upon holy subjects. According to the relation of thoughts to each other, one thought will suggest another, and another, until a long procession will have passed before the mind, out of which one or other will be the predestinated theme.[25]

Preachers constantly face the subtle temptation of imposing a topic on a text. This taints the very text upon which you will soon preach. As you spend extended time with the text, you will treasure the text more than any tantalizing topic or title. The title and/or topic of the sermon should be drawn from the heart of the text. Determining the topic within the text is not intended to be an exercise of creativity and cleverness. This should be accomplished through prayerful meditation upon the text. Spurgeon maintains, "The difficulty of settling upon a topic, if it makes you pray more than usual, will be a great blessing. Praying is the best studying . . . Pray over

---

24. Spurgeon, "Christian Minister's Private Prayer," 112–13.
25. Spurgeon, *Lectures to My Students*, 92–93.

Scripture; it is as the treading of grapes in the wine-vat, the threshing of corn on the barn floor, the melting of gold from ore. Prayer is twice blest; it blesseth the pleading preacher, and the people to whom he ministers."[26] Praying over Scripture assists you in working with the heart of the text. It also assists the text in working on the heart of the preacher. Spurgeon testifies to this reality: "I have searched the Word of God with the view of finding the most impressive texts—and I have prayed to God to guide me to subjects which might savingly affect you. These topics have often affected my own heart while I have been preparing for the pulpit."[27] Remember, the sermon-text is not just the source of a lesson to be delivered from the pulpit but rather the substance of a life that is to be lived by the preacher.

Prayerfully consider how the heart of the sermon-text can be highlighted in the title. The sermon title should simply introduce the sermon-text and identify its focus. It is this title/topic that should be tested and fashioned by the text, not vice versa. Spurgeon observes:

> I am quite certain that if we will wait upon God for our subjects and make it a matter of prayer that we may be rightly directed, we shall be led forth by a right way; but if we are puffed up with the idea that we can very easily choose for ourselves, we shall find that even in the selection of a subject, without Christ, we can do nothing. Wait upon the Lord, hear what He would speak, receive the word direct from His mouth, and then go forth as an ambassador fresh from the court of heaven. "Wait, I say, on the Lord"[28]

The prayerful selection of the text-based topic/title should be done after your exegesis is completed. Patiently waiting until this stage of preparation, the sermon-text will more likely be the foundation and touchstone of the title/topic of the sermon.

The sermon must be text-driven, not title- or topic-diverted. Your goal is to immerse your hearers in the scriptural text, not to impress them with a spectacular title. Seek to guide your hearers to worship in the text rather than attempting to wow them with a title. This demands that you train your eyes to look for the truth written in the text rather than its topic. A predetermined title or topic distracts hearers from the truth by distorting and misrepresenting the Word of God. Remember, the sermon-text is not dependent upon the sermon title for its power. There is a divinely inherent

---

26. Spurgeon, *Lectures to My Students*, 86.
27. Spurgeon, *Metropolitan Tabernacle Pulpit*, 53:283.
28. Spurgeon, *Lectures to My Students*, 96.

power placed by the Holy Spirit within the text by which he himself impacts the hearts of people. If you present your title with more energy than you have when reading the text, you may be encroaching on idolatrous thin ice.

## Practice Spirit-Led Exposition in the Atmosphere of Prayer

> I am sure that God measures much of our work according to the prayer we expend over it... A sermon that is prayed over is worth ten thousand that are merely prepared, or copied, or that spring out of a man's mind without being wrought by the Holy Spirit in his heart. Oh, to pray down the sermon, and then to pray up the sermon, and pray it all over, resting upon God alone![29]

You must faithfully receive from the Father to faithfully represent him. The primary question is not "What do the people need to hear?" but rather "What does the Father want me to say to His people on His behalf?" The Father must touch your lips before he can touch lives through you (Isa 6:1–8). Having practiced prayerful exegesis, it is important that you also practice prayerful exposition. This stage of sermon preparation is the task of building a bridge from the text into the hearts and lives of the hearers.

Your hearers need to hear what the sermon-text meant to the original hearers and then how it applies to them. The ultimate objective of your exposition is for your hearers to leave with the text at the forefront of their minds. Your goal is not to make the sermon memorable but rather to help hearers see that the text is applicable. Your most able assistant in this process will be an acute prayerfulness by which the illumination of the Holy Spirit is released.

It is essential for prayer to become much more than a launching pad toward your preparation of sermons. Rather than an opening and closing activity, prayer should become the atmosphere in which you commune with the Father over the message. Nurture a heightened prayerful sensitivity to the Holy Spirit. Spurgeon contrasts prayer-filled sermon preparation with that which is limited or nonexistent:

---

29. Spurgeon, *Metropolitan Tabernacle Pulpit*, 37:477.

> The way to make sermons is to work vital electricity into them, putting your own life and the very life of God into them by earnest prayer. The difference between a sermon that has been prayed over and one that has been prepared and preached by a prayerless man is like . . . the high priest before and after his anointing. You must anoint your sermons, brethren, and you cannot do it except by much private communion with God.[30]

God's desire is not for you to work *for* him. He wants to work *through* you. This is God's message to his people. He has chosen you to deliver his message. It is imperative that he be in the lead and at the center of all your preparation. The seriousness of your call should have a sanctifying influence on the preparation of your sermon. Spurgeon admonished his students:

> Brethren, avoid anything like trifling over sermon-making . . . Do not rush upon your holy duties without devout preparation for the hallowed service. Make your waiting upon God a necessity of your calling, and at the same time the highest privilege of it. Count it your joy and honour to have an interview with your Master. Get your message fresh from God. Even manna stinks if you keep it beyond its time; therefore, get it fresh from Heaven, and then it will have a celestial relish.[31]

To prepare your sermon apart from intimate interaction with God is not just an awful shame. It is an absolute sham.

## Prayerfully Outline the Sermon-Text and the Sermon

> The way to begin to make a sermon is to bend the
> knee and to cry to God for direction.[32]

The very best practices of exegesis can easily be wasted on an inadequate and improper arrangement of material in outlining the sermon. The outline of the sermon-text and the sermon itself should be virtually symmetrical. Remain dependent upon the Holy Spirit as you outline the sermon-text and ultimately your sermon. The Holy Spirit, the very one who inspired the writing of Scripture, is both able and willing to guide you toward the

---

30. Spurgeon, *Soul Winner*, 111.
31. Spurgeon, *All-Round Ministry*, 335–36.
32. Spurgeon, *Metropolitan Tabernacle Pulpit*, 7:222.

discovery of the divinely determined structure of the passage. When this stage of preparation is completed in the context of prayer, the Holy Spirit is given freedom to illuminate your mind.

Guard against feverishly and prayerlessly attempting to establish an outline. Outlining the text should be the outgrowth of Spirit-led exploration of its structure. This structure, in turn, will determine the structure of the sermon itself. Spurgeon reminisced about his experiences during this level of preparation:

> Much hard labour have I spent in manipulating topics, ruminating upon points of doctrine, making skeletons out of verses... Almost any Saturday in my life, I prepare enough outlines of sermons, if I felt at liberty to preach them, to last me for a month, but I no more dare to use them than an honest mariner would run to shore a cargo of contraband goods.[33]

Once you gain a clearer understanding of the structure of the text, you are better equipped to determine the wording and flow of the sermon outline. The text will almost preach itself when you explore the structure of the text with Spirit-led diligence.

## Prayerfully Add Flesh to the Skeleton of the Sermon Outline

Whether you are preparing to preach from an outline or a manuscript, you should prayerfully consider the extended content of each section of the sermon. Spurgeon highlighted the importance of prayer as the preparation continues: "Your prayers will be your tender assistants *while your discourses are yet upon the anvil*... If you can dip your pens into your hearts, appealing in earnestness to the Lord, you will write well; and if you can gather your matter on your knees at the gate of heaven, you will not fail to speak well."[34] Prayerful patience is necessary at this juncture of the sermon preparation process. Spurgeon further states, "Prayer supplies a leverage for the uplifting of ponderous truths... Waiting upon God often turns darkness into light. Persevering inquiry at the sacred oracle uplifts the veil and gives grace to look into the deep things of God."[35] The urgency of the rapidly ap-

---

33. Spurgeon, *Lectures to My Students*, 85.
34. Spurgeon, "Christian Minister's Private Prayer," 2:112.
35. Spurgeon, *Lectures to My Students*, 44.

## Shaping the Sermon

proaching hour of preaching demands perseverance instead of panic. You must proceed prayerfully and meditatively. Spurgeon stresses, "It is a waste of time, not an economy of it, to dispense with study, private prayer, and due preparation for your work."[36] Initially, your prayerful meditation must focus intently upon the message. This will be followed by compassionate intercession for the congregation whom the Lord will providentially assemble to hear the message.

God's Word must always take priority over the needs and/or preferences of the hearers. When this is not the case, the text easily becomes misrepresented and the message becomes misdirected. It is important that you value content consciousness over congregation consciousness. You should proceed with a humbling sense of dependence upon the illumination of the Holy Spirit in the hearts and minds of your hearers. This alone will result in obedience and application.

In this stage of sermon preparation, prayer must remain preeminent and pervasive. This will enable you to avoid any subtle temptation of imposing your opinions into the expositing God's truth. Although Spurgeon did lengthy exposition in the worship service apart from the sermon he preached, he upheld the great importance of developing an expository mind and ministry:

> Let us be thoroughly well acquainted with the great doctrines of the Word of God and let us be mighty in expounding the Scriptures. I am sure that no preaching will last so long, or build up a church so well, as the expository . . . If your ministries are to be lastingly useful, you must be expositors. For this purpose, you must understand the Word yourselves, and be able so to comment upon it that the people may be built up by the Word. Be masters of your Bibles, brethren; whatever other works you have not searched, be at home with the writings of the prophets and apostles. "Let the Word of God dwell in you richly."[37]

If the "Word of God dwells in you richly," it will also richly dwell within your sermons. Do not be deceived in your preaching: it is not your words which bring power to God's Word; it is God's Word which brings power to your preaching when you conscientiously allow it to take the lead role in your sermon. Emphasizing this reality, Spurgeon quotes Robert Murray McCheyne: "McCheyne somewhere says, 'Depend upon it, it is God's word,

---

36. Spurgeon, *All-Round Ministry*, 74.
37. Spurgeon, *All-Round Ministry*, 53.

not man's comment on God's word, which converts souls.' I have frequently observed that this is the case. A discourse has been the means of conviction or of decision; but usually upon close inquiry I have found that the real instrument was a Scripture quoted by the preacher."[38]

The Word of God must be recognized as preeminent. Your sermon is to simply shed light on this eternal reality.

Your words should flow from your heart as an expression of your walk with God. He has uniquely gifted you to communicate his unchanging Word with the people whom he has providentially placed in your congregation. It is within this unique setting that he will use you in a fresh way. "Be yourself, dear brother," Spurgeon said to his students, "for, if you are not yourself, you cannot be anybody else; and so, you see, you must be nobody . . . Do not be a mere copyist, a borrower and spoiler of other men's notes. Say what God has said to you, and say it in your own way, and when it is so said plead personally for the Lord's blessing upon it."[39] When you allow him to be himself among his people, this gives you great freedom to be yourself in presenting his Word to his people. Ultimately, you did not choose these people to be your congregation. Neither did this congregation ultimately choose you as their pastor. But you have been called and sent by God to this people at this time for his glory. You represent him with his Word in your life and in your sermon. Walking in this reality will bring great freedom and confidence to you regardless of the circumstances or challenges that you encounter.

## Pray Through the Finished Sermon

> Let the words of my mouth and the meditation of my heart be acceptable in Your sight, O Lord, my strength and my Redeemer (Ps 19:14).

When the sermon has been prepared, that is no time to lessen your praying. Instead, your praying should grow in intensity as you move closer to entering the pulpit. Praying through the finished sermon will stir the heart and focus the mind. This is an invaluable spiritual discipline within the sermon preparation process. You now position yourself to search your heart concerning the truths you will preach. Practicing persistent prayer at this stage

---

38. Spurgeon, *My Sermon Notes*, 23–24.
39. Spurgeon, *All-Round Ministry*, 73–74.

of the sermon also enhances your ability to cooperate with the Holy Spirit. Your preaching will be in answer to the multitude of prayers you have prayed throughout the sermon preparation process. This spiritual exercise of prayer has the potential to transform your message from an academic work to an act of worship.

Spurgeon speaks of travailing in prayer over the completed sermon as "steeping the seed" which the Holy Spirit is about to sow: "There is a distinct connection between importunate agonising and true success, even as between the travail and the birth, the sowing in tears and the reaping in joy. 'How is it that your seed comes up so soon?' said one gardener to another. 'Because I steep it,' was the reply. We must steep all our teachings in tears, 'when none but God is nigh,' and their growth will surprise and delight us."[40] Travailing in prayer will assist you in preaching heart-to-heart instead of head-to-head. When your sermon is prayed into your travailing heart, it is more likely to flow from your heart to the heart of your hearers. If the sermon cannot be prayed, it is not fit to be preached. Powerful preaching is truly the offspring of passionate praying. Praying over the finished sermon will bring great spiritual dividends to you and your hearers.

Make each point of the sermon a personal prayer focus:

- "Father, please speak to me about me . . ."
- "Father, please speak to me about my heart . . ."
- "Father, please speak to me about my walk with You . . ."
- "Father, please reveal any area of my life where I have yet to obey You . . ."
- "Father, please use this sermon-text to reveal any sin in my heart . . ."

Allow the sermon-text to guide you toward specific intercession for your hearers:

- "Father, please give Your people a heightened sensitivity to the Holy Spirit . . ."
- "Father, please nurture a contrite heart of receptivity within the hearers . . ."
- "Father, please give Your people a holy hunger for the truth of the text . . ."

---

40. Spurgeon, *Lectures to My Students*, 46.

- "Father, please increase reverence for Your Word among Your people..."
- "Father, please bring the hearers to a point of worship in the text..."

Pray through these heart-searching questions:

- Is there any command in your text which you have failed to obey?
- Is there any truth in your text which you have yet to appropriate in your personal life?
- Is there any sin in your text of which you have failed to repent?
- Is there any promise in your text that you have yet to claim?
- Is there any example in your text that you have not followed?
- Is there any warning in your text that you have failed to heed?
- Is there any error in your text that you have failed to avoid?
- Is there any doctrine in your text that you have avoided to explore/expound to your people?

Allow these questions to guide you in conversation with the Father about your sermon:

- How will this message exalt Jesus Christ?
- What attribute of Christ is emphasized in this message?
- How will this message challenge believers to pursue a deeper Christlikeness?
- What specific quality of Christlikeness in the congregation challenged to pursue?
- What attribute of Christ does this message emphasize?
- What teaching of Christ coincides with this passage?
- How will this message challenge believers to pursue obedience to Christ?

## Prayerfully Preach the Sermon to Yourself

I discipline my body and bring *it* into subjection, lest, when I have preached to others, I myself should become disqualified (1 Cor 9:27).

If the sermon does not move from your head to your heart, it will not move effectively from the pulpit to the people. Messages from God must come *to* you and then *through* you. A sermon that is not personally applied is seldom powerfully anointed. The message must come from your life as well as your lips.

> It is an excellent rule concerning a text, for the hearer as well as the minister, to apply himself to the text, and then, secondly, to apply the text to himself. Keep your thoughts to the text, and then when you have drawn out its meaning, let all that it has to say be spoken in your own ears as addressed personally to you. I pray that God the Holy Spirit may stir us up to self-examination, that if any strange sin or evil passion may have devoured our strength, at any rate we may know it and drive out the traitor at once.[41]

God desires to prepare his messenger and the message simultaneously. When both are well-prepared, it brings much glory to God and much good to his people. It is essential that you allow God to prepare you to prepare the sermon.

God's focus is as much on shaping his messenger as sculpting the message. This does not imply that God is unconcerned about your message, for a God-given message must flow through a God-made man. Spurgeon spoke of the impact his messages had on him personally:

> I have to bear my willing witness to the benefit received in the congregation of God's people. "What!" say you, "Why, you do not hear any sermons!" No, I hear very few except my own, and they are not the best; but preaching them is probably of more service to me than hearing them is to you, for there is a care of the Word of God that is necessary, and the searching of it in the preparation of the sermon, and the waiting upon God for help in the service; all these have been to me a means of grace.[42]

Sometimes, God speaks *through* and *to* the preacher simultaneously. The preaching of the Word of God addresses all who will hear, and that includes the one through whom it is delivered.

Preach the sermon to yourself at the completion of your preparation. When this exercise is done with a sensitive heart toward God, it produces much fruit in your life. It also deepens and strengthening the impact on your hearers. Only a repentant and obedient heart is adequately prepared

---

41. Spurgeon, *Metropolitan Tabernacle Pulpit*, 14:506.
42. Spurgeon, *Metropolitan Tabernacle Pulpit*, 39:355.

to call others to repentance and obedience. Spurgeon lamented occasions when he failed in personal application of God-given messages:

> I have read some of my own utterances and have trembled as I have read them, and afterwards I have wept over them, not wanting to alter them, not regretting them, but fearing and trembling lest I should have my own words used in judgment against me at the last great day... It will be a dreadful thing to have known how to use the bow, and yet not to win the victory oneself.[43]

To avoid this tragedy, it is helpful to deliver the sermon to yourself with heart-searching passion. The initial transformation brought about by every message should happen in your heart in the solitude of your study.

When preaching the sermon to yourself, it can be helpful to insert your first name every time you use the words "we" or "you." In doing so, you are simply personalizing the message by turning the sword of the Spirit upon yourself in order that God may deal with you in the depths of your heart.

> When a minister is studying a sermon, his best preparation comes through his feeling, himself, the power of his subject. He rehearses his discourse before the little audience of his own heart and conscience; and in observing the effect produced, he arrives at some idea of how the Word will operate upon others. He that has run the gauntlet of a truth, and felt all the heavy blows which it levels at his own conscience, is likely to deliver that truth to others with tender sympathy and full assurance. Such a preparation I think I have had, and I pray that you may be benefited by it.[44]

Another way you can preach and apply the sermon to yourself is to pray-eraphrase your finished sermon into heart-searching questions. Consider the following examples:

- Are you elevating any sin above your own?
- Are you attempting to preach the demons away from your own heart apart from confession, repentance and obedience?
- Does this message clearly echo the preaching of the apostles?
- Is the person and work of Christ central to this message or is it peripheral or absent?
- Are you prepared to preach this message in the power of the Holy Spirit?

43. Spurgeon, *Metropolitan Tabernacle Pulpit*, 12:343.
44. Spurgeon, *Metropolitan Tabernacle Pulpit*, 35:361.

Regardless of how you choose to accomplish this task of preaching the sermon to yourself, it is imperative that you do so. Spurgeon concludes, "The preacher who neglects to preach to himself has a very important part of his audience. He who never in his silent privacy speaketh a word to his own soul, doth not know where to begin his preaching. We must first address our own soul. If we can move that by the words we may utter, we may hope to have some power with the souls of others."[45] Unapplied truth quickly spoils and becomes unappetizing truth. Do not fail to assimilate what you preach into your own heart and life.

---

45. Spurgeon, *New Park Street Pulpit*, 3:293.

# 7

# Seeking the Spirit

> Oh, my brethren, think not that the preaching of the Word is on a level with mere lecturing or talking upon subjects that may be of thrilling interest. The moment a man preaches God's truth, if God has sent him, he is gifted with a power which no learning or eloquence can confer upon another man whom God has not called. A man preaches with the Holy Ghost sent down from heaven; his every word is a thunder stroke—one tremendous lightning blast amongst the sons of men—and God owns him, and God blesses him, or, if God does not own him and does not bless him, he has good reason to believe that God never sent him—that he is not a servant of God—that the Lord has not raised up nor qualified him for the salvation of the souls of men.[1]

WHEN SPURGEON PREACHED TO thousands, the Holy Spirit was the most important person in the vast room. He sought to bring the person, power, and manifest presence of the Holy Spirit with him to each service and every sermon. The cry of Spurgeon's heart was, "I believe in the Holy Spirit!" This was much more than a mental acknowledgement to his existence. It was an active recognition of, and reliance upon, the person and power of the Holy Spirit himself.

1. Spurgeon, *Metropolitan Tabernacle Pulpit*, 6:377.

> We need the Spirit in another manner, namely, as the live coal from off the altar, touching our lips, so that when we have knowledge and wisdom to select the fitting portion of truth, we may enjoy freedom of utterance when we come to deliver it. "Lo, this hath touched thy lips." Oh, how gloriously a man speaks when his lips are blistered with the live coal from the altar feeling the burning power of the truth, not only in his inmost soul, but on the very lip with which he is speaking![2]

To preach with this biblical perspective requires that you live in the perpetual awareness of your complete inadequacy. To attempt even a single sermon without utter desperate dependence upon the Holy Spirit is to fail.

The Holy Spirit is not dependent upon you as a messenger, rather you are dependent upon him for a message. As a heaven-sent messenger, you are barren at best. Without the person of the Holy Spirit, you are void of power and vulnerable to pride. You must develop a humble hesitancy to enter the study or proceed to the pulpit without death to self and deference to the Holy Spirit. The Holy Spirit will enable you to overcome pride and pretense to fill you with power. Death to the self! Alive to the Spirit!

Spurgeon sought to be filled, led, and empowered by the Holy Spirit, in and out of the pulpit. Following his example means pursuing the cultivated presence of God in private with a view to the manifest presence of God in public. Spurgeon provides helpful insight regarding the practice of cultivating the presence of the Holy Spirit in the study:

> Student in the school of Christ, wouldst thou be wise? Ask not the theologian to expound to thee his system of divinity; but, sitting down meekly at the feet of Jesus, ask that His Spirit may instruct thee ... Whenever thou readest the Bible, cry to the Spirit, "Open thou mine eyes, that I may behold wondrous things out of thy law." The Spirit gives eye-salve to the blind ... Those who are taught of the Spirit often surpass those who are taught of man. I have met with an entirely uninstructed clod-hopper, in the country, who never went to school for one hour in his life, who yet knew more about the Holy Scriptures than many a clergyman trained at the University ... If we would learn in the heart, and not merely in the head, we must be taught entirely by the Holy Spirit. What you learn from man, you can unlearn; but what you learn of the Spirit is fixed indelibly in your heart and conscience, and not even Satan himself can steal it from you.[3]

---

2. Spurgeon, *Metropolitan Tabernacle Pulpit*, 21:601.
3. Spurgeon, *Metropolitan Tabernacle Pulpit*, 53:342–43.

In your study, are you more focused on constructing a sermon, or on cultivating the Spirit? Are you motivated more by the urgency of Sunday or the unction of the Spirit? There is a subtle temptation to be more focused on finishing the sermon than on being filled the Spirit. You are a man of God, who will stand before the people of God, to expound the Word of God. This requires the blessing of the Spirit of God. Usefulness demands holiness from the Holy Spirit.

The Holy Spirit empowers men for ministry, not ministry for men. It is the activity of the Holy Spirit that is accompanied by the anointing of the Holy Spirit. Therefore, the most important reality in the pulpit is not a prepared sermon but the presence of the Spirit.

## Prayerfully Cultivate the Fruit of the Spirit in Your Life and Ministry

Fruit-bearing sermons are preached by fruit-bearing servants: "The fruit of the Spirit is love, joy, peace, longsuffering, kindness, goodness, faithfulness, gentleness, self-control" (Gal 5:22–23). Our fruitfulness begins and continues with the fruit of the Spirit. Does your pulpit ministry reflect the fruit of the Spirit? If the complete focus of your ministry is on the external, tangible, and measurable fruit which it produces, you have become short-sighted. It is the bearing of the fruit of the Spirit which gives birth to eternal and lasting fruit in your life and ministry. A gift of the Spirit, even the preaching of the Word, quickly becomes distorted when divorced from the fruit of the Spirit. Spurgeon explains:

> Perhaps "love" is put first not only because it is a right royal virtue, nearest akin to the divine perfection, but because it is a comprehensive grace and contains all the others. All the commandments are fulfilled in one word and that word is "love." And all the fruits of the Spirit are contained in that one most sweet, most blessed, most heavenly, most God-like grace of love. See that you abound in love to the great Father and all His family, for if you fail in the first point, how can you succeed in the second? Above all things put on love, which is the bond of perfectness![4]

The Spirit's fruitfulness in your life will determine your fitness for ministry! Consider your ministry under this scriptural searchlight: "Though I speak with the tongues of men and of angels, but have not love, I have become

---

4. Spurgeon, *Metropolitan Tabernacle Pulpit*, 27:73.

sounding brass or a clanging cymbal. And though I have the gift of prophecy, and understand all mysteries and all knowledge, and though I have all faith, so that I could remove mountains, but have not love, I am nothing (1 Cor 13:1–2). A loveless ministry is a lifeless ministry.

A crop failure of the fruit of the Spirit is an exposure of your heart. Spurgeon observes, "The Spirit of God is not barren! If He is in you, He must and will inevitably produce His own legitimate fruit."[5] Is your life and ministry producing legitimate fruit or artificial fruit? Consider the artificial fruit in a local church described by James: "Where do wars and fights come from among you? Do they not come from your desires for pleasure that war in your members. You lust and do not have. You murder and covet and cannot obtain. You fight and war. Yet you do not have because you do not ask. You ask and do not receive, because you ask amiss, that you may spend it on your pleasures" (Jas 4:1–3). It is obvious that this describes people who are better at *preying* on one another than they are at *praying* for one another.

Spirit-born prayer produces Spirit-birthed fruit! Flesh-born prayer produces the rotten fruit of the flesh. Spurgeon warns, "The worst enemy we have is the flesh ... All the fire which the devil can bring from hell could do us little harm if we had not so much fuel in our nature. It is the powder in the magazine of the old man which is our perpetual danger. When we are guarding against foes outside, we must not forget to be continually on our watch-tower against the foe of foes within."[6] He then emphasizes: "On the other hand, our best friend, who loves us better than we love ourselves, is the Holy Spirit."[7]

It is tragic when the preacher and people are *preying* on one another. Many pastors have been devastated by a back-biting campaign of cannibalistic carnality. Preachers can also carnally view their congregation as a necessary nuisance for his pulpit prowess. Both preacher and people are fully capable of grieving the Holy Spirit. The apostle Paul admonishes, "Let no corrupt word proceed out of your mouth, but what is good for necessary edification, that it may impart grace to the hearers. And do not grieve the Holy Spirit of God, by whom you were sealed for the day of redemption. Let all bitterness, wrath, anger, clamor, and evil speaking be put away from you, with all malice. And be kind to one another, tenderhearted, forgiving one another, even as God in Christ forgave you" (Eph 4:29–32). Grieving

---

5. Spurgeon, *Metropolitan Tabernacle Pulpit*, 27:73.
6. Spurgeon, *Metropolitan Tabernacle Pulpit*, 30:289.
7. Spurgeon, *Metropolitan Tabernacle Pulpit*, 30:289.

and quenching the Holy Spirit are simultaneous in the life of a local church. Is your pulpit ministry nurturing the fruit of the Spirit in your heart and in your hearers? Or is your pulpit ministry producing fleshly fruit which grieves and quenches the Holy Spirit? Jesus said, "Beware of false prophets, who come to you in sheep's clothing, but inwardly they are ravenous wolves. You will know them by their fruits. Do men gather grapes from thornbushes or figs from thistles? Even so, every good tree bears good fruit, but a bad tree bears bad fruit. A good tree cannot bear bad fruit, nor can a bad tree bear good fruit. Every tree that does not bear good fruit is cut down and thrown into the fire. Therefore, by their fruits you will know them" (Matt 7:15–20).

## Daily Bring Yourself under the Scrutiny of the Holy Spirit

> "I believe in the Holy Ghost." Having pronounced that sentence as a matter of creed, I hope we can also repeat it as a devout soliloquy forced to our lips by personal experience. To us the presence and work of the Holy Spirit are the ground of our confidence as to the wisdom and hopefulness of our life work. If we had not believed in the Holy Ghost we should have laid down our ministry long ere this, for "who is sufficient for these things?" Our hope of success, and our strength for continuing the service, lie in our belief that the Spirit of the Lord resteth upon us.[8]

What the Holy Spirit knows about you is much more important than what people assume about you. What the Holy Spirit sees in you is more significant than what people perceive about you. Be pleased with pleasing him every day! When you are cheered by people, quickly bring yourself back under the scrutiny of the Holy Spirit. When others criticize you allow the Holy Spirit to scrutinize you beyond the surface from which the critique of people springs. Allow him to probe the depths of your heart.

> The Holy Ghost is our Sanctifier, and when we feel sin raging within, how can we hope to conquer without His aid? . . . Holiness is too divine a work to be wrought in us by any inferior hand. He who made the first rough draft must put in the perfecting stroke, or all will remain incomplete. And He, also, is our power

---

8. Spurgeon, *Lectures to My Students*, 185.

> for practical service—the "power from on high" for which apostles tarried of old. If the Holy Ghost be not with the preacher, vain are his pleadings with men . . . I dread beyond all things the Spirit's withdrawal. Death has not half the terror of that thought. I would sooner die a thousand times, than lose the helpful presence of the Holy Ghost.[9]

The withdrawal of which Spurgeon speaks does not refer to the loss of salvation but to the withdrawal of the empowering of the Holy Spirit which rests upon his holy vessels. This is a dynamic of which every preacher is aware. Cherishing the active presence of the Holy Spirit should sensitize you to any hint of sin in your heart. It was this depth of piety and godliness that marked Spurgeon as a man of God.

Remember that you and the Holy Spirit will never be equal co-laborers in ministry. The Holy Spirit is the one who calls, shapes, equips, and empowers those whom he chooses for proclaiming the Word of God. It is only through submission to his divine nature and will that you are made fit to serve as his instrument. Spurgeon describes how the Holy Spirit uses his pruning process to prepare his servants: "A good man, who feels the power of the word pruning him of this and that superfluity, sets to work, in the power of the Holy Ghost, to do more for Jesus . . . The more he is pruned, the more he serves his Lord."[10] He further expounds upon the quantity of fruitfulness due to divine pruning: "One tree can only produce one kind of fruit usually, but the Lord's people can produce many . . . and the more they are pruned the more they will produce. There will be all kinds of fruits, both new and old, which they will lay up for their Beloved."[11] Perhaps the greatest blessing which Spurgeon recognized from pruning had to do with divinely produced quality. He asserts:

> There will be more in quality, too. The man may not pray more, but he will pray more earnestly; he may not preach more sermons, but he will preach them more thoroughly from his heart, with a greater unction. It may be that he will not be more in communion with God as to time, but it will be a closer communion; he will throw himself more thoroughly into the divine element of communion, and will become more hearty in all that he does.[12]

---

9. Spurgeon, *Metropolitan Tabernacle Pulpit*, 16:559.
10. Spurgeon, *Metropolitan Tabernacle Pulpit*, 13:563.
11. Spurgeon, *Metropolitan Tabernacle Pulpit*, 13:563.
12. Spurgeon, *Metropolitan Tabernacle Pulpit*, 13:563.

The Holy Spirit cultivates a hunger for holiness within us. To be filled with the Holy Spirit in your preaching requires the intentional removal of everything that corrupts and clutters your life. You must make way for the cultivated presence of the Holy Spirit. To be filled with the Spirit is to be emptied of that which is not of God in your life.

## Strive to be a Spirit-Filled Preacher of Christ-Filled Sermons

> He (the Holy Spirit) will glorify Me, for He will take of what is Mine and declare *it* to you. All things that the Father has are Mine. Therefore I said that He will take of Mine and declare *it* to you (John 16:14–15).

A Spirit-filled preacher will preach a Christ-filled message! Spurgeon resounds:

> It is the chief office of the Holy Spirit to glorify Christ. He does many things, but this is what He aims at in all of them, to glorify Christ. Brethren, what the Holy Spirit does must be right for us to imitate; therefore, let us endeavor to glorify Christ. To what higher ends can we devote ourselves, than to something to which God the Holy Spirit devotes Himself? Be this, then, your continual prayer "Blessed Spirit, help me to ever glorify the Lord Jesus Christ!"[13]

Spurgeon tenaciously kept Christ at the forefront of his pulpit ministry. He believed that to fail in this matter was to weaken and neutralize his preaching: "The Spirit of God bears no witness to Christless sermons. Leave Jesus out of your preaching, and the Holy Spirit will never come upon you."[14] Because of this deep conviction, he never diverted from preaching Christ. Preachers who are Spirit-led, and whose sermons are Scripture-bred, will exalt the person and work of Jesus Christ. A man may preach a sermon on Christ apart from the filling of the Holy Spirit, but a preacher cannot be filled with the Holy Spirit without preaching sermons that exalt Jesus Christ.

Contrary to popular notions, the preaching of the early church never shifted from preaching Christ to a primary emphasis on the Holy Spirit. On the Day of Pentecost, the coming of the Holy Spirit simply accelerated and

---

13. Spurgeon, *Metropolitan Tabernacle Pulpit*, 40:481.
14. Spurgeon, *Metropolitan Tabernacle Pulpit*, 26:315.

deepened their Christ-centered focus. Consider the following examples of the preaching of the early church:

- Peter: Men of Israel, hear these words: Jesus of Nazareth, a Man attested by God to you by miracles, wonders, and signs which God did through Him in your midst, as you yourselves also know—Him, being delivered by the determined purpose and foreknowledge of God, you have taken by lawless hands, have crucified, and put to death; whom God raised up, having loosed the pains of death, because it was not possible that He should be held by it (Acts 2:22–24).

- Peter: Men of Israel, why do you marvel at this? Or why look so intently at us, as though by our own power or godliness we had made this man walk? The God of Abraham, Isaac, and Jacob, the God of our fathers, glorified His Servant Jesus, whom you delivered up and denied in the presence of Pilate, when he was determined to let *Him* go. But you denied the Holy One and the Just, and asked for a murderer to be granted to you, and killed the Prince of life, whom God raised from the dead, of which we are witnesses. And His name, through faith in His name, has made this man strong, whom you see and know. Yes, the faith which *comes* through Him has given him this perfect soundness in the presence of you all (Acts 3:12–16).

- Then Peter, filled with the Holy Spirit, said to them, "Rulers of the people and elders of Israel: If we this day are judged for a good deed *done* to a helpless man, by what means he has been made well, let it be known to you all, and to all the people of Israel, that by the name of Jesus Christ of Nazareth, whom you crucified, whom God raised from the dead, by Him this man stands here before you whole. This is the 'stone which was rejected by you builders, which has become the chief cornerstone.' Nor is there salvation in any other, for there is no other name under heaven given among men by which we must be saved" (Acts 4:8–12).

- The apostles: And daily in the temple, and in every house, they did not cease teaching and preaching Jesus *as* the Christ (Acts 5:42).

- Then Philip opened his mouth, and beginning at this Scripture, preached Jesus to him . . . Then Philip went down to the city of Samaria and preached Christ to them (Acts 8:5, 35).

- Paul: "Men *and* brethren, sons of the family of Abraham, and those among you who fear God, to you the word of this salvation has been sent. For those who dwell in Jerusalem, and their rulers, because they did not know Him, nor even the voices of the Prophets which are read every Sabbath, have fulfilled *them* in condemning *Him*. And though they found no cause for death *in Him*, they asked Pilate that He should be put to death. Now when they had fulfilled all that was written concerning Him, they took *Him* down from the tree and laid *Him* in a tomb. But God raised Him from the dead" (Acts 13:26–30).

- Then Paul dwelt two whole years in his own rented house, and received all who came to him, preaching the kingdom of God and teaching the things which concern the Lord Jesus Christ with all confidence, no one forbidding him (Acts 28:30–31).

It was also this preaching of Christ, and his resurrection, which the enemies of the gospel bitterly opposed:

- Now as they spoke to the people, the priests, the captain of the temple, and the Sadducees came upon them, being greatly disturbed that they taught the people and preached in Jesus the resurrection from the dead (Acts 4:1–2).

- Now when they saw the boldness of Peter and John, and perceived that they were uneducated and untrained men, they marveled. And they realized that they had been with Jesus. And seeing the man who had been healed standing with them, they could say nothing against it. But when they had commanded them to go aside out of the council, they conferred among themselves, saying, "What shall we do to these men? For, indeed, that a notable miracle has been done through them *is* evident to all who dwell in Jerusalem, and we cannot deny *it*. But so that it spreads no further among the people, let us severely threaten them, that from now on they speak to no man in this name." So they called them and commanded them not to speak at all nor teach in the name of Jesus (Acts 4:17–18).

- And the high priest asked them, saying, "Did we not strictly command you not to teach in this name? And look, you have filled Jerusalem with your doctrine, and intend to bring this Man's blood on us!" (Acts 5:27–28).

- When they heard *this,* they were furious and plotted to kill them. Then one in the council stood up, a Pharisee named Gamaliel, a teacher of the law held in respect by all the people, and commanded them to put the apostles outside for a little while. And he said to them: "Men of Israel, take heed to yourselves what you intend to do regarding these men. For some time ago Theudas rose up, claiming to be somebody. A number of men, about four hundred, joined him. He was slain, and all who obeyed him were scattered and came to nothing. After this man, Judas of Galilee rose up in the days of the census, and drew away many people after him. He also perished, and all who obeyed him were dispersed. And now I say to you, keep away from these men and let them alone; for if this plan or this work is of men, it will come to nothing; but if it is of God, you cannot overthrow it—lest you even be found to fight against God." And they agreed with him, and when they had called for the apostles and beaten *them*, they commanded that they should not speak in the name of Jesus, and let them go (Acts 5:33–40).

- When they heard these things they were cut to the heart, and they gnashed at him with *their* teeth. But he, being full of the Holy Spirit, gazed into heaven and saw the glory of God, and Jesus standing at the right hand of God, and said, "Look! I see the heavens opened and the Son of Man standing at the right hand of God!" Then they cried out with a loud voice, stopped their ears, and ran at him with one accord; and they cast *him* out of the city and stoned *him*. And the witnesses laid down their clothes at the feet of a young man named Saul (Acts 7:54–58).

The person and work of Jesus Christ were conspicuously obvious in the preaching of the early church, and the power of the Holy Spirit rested upon their Christ-centered messages.

This example of the early church left an indelible imprint upon the preaching of Spurgeon: "He who can preach Christ is the true minister. Let him preach anything else in the world, he has not proved his calling, but if he shall preach Jesus and the resurrection, he is in the apostolical succession. If Christ crucified be the great delight of his soul, the very marrow of his teaching, the fatness of his ministry, he has proved his calling as an ambassador of Christ."[15] To be a *true* minister with a *true* ministry, you must allow the Holy Spirit to magnify Christ in your messages. Spurgeon reiterates, "This makes all the difference in preaching. Ministers may preach sound doctrine by itself, and be utterly without unction; but those who preach it in connection with the person of the blessed Lord have an

---

15. Spurgeon, *Metropolitan Tabernacle Pulpit*, 13:209.

anointing which nothing else can give. Christ Himself, by the Holy Ghost, is the savor of a true ministry."[16] In light of these statements, "Are you a true minister?" and "Do you have a true ministry?"

When you are true to Christ in your walk and in your work, then the Holy Spirit will be true to you. Spurgeon expressed great confidence in this reality: "If I preach, and the Holy Spirit is with me, Christ will be glorified; but if I were able to speak with the tongues of men, and of angels, but without the power of the Holy Spirit, Christ would not be glorified . . . It is not merely we who speak, but the Spirit of the Lord, who speaks by us."[17] To attempt to effectively preach Christ apart from the filling and empowering of the Holy Spirit is to attempt the impossible. It would be just as impossible as driving an automobile without any fuel, or even worse, without any engine. But, when you are filled with the Spirit, there is a freedom and fullness in your preaching. Spurgeon asserts, "Where there is nothing of Christ, brethren, there is nothing of unction, nothing of savor . . . Leave Christ out of your preaching, and you have taken the milk from the children, you have taken the strong meat from the men."[18] He then avows, "But if your object as a teacher or preacher is to glorify Christ, and to lead men to love Him and trust Him, why, that is the very work upon which the heart of God himself is set. The Lord and you are pulling together, and God the Holy Ghost can set his seal to a work like that."[19] Are you preaching contrary to the Holy Spirit or in cooperation with him? To concentrate on Christ is to comply with the Holy Spirit:

> Just preach a sermon that is full of Christ, and throw it unto your congregation, as you throw a net into the sea—you need not look where they are, nor try to fit your sermon to different cases; but, throw it in, and as sure as God's Word is what it is, it shall not return to Him void; it shall accomplish that which he pleases, and prosper in the thing whereto he hath sent it. The gospel never was unsuccessful yet, when it was preached with the demonstration of the Spirit and of power.[20]

If you have ever preached "with the demonstration of the Spirit and of power," you know that nothing less is sufficient or satisfying.

16. Spurgeon, *Metropolitan Tabernacle Pulpit*, 35:206.
17. Spurgeon, *Metropolitan Tabernacle Pulpit*, 40:484.
18. Spurgeon, *Metropolitan Tabernacle Pulpit*, 41:187.
19. Spurgeon, *Metropolitan Tabernacle Pulpit*, 41:187.
20. Spurgeon, *Metropolitan Tabernacle Pulpit*, 3:259.

SEEKING THE SPIRIT

## Plead in Prayer for the Unction and Anointing of the Holy Spirit

> We often speak about this, but in truth, it is unspeakable—the power of the Holy Spirit ... The minister studies his text; but does he ask for a baptism of the Holy Ghost? I am afraid that this spiritual qualification, the most essential of all, is frequently overlooked. Then, the Lord have mercy upon us ... It were better to be dumb than to speak only in the power of our own spirit. It were better to lay the finger on the lip than to begin to talk before our message has been burnt into us by the Holy Ghost. Wait for the live coal from off the altar to blister thy lip, for then only canst thou speak with power when thou thyself hast felt the fire of the Spirit.[21]

Through the annals of church history, unction was a word commonly used in reference to preaching. But it seems to be missing in many contexts about preaching today. A biblical definition of *unction* is preaching "in demonstration of the Spirit and of power" (1 Cor 2:4). Unction is the Spirit's seal upon the servant and the sermon. Spurgeon declares, "The man of God is nothing without the Spirit of God. It is the sine qua non of a ministry from God that it should be in the power of the Spirit."[22] It is unction that distinguishes the delivery of a sermon from the delivery of a common speech or lecture. There is a vast difference between delivering a well-crafted sermon and a Spirit-anointed message from God. Unction empowers you to be useful. To be filled with the Holy Spirit is to be fueled for holy service! The unction of the Holy Spirit will make your intimate walk with God conspicuous and contagious.

Unction is the supernatural enabling of the Holy Spirit within the servant and upon the sermon. Unction is critical, crucial, and costly. Spurgeon emphasizes that unction is indispensable and non-negotiable:

> The Holy Spirit must inflame the minister. The man who never takes fire, how is he sent of God? He who never glows and burns, what knows he of the baptism of the Holy Spirit, which is also the baptism of fire? Pray, therefore, for the supply of the Spirit. Without the Spirit every ministry lacks that subtle, I was about to say indescribable, something which is known by the name of unction. Nobody here can tell what unction is. He knows that the Spirit of

---

21. Spurgeon, *Metropolitan Tabernacle Pulpit*, 39:497–98.
22. Spurgeon, *Metropolitan Tabernacle Pulpit*, 19:609.

> God gives it, and he knows when it is in a discourse, and when it is absent. Unction is, in fact, the power of God.[23]

Although the presence of unction is unexplainable, its absence is undeniable and inexcusable. Most parishioners are more aware of a functionless ministry than they are of an unctionless ministry. However, God is more concerned with *unctionality* than he is with functionality, because an unctionless ministry is a dysfunctional ministry.

When church members reflect on the demands of pastoral ministry, they tend to focus on the heavy schedule and emotional load a pastor carries. However, the greatest weight upon a pastor's life is his desperate need for the filling and empowering of the Spirit of God. This should weigh heaviest upon your heart and mind as you weekly contemplate your responsibility of entering the pulpit as an ambassador for Christ. No matter what kind of week you have, you will be required to get in the pulpit with a message from God. The unction of the Holy Spirit must rest upon you as well as your message. To be called by God is to be consecrated and controlled by the Spirit of God. This requires a crucifying of self through surrender and submission to the Holy Spirit. The choice is either death to self or death to your ministry:

> Imagine a dead preacher preaching a dead sermon to dead sinners: what can possibly come of it? Here is a beautiful essay which has been admirably elaborated, and it is coldly read to the cold-hearted sinner. It smells of the midnight oil, but it has no heavenly unction, no divine power resting upon it, nor, perhaps, is that power even looked for. What good can come of such a production? . . . It is only as the Spirit of God shall come upon God's servant and shall make, the word which he preaches to drop as a living seed into the heart that any result can follow his ministry; and it is only as the Spirit of God shall then follow that seed and keep it alive in the soul of the listener that we can expect those who profess to be converted to take root and grow to maturity of grace, and become our sheaves at the last.[24]

The spiritually decaying preacher can only deliver sermons that carry the putrid scent of death. These sermons are nothing more than a carnal carcass. Spurgeon observes:

> The same sermon may be preached, and the same words uttered, but without unction there is nothing in it. The unction of the Holy

---

23. Spurgeon, *Metropolitan Tabernacle Pulpit*, 19:609.
24. Spurgeon, *Metropolitan Tabernacle Pulpit*, 23:16.

## Seeking the Spirit

> One is true power. Therefore, brethren, we need your prayers that we may obtain the supply of the Spirit upon our ministry, for otherwise it will lack unction, which will amount to lacking heart and soul. It will be a dead ministry, and how can a dead ministry be of any service to the people of God?[25]

Spurgeon made himself accountable to his congregation by urging them to pray toward a living ministry among them. The Holy Spirit must breathe life *into* you to breathe life *through* you.

This filling of the Holy Spirit will fill a preacher with insight and power unknown to the intellectual orator. Do you trust the Holy Spirit to fill the "white spaces" in your sermon manuscript or sermon notes during the delivery of your message? The very same trust which you place in the Holy Spirit when contemplating the blank white page upon which you will write the sermon is required for the "white spaces" during its delivery. You never come to a point of independence in the preparation and/or preaching of sermons. Your dependence upon the Holy Spirit should remain active from before the first stroke of the pen through and beyond the final "Amen."

## Refuse to Enter the Pulpit without the Filling of the Holy Spirit

> Pray in the Holy Ghost, preach in the Holy Ghost, and do not believe in the conversion of a single soul apart from the Spirit of God. Go and preach, "Believe on the Lord Jesus Christ, and thou shalt be saved," as fully and as freely as you can, but remember that your preaching cannot, of itself, raise one soul out of its lost estate. This will be your comfort, that the Spirit of God will work with you and through you if you rely upon Him and depend wholly upon Him.[26]

The preacher must be distinguished by a terrifying fear of entering the pulpit without the empowering and enabling of the Holy Spirit. In your preaching ministry you should settle for nothing less than a passionate pursuit of the presence of the Holy Spirit. Spirit-filled preaching is born in the study. You will never be more Spirit-filled in the pulpit than you have been Spirit-focused in your study. An atmosphere of dependence upon the

---

25. Spurgeon, *Metropolitan Tabernacle Pulpit*, 19:60.
26. Spurgeon, *Metropolitan Tabernacle Pulpit*, 54:588.

Holy Spirit must permeate the entire preparation process. Spurgeon speaks to this:

> There is a way of preaching, in which a great divine has evidently displayed his vast learning and talent; and there is another way of preaching, in which a faithful servant of Jesus Christ, depending upon his Lord, has spoken in his Master's name, and left a rich unction behind . . . May the Lord do unto us according to His word, "I have put my words in thy mouth, and I have covered thee in the shadow of my hand."[27]

The person and power of the Holy Spirit is not an optional additive for your ministry. He is your essential ally. This is to be your primary and prized relationship within the study and the pulpit. Spurgeon sheds light on just how real this relationship should be:

> You have heard the story of the Welsh preacher who had not arrived when the service ought to have been begun, and his host sent a boy to the room to tell him that it was time to go to preach. The boy came hurrying back, and said, "Sir, he is in his room, but I do not think he is coming. There is somebody in there with him. I heard him speaking very loudly, and very earnestly, and I heard him say that if that other person did not come with him, he would not come at all, and the other one never answered him, so I do not think he will come." "Ah!" said the host, who understood the case, "he will come, and the other one will come with him." Oh! it is good sowing when the sower goes forth to sow, and the Other comes with him! Then we go forth with steeped seed, seed that is sprouting in our hands as we go forth. This does not happen naturally, but it does happen spiritually. It seems to grow while we are handling it, for there is life in it; and when it is sown, there will be life in it to our hearers.[28]

You should desire a pulpit ministry filled and fueled by the Holy Spirit. To be full of the Holy Spirit, you must be wholly his! This surrender to the Spirit should increase the freedom with which you develop and deliver the sermon. It should strengthen you rather than stifle you. If your sermon delivery is not balanced with the guidance of the Holy Spirit, your preaching will quickly become carnal and powerless. Your goal is to spend the

---

27. Spurgeon, "Under His Shadow," 47.
28. Spurgeon, *Metropolitan Tabernacle Pulpit*, 49:368.

week emptying yourself of sin and self, that you may be filled with the Holy Spirit. To be pure is to be prepared. Purity is the pathway to power!

The preacher should become a fountain overflowing with the power and authority of God. Without the Holy Spirit, your messages are a mere trickling of living water at best and a barren desert at worst. Spurgeon laments, "I know that it is dreadful work to be bound to preach when one is not conscious of the aid of the Spirit of God! It is like pouring water out of bottomless buckets, or feeding hungry souls out of empty baskets."[29] Empty messengers deliver empty messages! You must be filled to overflowing with the Spirit of God! When you are full of the Spirit of God, your mind will be full of the Word of God, and your preaching will fully exalt the Son of God. Spirit-filled preaching fosters Spirit-convicted listening.

Because you are an instrument of the Holy Spirit, your spiritual preparation should exceed your mental preparation for the pulpit. The Spirit of God longs to feed the people of God upon the Word of God through you. He alone can satisfactorily sustain his people with a proper diet of truth. A Spirit-bred and Spirit-led pulpit ministry produces a Spirit-fed church. If your sermons are to have spiritual nutritional value, the Word of God and the Spirit of God must be at the heart of the preparation process. Failing at this point can cause your preaching to cater to congregational carnality and cater to congregational cravings.

A Spirit-less preacher quickly becomes a spineless preacher. Listen to the testimony of the apostles and the early church: "And when they had prayed, the place where they were assembled was shaken; and they were all filled with the Holy Spirit, and they spoke the Word of God with boldness" (Acts 4:31). It is the Spirit himself that births boldness within his messengers! To be filled is to be fearless!

Much confusion has swirled around the filling of the Holy Spirit. How can a man know if he is a Spirit-filled preacher? There is one sure and certain evidence of the filling of the Holy Spirit in the preacher's life and ministry: if you are filled with the Holy Spirit, your message will be filled with Jesus Christ. If your message is filled with the Savior, it will be fueled by the Spirit. "With great power the apostles gave witness to the resurrection of the Lord Jesus. And great grace was upon them all" (Acts 4:33).

---

29. Spurgeon, *Metropolitan Tabernacle Pulpit*, 22:354.

## Wield the Sword of the Spirit in the Power of the Spirit

The Holy Spirit is intimately identified with prayer and the ministry of the Word: "And take the helmet of salvation, and the sword of the Spirit, which is the word of God; praying always with all prayer and supplication in the Spirit, being watchful to this end with all perseverance and supplication for all the saints—and for me, that utterance may be given to me, that I may open my mouth boldly to make known the mystery of the gospel, for which I am an ambassador in chains; that in it I may speak boldly, as I ought to speak" (Eph 6:17–20). Praying in the Holy Spirit and preaching from the sword of the Spirit are non-negotiable in your pulpit ministry. Spurgeon says, "We do not stand up in our pulpits to display our skill in spiritual sword play, but we come to actual fighting: our object is to drive the sword of the Spirit through men's hearts."[30] When prayerfully wielded, the sword of the Spirit is a battle-ready blade: "For the word of God *is* living and powerful, and sharper than any two-edged sword, piercing even to the division of soul and spirit, and of joints and marrow, and is a discerner of the thoughts and intents of the heart. And there is no creature hidden from His sight, but all things *are* naked and open to the eyes of Him to whom we *must give* account" (Heb 4:12–13). Are you wholly consecrated to the Holy Spirit and committed to the sword of the Spirit?

Not only does the Holy Spirit inspire and illumine Scripture, but he also endeavors to influence your grip upon it. Men who allow the Spirit to intensify their grip on the Word of God in private will not grope for truth in the pulpit. Jesus told the apostles, "The Holy Spirit, whom the Father will send in My name, He will teach you all things, and bring to your remembrance all things that I said to you" (John 14:26). As you relinquish control of your life to the Holy Spirit, he powerfully recalls the Word of God to your mind. The Holy Spirit is faithful to those who are faithful to God's Word. Spurgeon offers these encouraging words:

> There are times, beloved, when the ordained servant of the living God will have nothing to do in preaching, but just to open his mouth and allow the words to flow. He will scarcely need to think; but the thoughts will be injected into his mind, and while he preaches he will feel there is a power accompanying his word. His hearers too will discern it . . . It will often happen that God's children will find an influence and a might irresistible going with the word. They have heard that minister before, they were delighted

---

30. Spurgeon, *Lectures to My Students*, 194.

with him, they trusted that they had been edified and profited, but on that day there was a special striking home, every word fell on good soil, every blow hit the mark, there was no arrow shot which did not go into the center of the soul—there was not a syllable uttered which was not like the word of Jehovah Himself, speaking either from Sinai, or Calvary.[31]

Ultimately, your grip on the sword of the Spirit is equal to the Holy Spirit's grip on you. You must be fashioned by him for him to fuel your preaching as you wield his sword.

The sword of the Spirit is spiritual in nature. It is not to be wielded with conceited motives or carnal methods. The apostle Paul contends, "For though we walk in the flesh, we do not war according to the flesh. For the weapons of our warfare *are* not carnal but mighty in God for pulling down strongholds, casting down arguments and every high thing that exalts itself against the knowledge of God, bringing every thought into captivity to the obedience of Christ" (2 Cor 10:3–5). Spurgeon emphasizes:

> The spiritual weapons which can be wielded by the Christian minister . . . are not to be despised, for while not fleshy, they are mighty through God. God is in them. God is with those who use them. The sword of the Spirit, which is the Word of God; the arrows of truth which pierce the consciences of men; the weapon of all-prayer; the influence of the Holy Spirit—that divine power—such weapons as these are by God's power made mighty to the overthrow of spiritual principalities and powers. Truth and holiness are the appointed engines for the pulling down of the castles of evil.[32]

Spiritual warfare demands spiritual weapons. Never is this more obvious than when the Word of God is preached. Only that which comes from God's armory equips the preacher for Satan's arsenal. Consider God's powerful armory paired against Satan's persistent arsenal:

- For Satan's arsenal of deception, the believer has been armed with the *belt of truth*.

- For Satan's onslaught of defilement, the believer is protected by the *breastplate of righteousness*.

- For Satan's device of despair, the believer has been fitted with *the footwear of the preparation of the gospel of peace*.

---

31. Spurgeon, *New Park Street Pulpit*, 2:163.
32. Spurgeon, *Metropolitan Tabernacle Pulpit*, 25:266.

- For Satan's bombardment of doubt, the believer has the sure protection of *the shield of faith*.
- For Satan's devilish destruction, the believer is fitted with the *helmet of salvation*.
- For Satan's defiance, the sharp blade of *the Spirit's sword* is living and active.

As you ascend the pulpit in the armor of God, you will experience the Holy Spirit wielding his sword through you. The victory is as sure as the battle!

## Prepare and Preach in the Awareness of the Holy Spirit's Intercession

> Likewise the Spirit also helps in our weaknesses. For we do not know what we should pray for as we ought, but the Spirit Himself makes intercession for us with groanings which cannot be uttered. Now He who searches the hearts knows what the mind of the Spirit *is*, because He makes intercession for the saints according to *the will of* God (Rom 8:26–27).

The Holy Spirit illuminates the Word of God to you as he intercedes according to the will of God for you. His illumination and intercession are supernaturally and simultaneously at work when you humbly follow his guidance in sermon preparation. You have been invited into a prayer partnership with the Holy Spirit himself on behalf of those to whom he will preach. Consider the fact that the Holy Spirit already knows those who will be in attendance to hear the sermon which you are in the process of preparing. This is not to make a mystical exaggeration. It simply is to enlarge your view of how the Holy Spirit works in and through you as his messenger. Not only do we "not know what we should pray for as we ought," but we do not know what we should preach as we ought. It is at this intersection of praying and preaching that you must place your ultimate confidence in the intercession of the Holy Spirit.

Just as the Holy Spirit prays for you, he longs to preach through you. The Holy Spirit desires that you walk in the Spirit, pray in the Spirit, and preach in the Spirit.

As you are preparing, the Holy Spirit is praying. When you are in the pulpit pleading with the people, the Holy Spirit is interceding with the Father! Your exposition is undergirded by his intercession. Pause and meditate on the intercession of the Holy Spirit in connection with the delivery of your sermon. "He who searches the hearts knows what the mind of the Spirit *is,* because He makes intercession for the saints according to *the will of* God" (Rom 8:27). While you are representing the Father before the people, the Holy Spirit is representing you before the Father! As you are preaching the Word of God, the Holy Spirit is interceding according to the will of God! The very one who is indwelling you is interceding for you! Spurgeon describes this intercessory role of the Holy Spirit regarding prayer and preaching:

> We need the Hoy Spirit, as an assistant Spirit, in all the duties we have to perform. The most common Christian duty is that of prayer . . . The Holy Spirit is the chariot wheel of prayer. Prayer may be the chariot, the desire may draw it forth, but the Spirit is the very wheel whereby it moveth. He propels the desire, and causeth the chariot to roll swiftly on, and to bear to heaven the supplication of the saints, when the desire of the heart is "according to the will of God." Another duty, to which some of the children of God are called, is that of preaching; and here too we must have the Holy Spirit to enable us. Those whom God calls to preach the gospel are assisted with might from on high. He has said, "Lo, I am with you alway, even unto the end of the world." It is a solemn thing to enter upon the work of the ministry . . . The only endowment necessary for success in the ministry is the endowment of the Holy Ghost.[33]

Contemplate the intercession of the Holy Spirit for you as he wields the sword of the Spirit through you. As you are tightening your grip on his sword, he is tightening his grip on you! As you preach, the unspoken groanings of your heart as you preach are brought before the Father by the intercession of the Holy Spirit. In your pulpit ministry, the Holy Spirit reinforces his illumination with his intercession.

There are two realties at work as you enter the pulpit: (1) the intercession of the Holy Spirit before the Father, (2) the conviction of the Holy Spirit among your hearers. This hidden work of the Spirit of God accompanies the preaching of the Word of God. If you are fashioned by the Holy Spirit, your message will be fortified and fueled by the Holy Spirit. The interference of the enemy is countered, confounded, and conquered by the intercession of the Holy Spirit.

---

33. Spurgeon, *Metropolitan Tabernacle Pulpit*, 53:340.

# 8

# Stirring the Soil

> I was reading yesterday a book by Father Faber, late of the Oratory, at Brompton, a marvellous compound of truth and error. In it he relates a legend to this effect. A certain preacher, whose sermons converted men by scores, received a revelation from heaven that not one of the conversions was owing to his talents or eloquence, but all to the prayers of an illiterate lay-brother, who sat on the pulpit steps, pleading all the time for the success of the sermon. It may in the all-revealing day be so with us. We may discover, after having laboured long and wearily in preaching, that all the honour belongs to another builder, whose prayers were gold, silver, and precious stones, while our sermonisings being apart from prayer, were but hay and stubble.[1]

FOR SPURGEON, TO PRAY well was to preach well. He understood that intercession empowered instruction and that passionate supplication preceded powerful sermons. Hence, he spent focused time stirring the soil of his own heart and pleading with the Holy Spirit to do the same in the hearts of his hearers:

---

1. Spurgeon, *Lectures to My Students*, 46.

> It is in vain to sow unto yourselves till the soil has been prepared by our Father, who is the Husbandman. Even Christ's own seed of the Word, pure from His own hand, brings forth no fruit when it falls on unprepared hearts. His ministers are bound to scatter the seed in all places—on the hard rocks, on the highways and amongst thorns—but still no harvest ever comes till the soil is broken up and made receptive of truth, by the Spirit of God . . . Some soils need plowing and cross plowing.[2]

Spurgeon depended upon the activity of the Holy Spirit in the hearts of those to whom he preached. He refused to substitute his own talent for what only the Holy Spirit could accomplish. He preached in partnership with the Holy Spirit, and the Holy Spirit was the controlling partner!

Without the convicting work of the Holy Spirit, you labor in vain, but in the wake of the work of the Holy Spirit, you labor toward victory. Spurgeon decries the powerless reality of preaching apart from the stirring of the soil of the hearer's heart by the Holy Spirit:

> We have seen too much of trying to sew without the sharp needle of the Spirit's convicting power . . . It is the work of the Spirit of God to convict men of sin, and until they are convicted of sin, they will never be led to seek the righteousness which is of God by Jesus Christ. I am persuaded that wherever there is a real work of divine grace in any soul, it begins with a pulling down—the Holy Spirit does not build on the old foundation![3]

Cooperation with the Holy Spirit makes the preaching of the Word take effect on the human heart. You should consistently plead in prayer for the activity of the Holy Spirit in your preaching.

Spurgeon not only prayed to this end, but he also preached to this end. He talked to God about the heart-condition of his hearers, and he also talked to his hearers about their desperate need for the Holy Spirit to condition their heart toward receptivity to the Word: "There is nothing for men to eat where there are no oxen to plow. And where there are no prayers to plow the soil, you have little to feed upon. We must be more earnest in prayer . . . If you were to compare the Christian to a steam engine, you must make his prayers, fed by the Holy Spirit, to be the very fire which sustains his motion. Prayer is God's chosen vehicle of grace, and he is unwise who

---

2. Spurgeon, *Metropolitan Tabernacle Pulpit*, 21:601.
3. Spurgeon, *Metropolitan Tabernacle Pulpit*, 17:376.

neglects it."[4] Spurgeon prayerfully depended on the Holy Spirit to stir the soil at the outset of entering the study:

> Now the preacher of the Gospel is like the sower. He does not make his seed; the seed is given him by his Master. It would not be possible for a man to make the smallest seed that ever germinated upon the earth, much less that celestial seed of eternal life. The minister goes to his Master in secret, and asks Him to teach him His truth, and thus he fills his basket with the good seed of the kingdom. What the minister has to do is go forth in his Master's name and scatter precious truth.[5]

It is not your responsibility to select the seed or to determine which soil the seed should be sown upon. This is the work of the Holy Spirit. You sow the seed, and the Holy Spirit brings the harvest. When the soil has been prayerfully stirred, and the seed prayerfully received, the Spirit is not quenched in the harvest which he desires. Scatter the seed from hands full of supplication.

## Spend More Time in Secret Supplication Than in Public Proclamation

> Imitate Jesus in secret. When no eye seeth you except the eye of God, when darkness covers you, when you are shut up from the observation of mortals, even then be ye like Jesus Christ. Remember his ardent piety, his secret devotion—how, after laboriously preaching the whole day, he stole away in the midnight shades to cry for help from his God. Recollect how his entire life was constantly sustained by fresh inspirations of the Holy Spirit, derived by prayer. Take care of your secret life... O, my brethren, strive to be more like Jesus Christ. These are times when we want more secret prayer.[6]

Do you spend more time in your study praying than you do in the pulpit preaching? Consider how many times you have spent less time praying about your message than it took you to deliver it. The power of your preaching will never rise above your praying. These two will always move

---

4. Spurgeon, *New Park Street Pulpit*, 1:391.
5. Spurgeon, *New Park Street Pulpit*, 6:173.
6. Spurgeon, *New Park Street Pulpit*, 1:161–62.

parallel with each other. Your praying must outdistance your preaching. The time you spend in prayer is being invested not wasted. "Prayer will singularly assist you in the delivery of your sermon; in fact, nothing can so gloriously fit you to preach as descending fresh from the mount of communion with God to speak with men. None are so able to plead with men as those who have been wrestling with God on their behalf."[7] Value prayer as a vital necessity.

Pray for your hearers with the intensity with which you want them to listen to you. This will ignite and intensify your pastoral intercession. Pray that the work of the Holy Spirit within your heart during preparation will also be accomplished within your hearers during proclamation. This will deepen your compassion for the hearers, and it will heighten your passion for the Father. Spurgeon testifies: "I see some before me who do not often hear me; and yet I can say concerning them, they have been the subject of my private prayers; and often, too, of my tears, when I see them going on in their iniquities."[8] Desperate dependence upon the Holy Spirit through faithful intercession frees you from fearing failure. It also liberates you in knowing that all success will come from God, not from your best efforts on his behalf.

## Intercede for Your Congregation from the Knee-Prints of the Apostle Paul

> For this reason I bow my knees to the Father of
> our Lord Jesus Christ ... (Eph 3:14).

The apostle Paul undergirded his messages with intercession for the recipients. Some of Paul's most intimate epistles were prayer letters to those whom he loved.[9] He prayed with depth and discernment for spiritual things. His intercession was spiritual and strategic. Could your intercession be described in the same way? Spurgeon observes, "Paul used much prayer. The gospel alone will not be blessed; we must pray over our preaching . . . Prevail with God, and you will prevail with men. Fresh from the closet to the pulpit let us come, with the anointing oil of God's Spirit fresh

---

7. Spurgeon, *Lectures to My Students*, 45.
8. Spurgeon, *New Park Street Pulpit*, 6:31.
9. Eph 1:15–21; 3:14–21; Phil 1:3–11; Col 1:3–4, 9–12, 15–21.

upon us . . . Let us never venture to speak for God to men, until we have spoken for men to God."[10] How many times has the length of your sermon exceeded the time which you spent with the Father praying over that sermon and interceding for those who would hear it?

Instruction without intercession can quickly become insensitive and insincere. Paul prayed nothing for those whom he addressed that he was not personally pursuing himself. In order for your hearers to be granted "the spirit of wisdom and revelation in the knowledge of Christ, and the eyes of their understanding being enlightened" (Eph 1:17–18), the same must become your personal prayer focus as you prepare to address them: "Lord, please enlighten the eyes of my understanding that you may enlighten the eyes of Your people with Your Word through me as Your messenger."

It was within the atmosphere of intimacy with the Father that Paul practiced intercessory prayer. The focus of Paul's intercession was that people would come to know the Lord (Rom 9:1–3; 10:1) and that they would come to know him intimately (Eph 1:15–21; 3:14–21). Paul prayed Father-focused, Christ-centered, Spirit-led prayers of intercession.

Paul's intercession was also instant. Spurgeon states, "Intercessory prayer will be all the more valuable if it is our immediate resort. The apostle says, 'Since the day we heard it, we do not cease to pray for you.' He began to pray at once. Whenever you perceive the work of the Spirit in any heart, pray at once, that the holy change may proceed with power . . . Linger not a minute, speed thee to the mercy-seat."[11] Paul's intercession was intensely instant and instantly intense. Like Christ, he interceded for others within the atmosphere of intimacy with the Father.

The apostle Paul was instant and constant in intercession for individuals (2 Tim 1:2–3) and for congregations (Eph 1:15–23; 3:14–21; Phil 1:9; Col 1:9). Spurgeon observes:

> Intercessory prayer, again, is most valuable, because it is an infallible means of obtaining the blessings, which we desire for our friends . . . The unselfish devotion which pleads as eagerly for others as for itself is so pleasing to the Lord that he puts great honor upon it . . . The instruction which we offer will be of no service unless we first bring down the blessing of God upon it, that thereby

---

10. Spurgeon, *Metropolitan Tabernacle Pulpit*, 25:682.
11. Spurgeon, *Metropolitan Tabernacle Pulpit*, 29:531.

## Stirring the Soil

our friends may be made willing to learn, and may receive the truth not as the word of man, but as from the Lord Himself.[12]

It is important that you make an intercessory investment on behalf of your congregation collectively and individually. Do not hesitate to bring names and needs before the throne of God with compassionate expectancy.

You can implement the practice of the apostle Paul by prayeraphrasing your sermon-text into a prayer of intercession. First pray for the congregation. Also, ask the Father to bring individuals to mind as you intercede. This will heighten your sense of his compassion and activity in the lives of people to whom you will preach. Remember, the sermon will be delivered on a spiritual battleground. Upon this battleground, eternal souls are at stake. The people of God to whom you will preach are weary and wounded soldiers who have come from intense spiritual battle behind enemy lines. They are desperate to receive fresh instructions from the Savior. The sword of the Spirit must be wielded contritely and compassionately. Consider the compassion which marked this prayer by Spurgeon:

> O God, save my people! Save my people! A solemn charge hast thou given to thy servant . . . Help him; help him, by thine own grace to discharge it as he ought. O Lord, let thy servant confess that he feels that his prayers are not as earnest as they should be for his people's souls; that he does not preach as frequently as he ought with that fire, that energy, that true love to men's souls . . . O God thou knowest that I lie not. How have I strived for them that they might be saved! But the heart is too hard for man to melt, and the soul made of iron too hard for flesh and blood to render soft. O God, the God thou canst save! There is the pastor's hope; there is the minister's trust. He cannot but thou canst, Lord; they will not come, but thou canst make them willing in the day of thy power. They will not come unto thee that they may have life; but thou canst draw them, and then they shall run after thee.[13]

Pastoral care and pastoral prayer are but two sides of a single coin in the life of a serious and sensitive pastor.

---

12. Spurgeon, *Metropolitan Tabernacle Pulpit*, 29:530–31.
13. Spurgeon, *New Park Street Pulpit*, 2:43–44.

## Approach Your Preaching Assignment as Delivering the Burden of the Lord

> I have come forth some Sunday mornings with the burden of the Lord upon my heart, till I have been bowed down with the weight... under the terror and the weight of the awful responsibility of having to preach to such a crowd as this.[14]

Each week you must bear up under the burden of the Lord to bless the people of the Lord. No burden, no blessing! The heavier the weight, the deeper the worship and the greater the wonder in the presence of the God of the Word. The preaching of the Word is not an exercise of levity but rather an expression of the gravity of the glory and grace of God. There is a heaviness in proclaiming holiness. Allow the weight of Spurgeon's prayer to rest upon your mind and heart:

> Thy servant Moses could not carry the burdens of the people which Thou broughtest up out of Egypt; much less can we carry the burden of this host upon us. O God, Thy servant feels His own inability every day, more and more, till sometimes his heart is ready to break with a sense of the overwhelming responsibilities which Thou hast laid upon one of the weakest creatures whom Thou didst ever honour in Thy service. But O God, wilt Thou not be the Pastor of this people? Wilt Thou, Jesus, not be the great Shepherd and Bishop of these souls?[15]

The Word of God is a crushing weight upon the heart of a man who mediates the master's message. There is a weightiness to God's Word. You must experience the weight of the Word to worship in the Word. A divinely appointed ambassador must live in awe of the almighty.

In the act of preparation and preaching, there is a heaviness which precedes harvest. Spurgeon graphically clarifies the nature of the burden which a conscientious preacher bears:

> The true preacher, the man whom God has commissioned, delivers his message with awe and trembling, because "The mouth of the Lord hath spoken it." He bears the burden of the Lord and bows under it... Woe unto us if we handle the Word as if it were an occasion for display!... No work is so important or honorable

14. Spurgeon, *Metropolitan Tabernacle Pulpit*, 7:557.
15. Spurgeon, *Behold the Throne of Grace*, 42.

as the proclamation of the gospel of our Lord Jesus, and for that very reason it is weighted with a responsibility so solemn that none may venture upon it lightly, nor proceed in it without an overwhelming sense of his need of great grace to perform his office aright.[16]

There is a heaviness of heart when you embrace God's message as a priceless treasure of truth. You are bearing the burden of blessing from the bridegroom to his bride. Spurgeon states, "We must ourselves feel the weight of that burden of the Lord which we proclaim to others, or we shall not be ministers of the apostolic sort, but rather shall be descendants of the hypocritical Pharisees who bound heavy burdens, grievous to be borne, upon other men's shoulders, but were not willing to touch them with so much as one of their fingers."[17] To preach flippantly is to deal with God's people falsely. This brings hurt rather than healing to God's people: "From the least of them even to the greatest of them, everyone *is* given to covetousness; and from the prophet even to the priest, everyone deals falsely. They have also healed the hurt of My people slightly, saying, 'Peace, peace!' when *there is no peace*" (Jer 6:13–14). Spurgeon admonishes, "Ministers should be much in prayer for their people . . . It is, perhaps, the great fault of this age that so many, who do preach, yet preach with so little earnestness, and are not sufficiently alive to the value of immortal souls. Oh, that the Holy Spirit would make our ministry to be 'the burden of the Lord' upon us."[18] Superficial sermons beget sickly saints!

You must come under the weightiness of the Word in order that the Father may bring blessing from his burden. Preaching is an exercise of extremity and exertion. Spurgeon observes:

> The Word of God is a burden; in the delivery of it. Do you think it an easy thing to stand before the people and deliver a message which you believe you have received from God? . . . To speak aright God's Word beneath the divine influence is, in the speaking as well as in the getting of the message, the burden of the Lord . . . Oh, that we may have, in all pulpits, ministers who bear the burden of the Lord in the study, in the pulpit, and when the discourse is

---

16. Spurgeon, *Metropolitan Tabernacle Pulpit*, 34:146–47.
17. Spurgeon, *Metropolitan Tabernacle Pulpit*, 11:493.
18. Spurgeon, *Metropolitan Tabernacle Pulpit*, 52:312.

finished! Once truly a minister you are always a minister; your burden clings to you.[19]

Effectively bearing this burden brings physical exhaustion and spiritual depletion. Yet the burden never lifts. Its weight demands an ever-deepening dependence upon divine empowerment and replenishment. To faithfully bear his burden is to experience his blessing.

Handling the holy infallible Word of God with levity is an abomination to the almighty and borders on blasphemy. You must be enveloped in the magnitude of the message. Dwelling under the weight of the burden of the Lord should lead to brokenness (Ps 126:6). The Word is fitly spoken through a messenger who is deeply broken. The matters of the Father's heart must weigh heavily upon your heart. Are you motivated by faithfulness to God or by flattery from people? Do you preach from a heart marked by God-given gravity or lukewarm levity?

> The prophets of old were no triflers. They did not run about as idle tellers of tales, but they carried a burden. Those who at this time speak in the name of the Lord, if they are indeed sent of God, dare not sport with their ministry or play with their message ... In the old times, those whom God sent did not borrow their messages. They had their message directly from God Himself, and that message was weighty—so weighty that they called it "the burden of the Lord."[20]

Spurgeon despised a shallow pulpit ministry that paraded knowledge, education, and mental prowess at the high cost of genuine heartfelt exposition of the holy infallible Word of God. Preachers can make high-sounding confessions regarding the nature of God's Word, but to have a pulpit ministry that constantly bears the weight of that Word with solemn seriousness is something entirely different. Your view of the nature of God and his Word will be reflected in the way in which you approach your God-given preaching assignment:

> The servants of God mean business; they do not play at preaching, but they plead with men. They do not talk for talking's sake; but they persuade for Jesus' sake. They are not sent into the world to tickle men's ears, nor to make a display of elocution, nor to quote poetry: theirs is an errand of life or death to souls immortal. They have a something to say which so presses upon them, that they

---

19. Spurgeon, *Metropolitan Tabernacle Pulpit*, 35:615–16.
20. Spurgeon, *Metropolitan Tabernacle Pulpit*, 35:613.

must say it . . . The servants of God have no feathers in their caps, but burdens on their hearts.[21]

Are you a burden-bearer for the one who bore your greatest burden to Golgotha? If not, the distance between a calloused heart and contrite heart is the distance between your knees and the floor. Fall before him. Call upon him.

## Weep over Those to Whom You Will Preach

> I am afraid that some sermon preaching is playing—fine words and oratorical fireworks, but no agony for souls.[22]

Jesus wept on the mountaintop before he whipped the moneychangers in the temple. His boldness was born out of brokenness. May the same be true of you. The seeds of the gospel are watered best with the tears of those who sow them. Prayerfully visualize the raw open wounds that ravenous wolves have inflicted upon the sheep whom you shepherd. Weep over them as you prepare to bring healing to them from the Word. Sheep with contusions need a shepherd with compassion. A bleeding sheep needs a feeding shepherd.

Spurgeon preached from a heart that was broken over the broken lives of those whom he addressed. He maintained a proper balance between mental exertion and emotional expression. Spurgeon had sobering and condemning words for any preacher who would dare to preach with a calloused heart with eternity in the balance:

> An idler has no right in the pulpit. He is an instrument of Satan in damning the souls of men. The ministry demands brain labor . . . To stand and drone out a sermon in a kind of articulate snoring to a people who are somewhere between awake and asleep must be wretched work . . . To promulgate a dry creed, go over certain doctrines, and expound and enforce them logically, but never to deal with men's consciences, never to upbraid them for their sins, never to tell them of their danger, never to invite them to a Savior with tears and entreaties! What a powerless work is this! What will become of such preachers? God have mercy upon them![23]

---

21. Spurgeon, *Metropolitan Tabernacle Pulpit*, 35:613–14.
22. Spurgeon, *Metropolitan Tabernacle Pulpit*, 22:530.
23. Spurgeon, *Metropolitan Tabernacle Pulpit*, 19:462.

Spurgeon warned against becoming a mere professional to the complete demise of emotional empathy for those to whom one preaches: "Does the tear tremble in your eye, now, as it once did for lost souls, perishing without Christ? Alas, upon how many has a hardening influence operated. Ah, and this is true even of us, ministers. We have grown professional in our service, and now we preach like automatons, wound up for a sermon, to run down when the discourse is over, and we have little more care for the souls of men than if they were so much dirt."[24] Personal contrition is indispensable in the life and ministry of the preacher. Contriteness produces compassion for the people. To weep over souls is to steep the seed of the Word of God with your tears.

Compassionately pray that your message will not provide superficial healing in the lives of your hearers. Spurgeon clarified the place of tears to express concern over souls: "We ought not to look upon this city of London without tears, nor even upon a single sinner without sorrow."[25] This attitude was also expressed by the apostle Paul: "I tell the truth in Christ, I am not lying, my conscience also bearing me witness in the Holy Spirit, that I have great sorrow and continual grief in my heart. For I could wish that I myself were accursed from Christ for my brethren, my countrymen according to the flesh" (Rom 9:1–3). Ultimately Spurgeon looked to Jesus as his example of the compassionate mixture of working and weeping: "Think of the Prince of preachers,—what a wonderful 'going' was his! Ah, and what wonderful 'weeping,' was his,—at the grave of Lazarus; and over the Jerusalem sinners! How deeply He loved even those who rejected Him! Oh, that we, who profess to be His servants, had tenderer hearts!"[26] A meek tender heart bursts forth with Christlike, tear-filled intercession over timely messages. Spurgeon laments, "We have no eyes now like the eyes of the Saviour, which could weep over Jerusalem; we have few voices like that earnest impassioned voice which seemed perpetually to cry, 'Come unto me, and I will give you rest.'"[27] If you preach a God-given message, you will shed God-given tears over a heedless congregation. Spurgeon contends, "These two things, 'going and weeping,' ought to be characteristic of every true preacher of the Word . . . They who win most from God are those whose hearts are most deeply affected,—those in whom there is the 'weeping' as

---

24. Spurgeon, *Metropolitan Tabernacle Pulpit*, 17:524.
25. Spurgeon, *Metropolitan Tabernacle Pulpit*, 26:667.
26. Spurgeon, *Metropolitan Tabernacle Pulpit*, 53:353–54.
27. Spurgeon, *New Park Street Pulpit*, 2:178.

well as the 'going.'"[28] Tears shed in preparation will become showers of God's blessing in preaching. "Those who sow in tears shall reap in joy. He who continually goes forth weeping, bearing seed for sowing, shall doubtless come again with rejoicing, bringing his sheaves *with him*" (Ps 126:5–6).

28. Spurgeon, *Metropolitan Tabernacle Pulpit*, 53:354–55.

# 9

# Sowing the Seed

> Ministers labor to break up men's hearts. This is the first effort of the wise preacher. The servant of Christ who teaches the gospel, whatever he may be called, is a sower of seed; and though it may appear useless to sow seed upon rocks, we are bound while acting as evangelists to sow our seed everywhere. Broadcast is our Master's rule: "Go ye into all the world and preach the gospel to every creature."[1]

THE PREACHER IS DESPERATELY dependent upon the activity of the Holy Spirit before, during, and after the delivery of the sermon (John 16:8–11). Long before entering the pulpit, you should have carefully handled the text and spent extensive time prayerfully preparing to sow the seed of God's Word. The germination of the seed in your heart creates urgency for sowing the seed in the hearts of others. You will find great freedom from the Holy Spirit as you preach from your heart to the hearts of your hearers.

---

1. Spurgeon, *Metropolitan Tabernacle Pulpit*, 25:231.

## Simultaneously Practice Supplication and Seed-Sowing

Spurgeon was not only an intense student of the Word of God, but he was also a perceptive student of the human heart. He embraced his identity of a sower and paid close attention to the seed which he sowed and the soil into which it was sown. This intensity of seed-sowing demands incessant supplication. Foster an expository/intercessory atmosphere in your pulpit ministry. As you sow the seed, it is good to focus specific intercession specifically on the types of hearers in Jesus' explanation of the parable of the sower and the seed:

> Therefore hear the parable of the sower: When anyone hears the word of the kingdom, and does not understand it, then the wicked one comes and snatches away what was sown in his heart. This is he who received seed by the wayside. But he who received the seed on stony places, this is he who hears the word and immediately receives it with joy; yet he has no root in himself, but endures only for a while. For when tribulation or persecution arises because of the word, immediately he stumbles. Now he who received seed among the thorns is he who hears the word, and the cares of this world and the deceitfulness of riches choke the word, and he becomes unfruitful. But he who received seed on the good ground is he who hears the word and understands it, who indeed bears fruit and produces: some a hundredfold, some sixty, some thirty."[2]

Interceding for these groups of hearers will enable you to intercede scripturally, specifically, and strategically for those to whom you will preach. It will also sensitize you to the variety of spiritual conditions among your hearers. Consider Spurgeon's comments on the soil samples contained in this parable:

- *When anyone hears the word of the kingdom, and does not understand it, then the wicked one comes and snatches away what was sown in his heart. This is he who received seed by the wayside* (Matt 13:19). Roadways, which have been long used, become very bad for sowing ... In a similar manner, there are many persons into whom we cannot get the gospel because they are too much occupied. There is too much traffic over them. They are not occupied with deep thought but with

---

2. Spurgeon, *New Park Street Pulpit*, 6:174.

multitudes of frivolous thoughts, which are well imaged by travelers who just pass along a road continually.[3]

- *He who received the seed on stony places, this is he who hears the word and immediately receives it with joy; yet he has no root in himself, but endures only for a while. For when tribulation or persecution arises because of the word, immediately he stumbles* (Matt 13:20–21). Those people, who are represented by this soil which has no deepness of earth, very soon make the good seed to appear to grow in them. They hear a sermon, are apparently converted directly, and they fancy that they are saved, or there is a revival meeting, where some earnest addresses are given by different speakers, and they at once profess to be believers. They are brought forward as converts, and there is great rejoicing over them, but after a very little while, days of trial arise, and there being no depth in them, they wither away and their names are struck from the church roll. The hopeful success, as it seemed, becomes a bitter failure. Men ask, "Where are those converts?" and echo can only answer, "Where?" for nobody knows but the Lord, who was never deceived by them.[4]

- *He who received seed among the thorns is he who hears the word, and the cares of this world and the deceitfulness of riches choke the word, and he becomes unfruitful* (Matt 13:22). Now we have this class very largely among us ... They are not ignorant and unenlightened ... They even go the length of making a profession of religion. The wheat seems to bud and bloom and blossom; it will soon come to perfection. Be in no hurry, these men and women have a great deal to see after, they have the cares of a large concern, their establishment employs so many hundred hands, do not be deceived about their godliness—they have no time for it. They will tell you that they must live, that they cannot neglect this world, that they must anyhow look out for the present, and as for the future, they think they will be able to take care of that by and by.[5]

- *But he who received seed on the good ground is he who hears the word and understands it, who indeed bears fruit and produces: some a hundredfold, some sixty, some thirty"* (Matt 13:23). The preaching of the

3. Spurgeon, *Metropolitan Tabernacle*, 49:377–78
4. Spurgeon, *Metropolitan Tabernacle Pulpit*, 49:385.
5. Spurgeon, *Metropolitan Tabernacle Pulpit*, 6:178–79.

## Sowing the Seed

Gospel was THE thing to give comfort to this disturbed and ploughed soil. Down fell the seed, it sprung up. In some cases it produced fervency of love, a largeness of heart, a devotedness of purpose, like seed which produced a hundredfold . . . It fell into another heart of like character—the man could not do the most, still he did much . . . In his daily walk, he quietly adorned the doctrine of God his Savior—he brought forth sixtyfold. Then, it fell on another, whose abilities and talents were but small, he could not be a star, but he would be a glowworm, he could not do as the greatest, but he was content to do something, even though it were the least. The seed had brought forth in him tenfold, perhaps twentyfold. How many have I of such in this vast congregation today?[6]

Spurgeon was a very perceptive student of the soil of the human heart. This enabled him to address his hearers heart-to-heart. He recognized that at best, the preacher's understanding of the human heart is nothing compared to the perfect understanding of God. Thus, he also viewed this parable as a portrait of the task of the prayerful preacher:

> The minister goes to his Master in secret, and asks Him to teach him His truth, and thus he fills his basket with the good seed of the kingdom. What the minister has to do is go forth in his Master's name and scatter precious truth. If he knew where the best soil was to be found, perhaps he might limit himself to that which had been prepared by the plough of conviction. But not knowing men's hearts, it is his business to preach the Gospel to every creature—to throw a handful on the hardened heart yonder, and another handful on that overgrown heart, which is full of cares and riches and pleasures of the world. He has to leave the fate of the seed in the care of the Master who gave it to him, for well he understands that he is not responsible for the harvest, he is only responsible for the care, the fidelity, and the industry with which he scatters the seed, right and left with both his hands.[7]

The proper pattern is clear: intercession followed by instruction and instruction followed by intercession. The seeds you sow should be watered with plenteous supplication.

---

6. Spurgeon, *Metropolitan Tabernacle Pulpit*, 6:180.
7. Spurgeon, *Metropolitan Tabernacle Pulpit*, 6:173.

## Spurgeon

# Seek to Preach from the Overflow of Extensive Prayer and Intimacy with God

> In preparing a sermon, wait upon the Lord until you have communion with Christ in it, until the Holy Spirit causes you to feel the power of the truth which you are to deliver.[8]

Just as Christ has commanded you to pray in his name (John 14:13–14), he has commissioned you to preach in his name (Matt 28:20; Mark 16:15). This requires extended communion with God and careful obedience to his commands. Spurgeon testifies:

> It is always good for an ambassador to receive his orders fresh from court; and good for us it is when we come into the pulpit with a message all glowing from the Master's mouth. Oh, I can say, if no one else can, it is good for me to draw near to God! . . . I had long since been utterly confounded were it not that I have been taught by experience to draw near to God, and breathe the bracing air of heaven, before I come among you to talk of the things of God.[9]

Only an intimate walk with God will overflow with passionate preaching on his behalf. There is no substitute for being intimate with the one who has called you to preach. Consider his invitation: "Draw near to God and He will draw near to you" (Jas 4:8). The nearness of God is an indispensable necessity in your life and ministry.

A lack of intimacy with God is the root cause of passionless preaching. Sermons are to be fueled by a heart that is full. Intimate prayer should be the sure foundation of intellectual preparation. This is much more than a mental exercise or an academic accomplishment. Thus, extended time in prayer should precede the first stroke of your pen or the first tap on your keyboard. Extensive prayer should also permeate and transcend the entire preparation process. Spurgeon observes:

> It is the praying man that is the right preaching man, and if any of you long to do good to your fellow men, you must begin on your knees. You cannot have power with man for God until first you have power with God for man. Solitary prayer was the equipment for the Prince of preachers when He came forth among the

---

8. Spurgeon, *All-Round Ministry*, 189.
9. Spurgeon, *Metropolitan Tabernacle Pulpit*, 15:382.

crowds . . . Workers for God, I entreat you to be abundant in supplication, that if success comes you may not be elevated unduly by it, that if failure comes you may not be depressed unduly by it.[10]

Intimacy with God overflows with faithfulness and fruitfulness. As a result of Jesus' intimate earthly walk with the Father, he was able to pray, "I have glorified You on the earth. I have finished the work which You have given Me to do" (John 17:4). His intimacy was full and his obedience was complete. This should be the desire of every preacher when he comes to the end of his life and ministry.

## Repent of All Carnal Desire to Perform or Impress Your Hearers

> But as we have been approved by God to be entrusted with the gospel, even so we speak, not as pleasing men, but God who tests our hearts (1 Thess 2:4).

Many a preacher has preached with one eye on the hearers and the other on Christ. However, to remain faithful to Christ, you must preach to an audience of one:

> I fear we often forget to do all for Him. I know if I preach a sermon and have any recollection that such and such a passage might please a learned or wealthy hearer, I have failed to please God. If I have any consideration in my mind as to whether I shall gain esteem for excellence of speech I am weak directly; but if I preach for Jesus only, then whoever finds fault my work is sweet to Him.[11]

Never allow the flattery or fury of your congregation to detour you from the fulfillment of your call. Spurgeon states, "It is unfaithfulness to Jesus if we even preach sound doctrine with the view to be thought sound; or pray earnestly with the desire that we may be known as praying men. It is for us to pursue our Lord's glory with a single eye, and with our whole heart."[12] It is a dangerous to take glory for yourself that only belongs to Christ.

Faithfulness to Christ in your preaching begins in the study! Seeking the face of the Father will keep you from scanning the faces of people as

---

10. Spurgeon, *New Park Street Pulpit*, 6:230.
11. Spurgeon, *Metropolitan Tabernacle Pulpit*, 18:467.
12. Spurgeon, *Metropolitan Tabernacle Pulpit*, 59:186–87.

you preach. Your goal is to feed hungry hearts, not to tickle itching ears. Avoid people-pleasing preaching. Spurgeon declared his desire to preach a clear distinct gospel regardless of negative response or adverse repercussions: "Offend or please, as God shall help me, I will preach every truth as I learn it from the Word."[13] Through various battles for truth, he remained faithful to these words. He had a clear understanding that even doing the right thing for the wrong reasons was offensive to God:

> Remember that whatever we do in order that we may make ourselves the end and object of it, is spoiled in the doing, and is not pleasing to God. Indeed, we are not offering it to God; we are offering it to ourselves. May we never be swayed by the fear of man, or the wish to win human approbation! . . . and when we are rendering any service to the Master, let us never even wish for human eyes to see it. That is the true spirit of piety; may God grant that we may have it to the full![14]

To develop a *Spurgeonesque* ministry in the attempt to grow in the esteem of pastoral peers would be a tragedy. Die to conceit and live to Christ. Maintain your focus on living a God-pleasing life and having a Christ-honoring ministry. Spurgeon warns: "Of many a minister it might be said—he lived to preach splendid sermons, and to gain credit for fine oratory . . . Oh that my memorial might be: 'He preached Christ crucified!' You fall short of your design in life if Jesus is not as much your object as he is your confidence."[15] It will do you well to daily dwell on these things.

## Handwrite Prayers in the Margin of Your Manuscript or Sermon Notes

Express your humility and desire to exalt Christ alone by recording the cry of your heart in the margin of your message. This was something practiced by Spurgeon.[16] These prayers appear to have been recorded during the writing of his notes or were written as an urgent cry just prior to the preaching of the sermon. Regardless of *when* they were written, it is very clear *why*

---

13. Spurgeon, *Metropolitan Tabernacle Pulpit*, 8:399.
14. Spurgeon, *Metropolitan Tabernacle Pulpit*, 48:293.
15. Spurgeon, *Metropolitan Tabernacle Pulpit*, 34:525.
16. While doing research in the Spurgeon Center at Midwestern Baptist Theological Seminary, I had the privilege of looking through copies of the actual notes from which Spurgeon preached. On a sermon "Help Jesus Amen Amen."

they were written. They were an active expression of his desperate dependence upon God. Consider the following examples from the heart and pen of Spurgeon: "Help. Oh, my King."[17] "Come Spirit, Come. Thy worm begs it."[18] "Give me, oh great one, words to speak in thy name."[19] "Help, My Lord, I crave."[20] Spurgeon exemplified a variety of ways to express prayer in one's pulpit ministry: in speech, through thought, and also in pen.

There are a variety of ways by which you can follow Spurgeon's example. These handwritten prayers can be condensed heart-cries that echo the cry of your heart during the preparation of the sermon. They can also be abbreviated *prayer triggers* to express pastoral intercession. This becomes a visible, tangible, and permanent expression of your dependence upon God in the delivery of the message he has given you. Prayers that are penned can also become a lasting testimony of one's humility and trust in the anointing of God. The benefits of this practice are virtually endless. First, this practice combines prayers to the Father with your message from the Father. Second, these written prayers are a permanent reminder of the spiritual context in which the message was preached. Third, these penned prayers assist you in keeping the Father and his glory at the heart of your preaching.

## Pray while You Preach

> Especially is it the Holy Spirit's work to maintain in us a devotional frame of mind whilst we are discoursing. This is a condition to be greatly coveted—to continue praying while you are occupied with preaching; to do the Lord's commandments, hearkening unto the voice of His word; to keep the eye on the throne, and the wing in perpetual motion . . . Oh, to burn in our secret heart while we blaze before the eyes of others! This is the work of the Spirit of God. Work it in us, O blessed Comforter![21]

Spurgeon literally attempted to live a life of prayer, not just to maintain a prayer life. His thoughts were Godward, and his words naturally flowed heavenward. Spurgeon graphically described what he meant by living and

---

17. Duesing, *Lost Sermons*, 7:600.
18. Duesing, *Lost Sermons*, 6:307.
19. Duesing, *Lost Sermons*, 5:257.
20. Duesing, *Lost Sermons*, 4:309.
21. Spurgeon, "Inaugural Address," 409.

preaching in the spirit of prayer: "I cry to God, principally, because I cannot help doing so . . . Minute by minute, moment by moment, somehow or other, my heart must commune with my God. Prayer has become as essential to me as the heaving of my lungs, and the beating of my pulse . . . I pray because I cannot help doing so."[22] Saturate the sermon with prayer-filled desire during its delivery.

According to Spurgeon, it is possible to simultaneously express heart-cries to the Father as you expound his Word to his people: "Oh, it is good preaching when you lean on the Beloved as you preach and feel, 'he will help me, he will give me thoughts and words, he will bless the message, he will fill the hungry with good things, and make the Sabbath to be a delight to his people.'"[23] It is easy to overestimate verbal communication and to underestimate heart-communion. It appears that Spurgeon consistently carried an open-ended conversation with the Father into the pulpit. That is how he preached in the atmosphere of prayer.

There was an inseparable relationship between Spurgeon's praying and his preaching. For him, to preach was to pray: "Is not my sermon the continuation of my prayer, for am I not desiring and aiming at the same thing? Is it not a continuing to pray when we use the best means towards the obtaining of that which we pray for?"[24] Ultimately, prayer is the communing of your heart with the heart of God. Spurgeon said, "Draw a circle around my pulpit, and you have hit upon the spot where I am nearest heaven."[25] Intimacy with God in your study should accompany you to the pulpit. Heart-prayers during your preaching can simply be echoes of your prayers during preparation: "Be in preaching like a conduit pipe between the everlasting and infinite supplies of heaven and the all but boundless needs of men, and to do this you must reach heaven, and keep up the communion without a break. Pray *for* the people while you preach *to* them; speak with God for them while you are speaking with them for God."[26] Even a glance of intercessory concern during the act of preaching can become an unspoken prayer in the hands of the Holy Spirit.

Spurgeon further observes, "I always find I can preach the better if I can pray while I am preaching. And the mind is very remarkable in its

22. Spurgeon, *Metropolitan Tabernacle Pulpit*, 49:476.
23. Spurgeon, *Metropolitan Tabernacle Pulpit*, 15:354.
24. Spurgeon, *Metropolitan Tabernacle Pulpit*, 18:139.
25. Spurgeon, *Metropolitan Tabernacle Pulpit*, 59:82.
26. Spurgeon, *Lectures to My Students*, 316.

activities. It can be praying while it is studying: it can be looking up to God while it is talking to man; and there can be one hand held up to receive supplies from God while the other hand is dealing out the same supplies which he is pleased to give."[27] This rhythm of receiving and relaying must occur in the pulpit; receiving a message from the Father through his Word and relaying that message from the Word of God to the people.

### Pray Spontaneous Prayers during Your Sermon

> In our pulpits we need the spirit of dependence to be mixed with that of devotion, so that all along, from the first word to the last syllable, we may be looking up to the strong for strength ... Looking to the hills whence cometh your help all the sermon through, with absolute dependence upon God, you will preach in a brave confident spirit all the while.[28]

Spurgeon often interjected cries of public prayer during his sermons. He did this without pausing to say, "Let us pray." It was simply spontaneous sentence or phrase of prayer spoken between sentences in his sermon. Spurgeon explains this approach: "When engaged in any holy duties, you may even refrain from praise for a moment in order to present a prayer to God. Nor would it be amiss for us sometimes to break the thread of a sermon, that the people might pause, and join with the preacher in asking God's blessing upon the men of mercy, and upon all that hear it."[29] Spurgeon inserted spontaneous prayers during his sermon no less than 964 times. These prayers were natural outbursts during the sermon: at the height of passionate preaching, at low points of struggle in delivery, during difficult points concerning difficult truths, soliciting divine assistance in calling for commitment and repentance, or when pleading with sinners to come to Christ. Consider the following examples of these spontaneous prayers:

- The place whereon we stand is holy ground, and the subject whereof we speak demands our solemn thought. Come, Holy Spirit, and teach us the full meaning of this prayer for holiness![30]

---

27. Spurgeon, *Metropolitan Tabernacle Pulpit*, 23:718.
28. Spurgeon, *Lectures to My Students*, 193.
29. Spurgeon, *Metropolitan Tabernacle Pulpit*, 52:241.
30. Spurgeon, *Metropolitan Tabernacle Pulpit*, 32:145–46.

- Oh for the fire! We will have a blaze out of them yet. Come, Holy Spirit, heavenly Dove, brood over the dark, disordered church as once thou didst over chaos, and order shall come out of confusion, and the darkness shall fly before the light. Only let the Spirit be with us, and we have all that is wanted for victory. Give us His presence, and everything else will come in its due season for the profitable service of the entire church.[31]

- Come, Holy Spirit, and take of the things of Christ, and show them unto us.[32]

It was Spurgeon's prayerful desire to preach in harmony with the blessing of God. This also helped the hearers to maintain an awareness of the presence of God during the sermon.

In following Spurgeon's example, you must exercise caution lest this becomes nothing more than a premeditated performance of prayer. Spontaneous prayers should be in response to the leading of the Holy Spirit. When this is properly incorporated, the value of this practice is multifaceted. These prayers can be an expression of your intimacy with God. They can also be a reminder to the congregation that this message is ultimately from God. Praying in this fashion provides a tangible expression of your desperate desire for God's blessing upon your preaching. A secondary benefit of these cries to God is that of modeling prayerful application of the truth that is being preached. You are equipping your hearers with an awareness of the need to call upon God for his assistance in applying the truth which they hear.

## Express Godward Desires During Your Sermon

Like the spontaneous prayers in Spurgeon's sermons are his Godward desires, which expressed a desire to see God move in specific ways. These Godward desires were more prominent in Spurgeon's sermons than the spontaneous prayers. He expressed these Godward desires during his sermon no less than 7,700 times. They voiced Spurgeon's deep desire for divine assistance, and for divine activity among his hearers. Consider the following examples of these unique expressions of Godward desires in their context:

31. Spurgeon, *Metropolitan Tabernacle Pulpit*, 32:488.
32. Spurgeon, *Metropolitan Tabernacle Pulpit*, 32:590.

- Oh! May God awaken us all, and stir us up to pray, for when we pray we shall be victorious. I should like to take you this morning, as Samson did the foxes, tie the firebrands of prayer to you, and send you in among the shocks of corn till you burn the whole up. I should like to make a conflagration by my words, and to set all the churches on fire, till the whole has smoked like a sacrifice to God's throne. If you pray, you have a proof that you are a Christian; the less you pray, the less reason have you to believe your Christianity; and if you have neglected to pray altogether, then you have ceased to breathe, and you may be afraid that you never did breathe at all.[33]

- Though we plead with you, and pray for you, and weep over you, you still remain as hardened, as careless, and as thoughtless as ever you were. May God have mercy on you, and break up your hard hearts, that his word may abide in you.[34]

- May God grant that some here, who have been like the ox for perverseness and stubbornness, and whose final doom would be to be felled by the pole-axe of death, may be subdued by the great Lion-tamer, who can surely tame the ox. May Jesus come and put His yoke upon your necks, for "His yoke is easy and His burden is light;" and from this day forth may you serve in the kingdom of King Jesus, to the praise of the glory of his grace.[35]

- May God help you! May the eternal God deliver you; for this, this iron yoke, is often hard to break. Resolve now, and pray also in God's name that you may be free. Have done with the accursed thing. God can enable you to come clear of it. May He do so now![36]

This practice can contribute great value in your preaching ministry. For instance, Godward desires can be a natural expression of your recognition of humble dependence upon God. They can also be constant reminders that your confidence is not in your ability to be persuasive but in God's ability to perform his Word. This practice can challenge your hearers to obediently open themselves to the activity of the Holy Spirit in the application of his Word. Expressions of Godward desires could also be followed by a prayerful pause or silence for supplication.

33. Spurgeon, *New Park Street Pulpit*, 1:123.
34. Spurgeon, *New Park Street Pulpit*, 6:175.
35. Spurgeon, *Metropolitan Tabernacle Pulpit*, 12:497.
36. Spurgeon, *Metropolitan Tabernacle Pulpit*, 18:59.

## Spurgeon

# Develop a Prayer Partnership with Your Congregation

> And being let go, they (Peter and John) went to their own companions and reported all that the chief priests and elders had said to them. So when they heard that, they raised their voice to God with one accord . . . (Acts 4:23–24).

Spurgeon valued prayer over preaching. He refused to delegate the pastoral prayer in the worship service to any of his associates or elders. He believed that it was of utmost importance that the people hear him pray for them. This gave the people assurance *that* he prayed for them and insight into *what* he prayed for them. This pastoral prayer was vital in the nurturing of an intercessory partnership between Spurgeon and his people.

During his sermons, Spurgeon also communicated his focus of intercession *for* his hearers *to* his hearers. Consider these examples:

- I pray God the Holy Spirit guide these words which are meant to encourage you who have been seeking Jesus.[37]

- O, I pray you look at him who spared you, and weep and mourn for your sin. May the Spirit of God come down on you this morning and draw you to the foot of his dear cross, and as you see the blood which has spared your blood, and the death which has made you live until now, I do trust that the divine Spirit may make you fall down and say, "O Jesus, how can I offend thee? How can I stand out against thee? Accept me and save me for thy mercy's sake." For while I have thus spoken of the general interest. which Christ has in you all, I have good hope that Christ has *a special interest in some of you*; I hope that he has specially redeemed you from among men, and bought you not with silver and gold, but with his own precious blood, having loved you with an everlasting love, I trust he intends with the bands of his kindness to draw you this morning.[38]

- My prayer to-night is that many here present may take the words of our text and have them laid upon their souls like burning coals, and that then the smoking incense of holy prayer may go up to heaven, and the Lord may smell in it, through Jesus Christ, a sweet savor of rest.[39]

---

37. Spurgeon, *Metropolitan Tabernacle Pulpit*, 9:331.
38. Spurgeon, *Metropolitan Tabernacle Pulpit*, 11:527–28.
39. Spurgeon, *Metropolitan Tabernacle Pulpit*, 62:554.

These prayer focuses seem to be a summary of his ongoing spirit of prayer in the pulpit. He preached with an ongoing active awareness of God. Spurgeon preached in the atmosphere of prayer.

Spurgeon also provided suggestive prayer focuses for his hearers in his sermons. This was a practical way in which he modeled biblical prayer in response to that which was being expounded:

- There are times when the preacher feels that he is sowing on stony ground, but on other days when God's Spirit is abroad, the soil seems broken up, friable, ready to receive the grain, and the seed suddenly springs up, and a speedy harvest is produced . . . Pray that there may come a great cave of religious thought over the minds of the people. God can cause it; he has the keys of human hearts, and can secretly guide them according to his will.[40]

- With the open Bible before you to guide your understanding, kneel down, and say, "O God, graciously reveal Christ to me by thy Holy Spirit; bring me to know him, bring me this day to find him as my own Saviour!"[41]

- Look to him; and when you have so done, and have trusted him, then pray this prayer to the Lord, "Order my steps in thy word: and let not any iniquity have dominion over me, for Jesus Christ's sake! Amen."[42]

- I want all the dear members of this church especially to join with me in breathing the prayer, day by day, and hour by hour, that the well would spring up in our midst. Conversion work is not pausing, I hope . . . O that he would now make bare his arm! We have seen what the gospel can do in the salvation of souls, and in making God's people cleave close to him. Let us ask for a renewal of those blessed seasons, and the continuance of our long prosperity. Let us pray for ourselves that our religion, our piety, may spring up like a well . . . And let us pray that the ministry may be greatly blessed amongst us, and for all our works . . .[43]

This was yet another way in which prayer was prominently kept at the forefront of Spurgeon's preaching. With the expression of spontaneous prayer,

---

40. Spurgeon, *Metropolitan Tabernacle Pulpit*, 18:125.
41. Spurgeon, *Metropolitan Tabernacle Pulpit*, 40:400.
42. Spurgeon, *Metropolitan Tabernacle Pulpit*, 42:501.
43. Spurgeon, *Metropolitan Tabernacle Pulpit*, 13:588.

Godward desires, and specific prayer focuses, he modeled biblical prayer and mentored his congregation in a life of prayer.

Spurgeon followed the example of the apostle Paul by faithfully interceding for the flock with which God had entrusted him. He did this both privately and publicly. It was very common for Spurgeon to share with his hearers that which he was praying concerning them: "My dear brethren, I pray God that this may stir you up to seek a high grade of piety and to live in daily communion with a living Savior, and He will bless and keep you."[44] He clearly connected prayer with the ministry of the Word.

Spurgeon also pleaded with his hearers for their constant intercession on his behalf. In his sermons, he specifically called upon his congregation to intercede for him and his preaching no less than two hundred times.[45] He expressed his dependence on their prayers of intercession for him: "Oh! may God help me, if you cease to pray for me! Let me know the day, and I must cease to preach. Let me know when you intend to cease your prayers, and I shall cry, 'O my God, give me this day my tomb, and let me slumber in the dust.'"[46] On another occasion Spurgeon expressed his intense yearning for the prayer support of his hearers:

> God help His poor servant. I have often felt the sweet preaching of the gospel to be bitter work. I do not wonder that dark thoughts come over the earnest preacher. I wish his hearers would partake with him in his anxieties. May we unite in deep concern tonight, I will pray for God's blessing upon every one of you, and you pray earnestly that no word of mine may be unprofitable to you. When preacher and hearer draw the same way the chariot wheels move to music, and that music is salvation. Come, Spirit of the living God, and make it be so.[47]

He consistently encouraged on-site intercession for him as he preached. Spurgeon knew that his preaching was strengthened by their praying: "My preaching will be poverty-stricken if you cease to pray for me."[48] Preachers often overestimate their ability to preach and underestimate the

---

44. Spurgeon, *Metropolitan Tabernacle Pulpit*, 10:520.

45. Spurgeon even devoted entire sermons to this matter: "The Minister's Plea" (Phil 1:19); "Pleading for Prayer" (Rom 15:33); "The Power of Prayer and the Pleasure of Praise" (2 Cor 1:11–12).

46. Spurgeon, *New Park Street Pulpit*, 3:256.

47. Spurgeon, *Metropolitan Tabernacle Pulpit*, 30:483.

48. Spurgeon, *Metropolitan Tabernacle Pulpit*, 30:483.

necessity for hearers to pray. Spurgeon viewed intercessory partnership with his congregation as indispensable: "'Oh, but,' say you, 'the pulpit is the great power of God, is it not?' I answer, it is so because of the prayers of God's people. One may speak, but what of that, unless the rest shall pray? Preaching is God's ordinance—his battle-axe and weapons of war; but, as far as the church is concerned, the arm that wields these weapons must be the prayer of the whole body of the faithful."[49] If Spurgeon recognized this need for a band of prayer warriors, how dare any preacher attempt ministry without it. Develop an army of intercessors around you! The Holy Spirit honors prayerful preaching accompanied by prayerful participation from the pews.

---

49. Spurgeon, *Metropolitan Tabernacle Pulpit*, 48:490.

# 10

# Silencing the Satanic

> For though we walk in the flesh, we do not war according to the flesh. For the weapons of our warfare *are* not carnal but mighty in God for pulling down strongholds, casting down arguments and every high thing that exalts itself against the knowledge of God, bringing every thought into captivity to the obedience of Christ (2 Cor 10:3–5).

> The devil never gives up to us; do not give up to him. He takes care to fight us with all his might; let us do the same to him.[1]

SATAN HATES THE TWO things that God values in the life of a preacher: prayer and the ministry of the Word (Acts 6:4). You been called into constant combat on the battlefield of ministry. Surrounded by innumerable casualties you must press forward. Divine anointing provokes satanic animosity. God's blessing brings Satan's bombardment. The more visible you are, the more vulnerable you are. Do not be surprised when divine victory provokes demonic venom!

---

1. Spurgeon, *Metropolitan Tabernacle Pulpit*, 14:332.

Before you preach, Satan will whisper into the ear of your conscience: "Who are you to preach?" He will proceed to do what he does so well, accusing you as one of God's saints (Rev 12:10). Satan will spew guilt and shame which will threaten to overtake your mind and weaken your heart. Stand on the Word clothed in spiritual armor, kneel before the Father, and allow the name and blood of Jesus to come to your defense. Having battled through to the pulpit, you may be tempted to assume Satan's silence means his absence. Nothing could be further from the truth.

As you descend the steps from the pulpit after you have preached, he will be waiting for you. This time, he is not armed with his arsenal of accusations but with his fiendish flattery: "You are an amazing communicator . . . You are a brilliant, gifted sermonizer . . . Even if God didn't come to your assistance, you would still be able to do what you have just done." Once again, it is imperative that you fall to your knees in rebuke of Satan's charm. Die to all pride and plead with God to deliver you from this deceptive delusion.

Satan will either jeer you with criticism or cheer you with compliments. He will seek to poison your ministry by puffing you up or by tearing you down! Satan can subtly chip away at your Christlike character through criticisms and/or compliments. Both are his weapons of choice. At your highest height and in your deepest depths, Satan is patiently preparing for his attack in his armory. Spurgeon warns:

> I believe that Satan has not often attacked a man in a place where he saw him to be strong; but he generally looks well for the weak point, the besetting sin. "There," says he, "there will I strike the blow;" and God help us in the hour of battle and in the time of conflict! We have need to say, "God help us!" for, indeed, unless the Lord should help us, this crafty foe might easily find enough joints in our armor, and soon might he send the deadly arrow into our souls, so that we should fall down wounded before him. And yet I have noticed, strangely enough, that Satan does sometimes tempt men with the very thing which you might suppose would never come upon them.[2]

In the heights, beware, pride is a sin which breeds other sins. In the depths, be on your guard, faithlessness subtly gives birth to unfaithfulness. You must maintain a Christ-centered perception of yourself and your ministry. You are a child of God whom he has called to be his messenger. To become

---

2. Spurgeon, *Metropolitan Tabernacle Pulpit*, 46:615.

self-centered and/or self-absorbed is to self-implode. Christ must be exalted above self continually and perpetually. Daily and moment by moment, "Put on the whole armor of God, that you may be able to stand against the schemings of the devil... that you may be able to withstand in the evil day, and having done all, to stand" (Eph 6:10, 13).

Spurgeon told his students, "I love to preach in such a mood, not as though *I* was about to preach at all, but hoping that the Holy Spirit would speak through me... Dependence upon God is the flowing fountain of success... Take care, brethren; for if we think we can do anything of ourselves, all we shall get from God will be the opportunity to try. He will thus prove us, and let us see our inability."[3] There is an atmosphere of anointing which rests upon the man who is desperate to bring glory to God.

## Daily Position Yourself as a Spiritual Soldier Equipped and Ready for Battle

> Finally, my brethren, be strong in the Lord and in the power of His might. Put on the whole armor of God, that you may be able to stand against the wiles of the devil. For we do not wrestle against flesh and blood, but against principalities, against powers, against the rulers of the darkness of this age, against spiritual *hosts* of wickedness in the heavenly *places*. Therefore take up the whole armor of God, that you may be able to withstand in the evil day, and having done all, to stand (Eph 6:10–13).

In the life of the preacher, the enemy unleashes a frontline assault on (1) the prayer closet and (2) the pulpit. Satan hates prayer and preaching done in the name of Christ. He persistently seeks to prevent communion with Christ and the conversion of sinners. He will use anything or anyone to keep you from the God-given priorities of prayer and the ministry of the Word. Count on it: when you exalt the Savior, you will encounter the satanic. To address sin is to awaken Satan. God's anointing provokes Satan's arrows. Christ is exalted through the preaching of the Word, and Satan's is enraged by the preaching of the Word. The messenger of God's Word must prepare and preach fully arrayed in the armor of God: "Do not simply look at the armor, and clean it up so as to keep it bright, but put it on, wear it, it is meant for you to use in the great battle for the right against the

---

3. Spurgeon, *All-Round Ministry*, 183.

wrong . . . Never go out without all your armor on, for you can never tell where you may meet the devil."[4] Satan is intimidated by the Word of God and infuriated with the man of God. He hates both the seed and the sower.

Satan majors on contaminating the soil and confiscating the seed. He doesn't fear the seed that enters the ears. But he does fear the seed that penetrates the heart. Satan will attack the seed between the head and the heart to prevent the harvest. Spurgeon reveals, "If you do hear the Gospel, even though it does not penetrate into your heart, yet still he does not like it to be there. So he comes and takes it away, makes you forget it, brings something fresh before you, so that you may fail to remember the good Word of God."[5] It is not your sermon which hearers are desperate to retain but God's Word from which it springs. The Word of God intimidates Satan and overwhelms his devices. Just as the Word of God is lethal to Satan, it is also loathsome to him. He has a dreaded fear and undying hatred for Scripture.

That which Satan fears is that which builds your faith. You must daily tighten your grip on the Word of God. When you tightly grip and confidently wield Scripture in the face of temptation, you are growing in Christlikeness: "And Jesus answered him, saying, 'It is written.' That is Christ's sword. Look how swiftly He drew it out of its sheath! What a sharp two-edged sword is this to be used against Satan! You also, believer, have this powerful weapon in your hand."[6] The strength of your sermon will be God's Word amidst an attempted ambush by the adversary. Have no confidence in your words but only in the Word of God.

## Daily Tighten Your Grip on the Sword of the Spirit and the Shield of Faith

> Above all, taking the shield of faith with which you will be able to quench all the fiery darts of the wicked one. And take the helmet of salvation, and the sword of the Spirit, which is the word of God (Eph 6:16–17).

Carnal weapons are no substitute for spiritual weapons. The sword of the Spirit and the shield of faith should be gripped tightly in the battleground of the pulpit. With truth in one hand and trust in the other, battle and

---

4. Spurgeon, *Metropolitan Tabernacle Pulpit*, 55:226.
5. Spurgeon, *Metropolitan Tabernacle Pulpit*, 49:381.
6. Spurgeon, *Metropolitan Tabernacle Pulpit*, 39:455.

believe! Satan's goal is nothing less than to devour and destroy your ministry. He hates exposition, and he is enraged with the expositor! Every time you enter the pulpit and unsheathe the sword of the Spirit, Satan unleashes his fiendish fury. He seeks to disorient you and derail your sermon. The prayer on your lips should be, "Father, please guard my heart, and guide my thoughts."

The adversary is no match for the almighty. You must live and preach with the sword of the Spirit in one hand and the shield of faith in the other. Satan will tempt you to rely on human reasoning instead of divine revelation. He will coax you to walk by sight and not by faith. This must be your mantra and mindset: "For though we walk in the flesh, we do not war according to the flesh. For the weapons of our warfare *are* not carnal but mighty in God for pulling down strongholds, casting down arguments and every high thing that exalts itself against the knowledge of God, bringing every thought into captivity to the obedience of Christ."[7] This requires an unshakable faith in the God of the Word. To question the Word is to quench the Spirit! Spurgeon states, "He must teach us how to grip this sword by faith, and how to hold it by watchfulness, so as to parry the adversary's thrust, and carry the war into the foeman's territory . . . It may take a long time to learn this art; but we have a right skillful Teacher."[8] He then prays: "Holy Spirit, teach us now feats of arms by this thy sword!"[9] Your effectiveness in wielding the sword of the Spirit is much more dependent upon your teachability than your capability.

Your grip on the shield of faith should be just as intense. The sword of the Spirit and the shield of faith will reinforce one another in your life and ministry. The sword of the Spirit pierces all doubts, and the shield of faith reinforces confidence in God and his Word. They are both mutually mandatory. Spurgeon states, "Do you but serve your Master zealously and diligently, and let but the Lord's blessing rest upon your labors, the Lord's blessing will entail Satan's curse, the smile of God will necessarily incur the frown of man."[10] Your faith in God and his Word must completely overshadow any fear of any foe. God's blessing is greater than the battle!

---

7. 2 Cor 10:3–5.
8. Spurgeon, *Metropolitan Tabernacle Pulpit*, 37:234.
9. Spurgeon, *Metropolitan Tabernacle Pulpit*, 37:234.
10. Spurgeon, *Metropolitan Tabernacle Pulpit*, 7:546.

Silencing the Satanic

# Battle the Enemy on Your Knees as a Shepherd-Watchman

Son of man, I have made you a watchman for the house of Israel; therefore hear a word from My mouth, and give them warning from Me (Ezek 3:17).

It is imperative that the shepherd-watchman discern and detect the devices of Satan among the flock of God. You are to grow in divinely imparted awareness of that which threatens the sheep with which God has entrusted you. The watchman is never off the clock. Just as the enemy prowls in search of his prey, the shepherd-watchman is to pray against his prowl. Spurgeon expounds:

> O shepherds, watch well the sheep that cost your Lord so dear. "Feed the flock of God which he hath purchased with his own blood." If we do not guard the truth of God once for all delivered to the saints, we are something worse than traitors . . . The service is seen to be responsible to the utmost degree when we see that it demands constant care: the Lord says of these watchmen, "they shall never hold their peace day nor night." . . . God's watchmen are not taken on by the hour, to watch by turns: but they are bound to be, throughout life, watchers for souls. We are never off duty.[11]

You must desperately depend upon the Holy Spirit for spiritual discernment and acute attentiveness. This will enable you to faithfully expound God's Word and expose Satan's devices. To deliver the truth is to dismantle the devil's deception. When you preach, you are standing on holy ground and entering enemy territory. To deliver the truth is to be despised by the devil. But a pastor who is unctionized by the Spirit is unintimidated by the satanic.

Jesus warned his followers, "Beware of false prophets, who come to you in sheep's clothing, but inwardly they are ravenous wolves" (Matt 7:15). False teaching is extremely attractive and easily accessible, and the wooing of these wolves has never been stronger. Satan's delicatessen of deception aims at every carnal craving. Your hearers spend each week surrounded by this false teaching and its adherents. Standing for truth exhausts them. They are worshiping through their wounded weariness and are desperate for hope and healing. You have been called by God to encourage, edify, and equip them for future battle. You must set the example of tenaciously holding to the sword of the Spirit, for the sheep will never grip the sword of the

---

11. Spurgeon, *Metropolitan Tabernacle Pulpit*, 37:87–88.

Spirit tighter than their shepherd does. Only the Word of God can expose the duplicity and disinformation of the devil.

Seductive wolves demand shepherd-watchmen. You must value the weapon of the Word in the prayer closet and study as much as you do in the pulpit. Satan knows that a swordless and prayerless preacher can only produce sickly sheep and gullible goats. If he can distract you from the Word of God in the presence of God, he can disarm the work of God. It is no coincidence that all of the spiritual armor builds up to the ministry of the Word (Eph 6:17) and prayer (Eph 6:18). The Word is the weapon and prayer the battleground. Just as God honors prayer and the ministry of the Word, Satan hates prayer and the ministry of the Word. He will stop at nothing to divide and destroy them. You will preach best from your knees.

## Pray Immediately After You Preach

> Be sober, be vigilant; because your adversary the devil walks about like a roaring lion, seeking whom he may devour. Resist him, steadfast in the faith, knowing that the same sufferings are experienced by your brotherhood in the world (1 Pet 5:8–9).

> It is always dangerous to be useful. It is to be desired above silver, and coveted above fine gold, and yet, when obtained, it has its measure of dangers, for Satan will whisper even if natural pride do not, "What an excellent man thou must be! What qualifications there must be in thee! What glory God gets out of thee!"... But, brethren, we need to be brought back to this, "Thou canst do nothing out of Christ; thou art, apart from him, a withered bough, to be gathered and cast into the fire." Yes, thou preacher, powerful, useful, honored of God, nothing but a withered bough, apart from Christ![12]

To preach is to engage in spiritual battle. When the sermon has been delivered, Satan does not depart. He will take advantage of your exhaustion. If he cannot get you to retreat, he will get you to relax. Spurgeon cautions those used by God: "Remember what Mr. Bunyan said on one occasion. After he had done preaching, a brother came to him, and said, 'You have preached an admirable sermon.' 'Ah!' said Bunyan, 'you are too late; the devil told me

---

12. Spurgeon, *Metropolitan Tabernacle Pulpit*, 14:369–70.

that before I got down the pulpit stairs.'"[13] Persistent prayerfulness is the requisite reinforcement after being used to God. You are most vulnerable when you are most victorious. To be used by God is to be abused by Satan.

Satan is most vicious when God is most victorious. The enemy will cunningly shower you with exaggerated praise. Spurgeon warns, "The head is peculiarly liable to the temptations of Satan, of self, and of fame. It is not easy, you know, to stand on a high pinnacle without the brain beginning to reel; and if God takes a man, and puts him on a high pinnacle of usefulness, he had need to have his head taken care of."[14] He further states, "Oh, to have a good, cool helmet to put on your brain when it begins to get a little hot with praise, so that you may still stand fast, and not be borne down by vanity. O Vanity, Vanity, Vanity, how many hast thou slain! . . . Take care of your heads, brethren."[15] Humble prayer immediately after the sermon is not optional. It is vital!

It is imperative that you prayerfully release all compliments to the Lord. Failure to do so could be fatal. Spurgeon soberly warns:

> How, careful, then, should we be when we do anything for God, and God is pleased to accept of our doings, that we never congratulate ourselves. The minister of Christ should unrobe himself of every rag of praise . . . The devil often tells God's servants a great many things which they should be sorry to hear . . . It is, perhaps, one of the hardest struggles of the Christian life to learn this sentence—"Not unto us, not unto us, but unto thy name be glory". . . Beware of vain glory![16]

Satan has dispatched an assassin for every preacher used of God. The assassin's name is Pride. His sight is set on your heart. He will inflict spiritually mortal wounds with much pleasure and delight.

> You must never forget that your goal is to bring pleasure praise to God alone. This was Spurgeon's objective: "A celebrated preacher was once told that he had pleased all his hearers. 'Ah!' said he, 'there is another sermon lost.' The most effective sermons are those which

---

13. Spurgeon, *Metropolitan Tabernacle Pulpit*, 44:484. This story deeply impressed Spurgeon and became a consistent warning to him amidst his fame. He also included it in the following sermons: "A Jealous God," "Paul: His Cloak and His Books," "Acceptable Service," "Non-Nobis, Domine," and "The Christian's Helmet."
14. Spurgeon, *Metropolitan Tabernacle Pulpit*, 55:507.
15. Spurgeon, *Metropolitan Tabernacle Pulpit*, 55:508.
16. Spurgeon. *Metropolitan Tabernacle Pulpit*, 9:188–89.

make opposers of the gospel bite their lips, and gnash their teeth. 'That preaching is worth little,' Rowland Hill used to say, 'that cannot make the devil roar. He preaches but very little truth who does not set the old lion roaring against him.'"[17] He continues, "But it is a good thing when we care little for the opinion of men, and when we have learnt to live above the world."[18] Divine power and human pride cannot coexist! Perhaps, of all forms of pride, none is more offensive to God than preacherly pride which robs praise from Him. Spurgeon speaks of this persistent battle: "When he has preached a sermon and has got on pretty well, the devil will come up the pulpit stairs and say 'Well done' . . . Ay, and even in his hallowed moments, when he is on the top of the mountain with his Lord, he will have to watch even there, lest self-congratulation should suggest—'Oh, man, greatly-beloved, there must surely be something in thee, or else God would not have done thus unto thee.'"[19]

God's hand of blessing only rests upon a humble heart. He only "exalts" those who only exalt him! "God resists the proud, but gives grace to the humble. Therefore humble yourselves under the mighty hand of God, that He may exalt you in due time, casting all your care upon Him, for He cares for you" (1 Pet 5:5–7). Constantly clothe yourself with humility. The following prayer focuses can be very helpful.

- Release all glory to the Father (Eph 3:20–21).
- Praise the Father as the God of the Word (2 Tim 3:16).
- Magnify God's Word as the source of power in the pulpit (Eph 6:17).
- Extol God's omniscience and providence in the lives of your hearers, rather than basking in your eloquence (Heb 4:12).
- Rejoice in the presence of God that his Word does not return void or empty (Isa 55:11).

---

17. Spurgeon, *Metropolitan Tabernacle Pulpit*, 44:524.
18. Spurgeon, *Metropolitan Tabernacle Pulpit*, 44:524.
19. Spurgeon, *Metropolitan Tabernacle Pulpit*, 8:30.

## Labor Fervently in Intercession for Your Hearers After You Preach

> God will not send a harvest of souls to those who never watch or water the field which they have sown. When the sermon is over we have only let down the net which afterwards we are to draw to shore by prayer and watchfulness.[20]

Jesus invested extensive time in focused prayer after his preaching and teaching.[21] Immediately after Jesus had delivered his final discourse to the apostles, he "lifted up his eyes to heaven, and said, Father, the hour is come; glorify thy Son, that thy Son also may glorify thee" (John 17:1). His instruction *to* the apostles was followed by intercession *for* the apostles: "I pray for them. . ." (John 17:8). Concerning this high priestly prayer of Jesus, Spurgeon verifies, "This was a prayer after a sermon. These words spake Jesus, and then he lifted up his eyes to heaven in supplication. No discourse should be unattended by prayer, for how can we expect a blessing on what we have heard or spoken unless we ask it of the Lord. The sower should water with many a supplication the seed that he has sown."[22] Prayer is a vital aspect of every stage of pulpit ministry. To pause from prayer is to sever your preaching from God's power. Satan longs to barricade the door of your prayer closet at every stage of your preaching ministry! He will stop at nothing to steal the seed and impede your intercession. Spurgeon describes this incessant spiritual siege: "Notice how zealous the devil is. We may be careless about souls, but he never is . . . He does not like losing his servants, and, from long experience, he knows that every now and then one of them runs away at night, and never comes back. So he is always on the watch for would-be runaways."[23] Fervent prayer not only empowers the pulpit delivery, but it also counters and neutralizes the attack of the enemy. This requires both intentionality and intensity in your intercession. Plead with the Father to bring a harvest from the seed that has been sown. It is tragic when men stand in the pulpit to speak for God after briefly consulting him

---

20. Spurgeon, *Lectures to My Students*, 308.

21. "When He had sent the multitudes away, He went up on the mountain by Himself to pray" (Matt 14:23).

22. Spurgeon, *Metropolitan Tabernacle Pulpit*, 25:163.

23. Spurgeon, *Metropolitan Tabernacle Pulpit*, 49:380–81.

during the week. It would be alarming to know how little prayer comes from the lips of those who preach after they have delivered the sermon.

Satan knows that once the sermon is delivered you are very vulnerable. You may experience the paradox of being overcome with exhaustion and overwhelmed with exhilaration. Exhaustion can quickly give birth to depression. Exhilaration can easily turn to pride. Therefore, you should be just as urgent in prayer after preaching as you are prior to preaching! Consider the following prayer focuses for praying following your sermon:

- Ask the Father to enable your people to be doers of the Word and not hearers only (Jas 1:22); not forgetful hearers, but doers of the work (Jas 1:25).
- Intercede intensely that the enemy will not snatch the Word away (Matt 13:19).
- Pray that difficulties will not cause hearers to stumble and forget the Word (Matt 13:20–21).
- Pray that the Word will not be choked out by the cares of this world and the deceitfulness of riches (Matt 13:22).
- Pray that the Holy Spirit will use the message preached to guide your hearers into meditation and obedience (Ps 1:1–3).
- Thank the Father for revealing his strength in your weakness (2 Cor 12:9–10).

## The Servant in Battle

O Lord, I bless Thee that the issue of the battle between Thyself and Satan has never been uncertain, and will end in victory. Calvary broke the dragon's head, and I contend with a vanquished foe, who with all his subtlety and strength has already been overcome. When I feel the serpent at my heel may I remember Him whose heel was bruised, but who, when bruised, broke the devil's head. My soul with inward joy extols the mighty conqueror. Heal me of any wounds received in the great conflict; if I have gathered any defilement, if my faith has suffered damage, if my hope is less than bright, if my love is not fervent, if some creature-comfort occupies my heart, if my soul sinks under pressure of the fight. O Thou whose every promise is balm, every touch life, draw near to Thy weary warrior, refresh me, that I may rise again to wage the strife, and never tire until my enemy is trodden down.

Give me such fellowship with Thee that I may defy Satan, unbelief, the flesh, the world, with delight that comes not from a creature, and which a creature cannot mar. Give me a draught of the eternal fountain that lieth in Thy immutable, everlasting love and decree. Then shall my hand never weaken, my feet never stumble, my sword never rest, my shield never rust, my helmet never shatter, my breastplate never fall, as my strength rests in the power of Thy might.[24]

---

24. Bennet, *Valley of Vision*, 91. Reprinted with permission from Banner of Truth Trust. This prayer preceded Spurgeon's sermon, "Satan in a Rage," on November 2, 1879. It is printed in its entirety in *Spurgeon, Pastor in Prayer*, 100–105.

# 11
# Submitting in Suffering

> Lest I should be exalted above measure by the abundance of the revelations, a thorn in the flesh was given to me, a messenger of Satan to buffet me, lest I be exalted above measure. Concerning this thing I pleaded with the Lord three times that it might depart from me. And He said to me, "My grace is sufficient for you, for My strength is made perfect in weakness." Therefore most gladly I will rather boast in my infirmities, that the power of Christ may rest upon me. Therefore I take pleasure in infirmities, in reproaches, in needs, in persecutions, in distresses, for Christ's sake. For when I am weak, then I am strong (2 Cor 12:7–10).

SUFFERING SAFEGUARDED SPURGEON FROM self-deception and self-conceit. His personal pain gave him pastoral insight because it drew him to the Lord rather than driving him away. It also deepened the intensity and intimacy of his walk with God. He worshiped through his wounds. His brokenness enabled him to drink deeply from the passion and suffering of Christ. It caused him to lean into the reality of the intercession of the Holy Spirit on his behalf. When you experience trials, follow Spurgeon's example, and remember to drink deeply from the pool of pain. Suffering has eternal significance in your life as a man of God and as a preacher of the gospel. It will deepen your life-message as well as your preaching. Spurgeon's prayerfulness redeemed his suffering and reinforced his pulpit ministry. He discovered gems of truth at the intersection of painfulness and prayerfulness. These personal discoveries enhanced his public ministry.

Your spirituality in the pulpit will be proportionate to your spirituality in the furnace. As you pass through the furnace of suffering, the Father desires to demonstrate his supernatural ability to replace your weakness with his strength. Spurgeon shares a vivid contrast between a preacher who grows through suffering and one who does not:

> Look at the preacher who has no burdens. His sermon is in his pocket . . . he has rehearsed all his action, he is as safe as an automaton. He does need to pray for the Spirit of God to help him in his preaching, and though he uses the form one wonders what the prayer can mean . . . He has something to say, and he knows what it is going to be, every word of it . . . he says it with ease, and comes down the stairs as pleased with himself as heart could desire: the notion of trembling is far from him, he is not so weak. Yonder is a poor brother who has been tugging away with his brains, wrestling on his knees, and bleeding at heart . . . he is fearful that he will not reach the hearts of the people; but he means to try what can be done by the help of God. Be you sure that he will get at the people, and God will give him converts . . . The weak man is strong and the strong man is weak.[1]

Suffering can be a significant stream for your sanctification. Pain pierces the heart and prepares the preacher for an inpouring of the Holy Spirit. This painful inpouring is a promise of potential outpouring in ministry. View seasons of anguish as avenues of abundance. How can a preacher faithfully proclaim the *Suffering Servant* without being immersed in suffering himself? Suffering and sermons are very close friends, not distant acquaintances or strangers, as some prominent preachers would have you to believe. God uses the furnace of suffering to shape and sharpen his instruments. It is through pain that you are conformed to the image of Christ. Conforming requires a crushing and chiseling away of that which is carnal. Spurgeon describes this process: "Trials teach us what we are; they dig up the soil, and let us see what we are made of; they just turn up some of the ill weeds on the surface."[2] The exposure of these weeds that position you for their removal. Clearing away the carnal will bring fresh fertility and renewed hope for harvest.

---

1. Spurgeon, "Inaugural Address," 509.
2. Spurgeon, *New Park Street Pulpit*, 2:141.

Spurgeon

## Prayerfully Embrace Trials as Providential Means for Spiritual Growth and Maturity

> My brethren, count it all joy when you fall into various trials, knowing that the testing of your faith produces patience. But let patience have *its* perfect work, that you may be perfect and complete, lacking nothing (Jas 1:2–4).

> It is well to look beyond all second causes and instrumentalities. Do not get angry with those who are the nearer agents, but look to the First Cause . . . What have you to do with them? Your business is with God. See his hand, and bow before it. Say, "The Lord gave, and the Lord hath taken away." Come to that, for then you will be able to say, "Blessed be the name of the Lord." Though your trials be peculiar, and your way be hedged up, yet the hand of the Lord is still in everything; and it behooves you to recognize it for your strengthening and consolation.[3]

Painful trials are providential tools in the hands of the Father. He uses unique trials to shape his messengers in specific areas for enhanced effectiveness. These providential trials have the potential to pulverize your pride and perfect your piety. They surface sinfulness and unmask pride. Self-sufficiency must be crucified to produce complete dependence upon God. The deeper the pain, the greater the purpose. Spurgeon explains, "Trials which are not felt are unprofitable trials. If there be no blueness in the wound, then the soul is not made better; if there be no crying out, then there will be no emptying out of our depravity."[4] He further expounds, "It is just so much as we feel, that we are profited; but a trial unfelt must be a trial unsanctified, a trial under which we do not feel at all, cannot be a blessing to us, because we are only blessed by feeling it, under the agency of God's Holy Spirit."[5] Trials can purify your heart and "pietize" your perspective. They can also teach you the deep dialect of travailing prayer. Those who travail in prayer also prevail in prayer. Allow God to use trials to shake you from ministerial monotony.

Sanctified submission amidst trials enables you to stand and serve on the sure footing of consecrated character. View trials as a tool in the

3. Spurgeon, *Metropolitan Tabernacle Pulpit*, 34:3–4.
4. Spurgeon, *New Park Street Pulpit*, 2:141.
5. Spurgeon, *New Park Street Pulpit*, 2:141.

hand of the Father fashioning you into the man that he desires for you to become. Spurgeon specifies, "God is at the bottom of all your tribulation—look through the second causes to the great First Cause. It is a great mistake when we fret over the human instrument which smites us, and forget the hand which uses the rod. If I strike a dog with a stick, he bites my stick—that is because he is stupid; if he thought a little he would bite me, or else take the blow and bow in obedience. Now, you must not begin biting the stick."[6] When viewed in this perspective, trials can move you from *believing* to *knowing* the truth of God's Word. Trials can drive the truth from the top of your head to the depths of your heart.

Your trials should drive you to look both inward and upward. God will encircle your life with a trial that he might envelop you in his will. "It is hopeful when we find that all our ills lie within the ring-fence of omnipotent overruling. It is one comfort that we see a wall of fire round about us, a circle so complete that even the devil, malicious as he is, cannot break through it, to do more than the Lord allows."[7] Times of distress can make the Word of God clearer and dearer to you. They can fine-tune your personal and pastoral application of Scripture. This brings maturity and clarity to your pulpit ministry.

## Allow Trials to Produce and Perfect Christlikeness in You

For whom He foreknew, He also predestined *to be* conformed to the image of His Son, that He might be the firstborn among many brethren (Rom 8:29).

How different would your life and ministry be without trials and adversity? This could be the most detrimental thing that could happen. It completely would distract us from the truth and power of the gospel. False teachers commonly teach that to become more like Jesus Christ is to live a triumphant tranquil life. However, the reshaping of one's character, attitudes, and actions is anything but stress-free. Spurgeon clarifies this process: "Affliction gives us through grace the inestimable privilege of conformity to the Lord Jesus. We pray to be like Christ, but how can we be if we are not men of sorrows at all, and never become the acquaintance of grief? . . . A share

---

6. Spurgeon, *Metropolitan Tabernacle Pulpit*, 26:358.
7. Spurgeon, *Metropolitan Tabernacle Pulpit*, 38:5.

in His sorrow must precede a share in His glory."[8] Suffering is an eternal investment with which God entrusts you. He uses suffering to reveal his Son *to* you, *in* you, and *through* you. Trials confirm the Word of God as they conform you to the Son of God. Spurgeon was well-acquainted with the furnace of trials and suffering. "What are the benefits of the furnace? . . . One benefit to be derived from the furnace is, that it purifies us . . . The furnace is a good place for you, Christian; it befits you; it helps you to become more like Christ, and it is fitting you for heaven."[9] View suffering from a providential and eternal perspective. The hidden hand of God is always at work, shaping you for future usefulness.

Spurgeon's all-encompassing desire for Christlikeness kept him from despising suffering and enabled him to expectantly anticipate it:

> If I had but one prayer to pray, and might not pray another, it would be this, "Lord, make me like Christ". . . "Like Christ,"—O if that prayer should involve the lion's den, or the furnace fiery heat, 'twere well . . . Oh! what trial would you not endure with it even though you had the direst tribulation coupled therewith. Better to be like Christ in his poverty, in his wanting a place whereon to lay his head; better to be like him as despised and rejected of men, than to be like a Caesar, or the richest, and in the world's eye, the most happy of men . . . If, then, this be the universal prayer and cry of the Christian, shall not we, my brethren, as part of the same family, join in it and say, "Lord, make me to be conformed to the image of Christ, my Lord?"[10]

Until you embark on a lifestyle of Christlikeness, you are not fully fit to preach the gospel of Jesus Christ. He is to be the very essence of our lifestyle. Adversity fuels the intensity of our intimacy with Jesus.

The apostle Paul declares his desire for intimate acquaintance with Jesus:

> Yet indeed I also count all things loss for the excellence of the knowledge of Christ Jesus my Lord, for whom I have suffered the loss of all things, and count them as rubbish, that I may gain Christ and be found in Him, not having my own righteousness, which *is* from the law, but that which *is* through faith in Christ, the righteousness which is from God by faith; that I may know Him and the power of His resurrection, and the fellowship of His sufferings,

---

8. Spurgeon, *Metropolitan Tabernacle Pulpit*, 19:22.
9. Spurgeon, *New Park Street Pulpit*, 1:274.
10. Spurgeon, *Metropolitan Tabernacle Pulpit*, 7:61–62.

being conformed to His death, if, by any means, I may attain to the resurrection from the dead.[11]

Terms like *suffering* and *death* are countercultural concepts for reaching one's goals. To live a Christlike life is to live a life which goes against the grain of the culture around you. Spurgeon preached and prayed to that end: "We should do all in the name of the Lord Jesus, for he should be the element in which we live . . . Let the Lord Jesus Christ be so woven and intertwisted into your very self, that you cannot be otherwise than Christlike under any circumstances. Lord, grant us this."[12] Sadly, many preachers find themselves so interwoven with the culture that Christlikeness is virtually invisible.

A call to serve Christ is a call to suffer with Christ. When your service requires suffering you gain a fresh glimpse of the heart of Jesus. He was the *suffering servant*. Spurgeon observes, "I believe that there would be much more persecution than there is if there were more real Christians; but we have got to be so like the world, that therefore the world does not hate us as once it did. If we would but be more just, more upright, more true, more Christlike, more godly, we should soon hear all the dogs of hell baying with all their might against us."[13] Ultimately trials are the treasured tools by which the Father chips away at self and conforms us to the Savior.

## Welcome Trials as an Instrument of Developing Wisdom in Your Life and Ministry

> It is good for me that I have been afflicted, that I may learn Your statutes. The law of Your mouth *is* better to me than thousands of *coins of* gold and silver. Your hands have made me and fashioned me; give me understanding, that I may learn Your commandments. Those who fear You will be glad when they see me, because I have hoped in Your word. I know, O Lord, that Your judgments *are* right, and *that* in faithfulness You have afflicted me (Ps 119:71–75).

Suffering produces a deeper understanding of yourself. Your consecrated suffering will result in compassionate sensitivity and will grip the hearts

---

11. Phil 3:8–11.
12. Spurgeon, *Metropolitan Tabernacle Pulpit*, 16:67.
13. Spurgeon, *Metropolitan Tabernacle Pulpit*, 42:451.

of your hearers more deeply than the most eloquent sermon. Spurgeon's suffering equipped him to sympathize and empathize with those to whom he preached. He did not hide the reality of his trials. He preached about suffering with a host of emotional, physical, and spiritual trials on display in his life. His trials became an empathetic platform from which he preached. Wisdom is the offspring of affliction. It is birthed from the womb of sanctified suffering. Consider Spurgeon's perspective:

> If it be very sweet to see God in our mercies, it is most consoling to discern Him in all our trials. Say not these are evil times. No times are evil where God is, for his presence scatters all that is ill. Say not that you dwell in an evil place; there is no evil place to the man who dwells with God. Think not that evil circumstances have happened unto you; they seem to be big with evil, but those clouds shall break in blessings on your head.[14]

Spurgeon continues, "Oh, if you can but look at your troubles as sent from God, it will take the sharpness from them, and turn them from wasps that sting into bees that gather honey. . . Regard not the second causes but the first cause, not the trying creature but the supporting Creator."[15] People mistakenly give the second cause too much credit for good or too much blame for what they consider to be evil.

Regardless of your circumstances in life or ministry, it is God who is doing the greatest work *within* you and *around* you. There is a Trinitarian involvement in your life when you are afflicted:

> Likewise the Spirit also helps in our weaknesses. For we do not know what we should pray for as we ought, but the Spirit Himself makes intercession for us with groanings which cannot be uttered. Now He who searches the hearts knows what the mind of the Spirit is, because He makes intercession for the saints according to the will of God. And we know that all things work together for good to those who love God, to those who are the called according to His purpose. For whom He foreknew, He also predestined to be conformed to the image of His Son, that He might be the firstborn among many brethren (Rom 8:27–29).

When you are experiencing pain, God is unveiling his plan. This perspective will enable you to preach with great faith and hope when immersed in trials. Your hearers will be enveloped in this same reality. As you suffer

---

14. Spurgeon, *New Park Street Pulpit*, 6:320.
15. Spurgeon, *New Park Street Pulpit*, 6:320.

alongside your congregation, unity will be born and strengthened. This unique oneness cannot be accomplished in any other way.

## Allow God's Grace in Trials to Equip You to Preach Even Out of the Depths of Depression

> Whenever your hope seems to fail you and your joy begins to sink, the shortest method is to take to your knees. By remembering the promise in prayer hope will be sustained, and then joy is sure to spring from it, for joy is the first-born child of hope . . . Impatience will be sure to follow prayerlessness, but the endurance of the divine will grows out of communion with God in prayer.[16]

The gateway to great joy is often the long, dark, twisting tunnel of depression. Spurgeon reflects on these seasons of suffering and sadness: "I must confess here, with sorrow, that I have seasons of despondency and depression of spirit, which I trust none of you are called to suffer, and at such times I have doubted my interest in Christ, my calling my election, my perseverance, my Savior's blood, and my Father's love."[17] During this emotional excruciation and spiritual disorientation, Spurgeon despaired of ever being used by God again. However, when these dark clouds parted, the faithful lovingkindness of a good Father was blatantly present.

Preaching from the one's overflow is not preaching from the abundance of learning and education. Neither is it displaying your comprehension of great doctrines with complete confidence. It simply means that what the Father pours into your life will overflow into the lives of those to whom you preach. Everything of any consequence that you give to others must first be given to you by the Father. God has gifted you to gift others. You are to be a conduit of his comfort: "Blessed be the God and Father of our Lord Jesus Christ, the Father of mercies and God of all comfort, who comforts us in all our tribulation, that we may be able to comfort those who are in any trouble, with the comfort with which we ourselves are comforted by God. For as the sufferings of Christ abound in us, so our consolation also abounds through Christ" (2 Cor 1:3–5). When you are comforted and

---

16. Spurgeon, *Metropolitan Tabernacle Pulpit*, 25:349.
17. Spurgeon, *Metropolitan Tabernacle Pulpit*, 7:125.

strengthened by God, you are then equipped to comfort and strengthen your congregation.

Spurgeon was extremely acquainted with the onset of depression due to mental and emotional stress, spiritual conflict, physical exhaustion, and recurring illness. He was able to foresee these seasons approaching: "The times most favorable to fits of depression, so far as I have experienced, may be summed up in a brief catalogue."[18] Consider three entries in this "catalogue" that directly connect with pastoral and preaching ministry.

First, Spurgeon experienced intense depression during great victories in his ministry: "First among them I must mention the hour of great success when at last a long-cherished desire is fulfilled, when God has been glorified greatly by our means, and a great triumph achieved, then we are apt to faint."[19] Spurgeon knew very well that many men have thrived amidst great adversity who could not stand under the extreme weight of victory. "Another period of great need is after extraordinary exaltations and enjoyments, when it often happens that God's servants are greatly depressed . . . I am much tossed up and down, and although my joy is greater than the most of men, my depression of spirit is such as few can have an idea of."[20] He recognized that in some respects victory is more dangerous to one's ministry effectiveness and longevity than devastating defeat. Both have their unique dangers.

Second, Spurgeon found that these mists of melancholy loomed prior to a great outpouring of the power of God: "Before any great achievement, some measure of the same depression is very usual. Surveying the difficulties before us, our hearts sink within us."[21] This is not solely due to a lack of faith but also the prospect of the physical and emotional drain required to accomplish the task. Spurgeon further expounds, "This depression comes over me whenever the Lord is preparing a larger blessing for my ministry; the cloud is black before it breaks, and overshadows before it yields its deluge of mercy. Depression has now become to me as a prophet in rough clothing, a John the Baptist, heralding the nearer coming of my Lord's richer benison."[22] When you are in a season of depression, it is difficult to read this prophetic forecast of God's blessing and fruitful ministry. At the

---

18. Spurgeon, *Lectures to My Students*, 158.
19. Spurgeon, *Lectures to My Students*, 158.
20. Spurgeon, *Metropolitan Tabernacle Pulpit*, 14:188.
21. Spurgeon, *Lectures to My Students*, 158.
22. Spurgeon, *Lectures to My Students*, 160.

point of desperation, the Father many times will pour out unexpected and unanticipated blessing.

Third, Spurgeon found himself depressed when overextended and exhausted by ministry demands. This is not surprising when you consider the broad involvement he sustained in church life, education, church-planting, and social ministry. You may never face demands on your time and physical stamina like those of Spurgeon. However, whatever the ministry setting, it has the potential to stretch you beyond your ability to thrive and to cope. Consider the counsel of Spurgeon: "In the midst of a long stretch of unbroken labor, the same affliction may be looked for. The bow cannot be always bent without fear of breaking. Repose is as needful to the mind as sleep to the body ... Hence the wisdom and compassion of our Lord, when he said to his disciples, 'Let us go into the desert and rest awhile.'"[23] Spurgeon knew very well that there was only one Messiah and that this Messiah was not him. You must embrace this same understanding. Renew your trust in the Lord Jesus and release the ultimate responsibility for the ministry back to him. He is faithful to shoulder that burden. Spurgeon contends, "Prayer is the great cure-all for depression of spirit. 'When my spirit is overwhelmed within me, I will look to the rock that is higher than I.' There will be a breaking up altogether, and a bursting of spirit, unless you pull up the sluices of supplication, and let the soul flow out in secret communion with God."[24] Prayer redeems our struggle and restores our strength. Receive this encouragement from Spurgeon:

> There are times when a want of success or a withering of our cherished hopes will help to make us feel most keenly how barren and unfruitful we are until the Lord endows us with his Spirit ... I suppose there is no successful worker who is quite free from times of deep depression, times when his fears make him say, "Surely I took up this work myself through presumption, I ran without being called; I have willfully thrust myself into a position where I am subject to great danger and great toil, without having the strength which is required for the place." ... I am not sorry if you are passing through this fiery ordeal. If your strength is dried up like a potsherd, if your strength is shriveled like a skin-bottle that has been hanging up in the smoke, if you feel as though your personal power was altogether paralyzed, I do not regret it, for know you

---

23. Spurgeon, *Lectures to My Students*, 158.
24. Spurgeon, *Metropolitan Tabernacle Pulpit*, 12:308.

> not that it is in your weakness God will show His own strength, and when there is an end of you there will be a beginning of Him.[25]

When you are depressed and Sundays seem to be one day apart, take heart! On those days when you crawl into the pulpit to offer hope from what feels like a hopeless heart, take a deep breath. Before you ascend the stairs to the pulpit, silently proclaim the words of the psalmist: "My help *comes* from the Lord, Who made heaven and earth!" (Ps 121:2). From early in his ministry, Spurgeon spoke candidly about this struggle:

> He who has been long experienced in the things of the divine life will sometimes be overtaken with a dark night and a stormy tempest . . . I have to speak today to myself; and whilst I shall be endeavoring to encourage those who are distressed and downhearted, I shall be preaching, I trust, to myself, for I need something which shall cheer my heart . . . My soul is cast down within me, I feel as if I had rather die than live; all that God hath done by me seems to be forgotten, and my spirit flags and my courage breaks down with the thought of that which is to come. I need your prayers; I need God's Holy Spirit; and I felt that I could not preach today, unless I should preach in such a way as to encourage you and to encourage myself in the good work and labour of the Lord Jesus Christ.[26]

Spurgeon spoke openly about his chronic battle with depression. He embraced it as a means of being empowered for ministry. It was from a position of downcast weakness that he found his greatest strength and reliance upon God. He acknowledged, "The first qualification for serving God with any amount of success, and for doing God's work well and triumphantly, is a sense of our own weakness."[27] This was not just an opinion held by Spurgeon. It is a truth about the ways of God: "God hath said it; men must serve Him, they must serve Him in His own way, and they must serve Him in His own strength too, or He will never accept their service. That which man doth, unaided by divine strength, God never can accept . . . There must be a consciousness of weakness, before there can be any victory."[28] God comes to the aid of those who are pursuing him with unconditional obedience to his Word. It is the weakest whom he immerses in his ways.

---

25. Spurgeon, *Metropolitan Tabernacle Pulpit*, 13:6465.
26. Spurgeon, *New Park Street Pulpit*, 3:389–90.
27. Spurgeon, *New Park Street Pulpit*, 3:390.
28. Spurgeon, *New Park Street Pulpit*, 3:390.

Spurgeon forecasts, "God will have no strength used in His own battles but the strength which He Himself imparts: and I would not have you that are now distressed in the least discouraged by it. Your emptiness is but the preparation for your being filled, and your casting down is but the making ready for your lifting up."[29] God is faithful to lift the ones who lift their eyes to heaven in the darkest of days.

> I can always believe the past, and always believe the future, but the present, the present, the present, that is what staggers faith ... However troubled, downcast, depressed, and despairing, the Christian may be, all things are working now for his good ... The winter has not spared our branches, nor the lightnings ceased to scathe our trunk; yet here we stand; preserved by conquering grace. Hallelujah to the grace that makes all things work together for good![30]

---

29. Spurgeon, *New Park Street Pulpit*, 3:391.
30. Spurgeon, *New Park Street Pulpit*, 3:419.

# 12

# Self-Examining the Soul

> Search me, O God, and know my heart; try me, and know my anxieties; and see if there is any wicked way in me, and lead me in the way everlasting (Ps 139: 23–24).

> Every wise merchant will occasionally hold a stock-taking, when he will cast up his accounts, examine what he has on hand, and ascertain decisively whether his trade is prosperous or declining. Every man who is wise in the kingdom of heaven, will do the same by himself; he will always cry, "Search me, O God, and try me;" and he will frequently set apart special seasons for self-examination, to discover whether things be right between God and his soul."[1]

SELF-EXAMINATION POSITIONS YOU TO agree with God concerning what he already knows about you. People can easily be deceived by one's appearance and actions. But "the Lord does not see as man sees; for man looks at the outward appearance, but the Lord looks at the heart" (1 Sam 16:7). Biblical self-examination will start with the heart. "Keep your heart with

---

1. Spurgeon, *Metropolitan Tabernacle Pulpit*, 8:577.

## Self-Examining the Soul

all diligence, for out of it spring the issues of life" (Prov 4:23). Beginning with the symptoms of outward behavior becomes nothing more than sin management. The heart is the root; habits are the fruit. The heart produces habits and habits reveal the heart. God works from the inside out. He first changes the heart, which then produces the transformation of habits.

Your self-examination must go deep beneath the surface and symptoms to the source of self and sin. The deeper you commune with God, the deeper you will confess to God, and the deeper the confession, the deeper the cleansing. You will become acutely sensitized to sin. Spurgeon observes, "Whenever we get near to God, and really enter into fellowship with him, the sensations we feel are the very reverse of self-congratulation . . . We never see the beauty of Christ without at the same time perceiving our own deformity."[2] Ask God, "What in me is displeasing to You?" Quietly allow the Holy Spirit to reveal these things to you. Repent quickly and deeply when he does. Healthy self-examination must be the result of humbly and obediently cooperating with Spirit-exposure of the sins of self.

Intimacy with God is greatly enhanced by self-examination, honest confession, and genuine repentance. The more you humble yourself before his holiness, the heavier sin will weigh upon your heart. You will live in the awareness that you cannot fully follow your Savior unless you are fully forsaking your sin. The one who has called you longs to consecrate you. Spurgeon explains:

> When God calls us to ministerial labour we should endeavour to get grace that we may be strengthened into fitness for our position, and not be mere novices carried away by the temptations of Satan, to the injury of the church and our own ruin. We are to stand equipped with the whole armour of God, ready for feats of valour not expected of others: to us self-denial, self-forgetfulness, patience, perseverance, longsuffering, must be every-day virtues, and who is sufficient for these things? We had need live very near to God, if we would approve ourselves in our vocation.[3]

These "everyday virtues" are the foundation for building a prayerful preaching life. Many preachers preach from libraries filled with helpful resources. However, the most effective preachers are those who preach a self-examined heart of purity and passion for God. The power of God flows freshest through the vessel that is cleanest. Spurgeon instructs, "Let the prayer be

---

2. Spurgeon, *Metropolitan Tabernacle Pulpit*, 19:305.
3. Spurgeon, *Lectures to My Students*, 14.

breathed, 'Search me, O God, and know my heart: try me, and know my thoughts: and see if there be any wicked way in me, and lead me in the way everlasting.'"[4] He then asks, "Are ye earnest in secret prayer? Do ye love the reading of the Bible? Have ye the fear of God before your eyes? Do you really commune with God? Do you truly love Christ? Ask yourselves these questions often, for though we preach the free gospel of Jesus Christ, I hope as plainly as any, we feel it to be just as needful to set you on self-examination and to excite in you a holy anxiety."[5] Questions like these will foster within you a genuine unrest with that which is unholy. Instruments of holiness are interrogators of the heart.

Your self-examination of your heart-condition will purge your ministry motives and practices of sinful contaminants. Failing at self-examination creates a disconnect between the heart of the man and the habits of the ministry. This is a heightened form of hypocrisy. A preacher can vehemently condemn the impure practices of the Pharisees, while harboring hypocrisy in his heart. It is a very helpful practice to humbly read the *woes* which Jesus pronounced on the Pharisees, and after each *woe*, ask yourself the question, "Lord, is it I?"[6] Asking piercing and pointed questions assists you in examining your heart as and your ministry. Prayerfully consider these questions:

- What besetting sin in your personal life tends to create a power leakage in your preaching?
- Have you become complacently casual in your sermon preparation routine?
- In preparing to preach, do you focus more on sermon preparation than spiritual preparation?
- Do you spend more time focusing on *words* you will use than on the *worship* you will express through the message? God is looking for a worshiper, not a wordsmith!
- Are you more focused on sentence structure than you are on being a sincere servant?
- Is your personal consecration enhancing your sermon preparation?

---

4. Spurgeon, *Metropolitan Tabernacle Pulpit*, 16:393.
5. Spurgeon, *Metropolitan Tabernacle Pulpit*, 16:393.
6. See Matt 23:1–33.

## Self-Examining the Soul

- Is most of your confidence placed in the books you peruse or the Bible you proclaim?
- Does your preaching reflect the convictions and the compassion of Jesus?

### Take Heed Lest You Fall

Therefore let him who thinks he stands take heed lest he fall (1 Cor 10:12).

> Satan is very crafty; he knows the ins and outs of manhood. There is many an old castle that has stood against every attack, but at last some traitor from within has gone without, and said "I know an old deserted passage, a subterranean back way, that has not been used for many a-day. In such and such a field you will see an opening; clear away a heap of stones there, and I will lead you down the passage: you will then come to an old door, of which I have the key and I can let you in; and so by a back way I can lead you into the very heart of the citadel, which you may then easily capture." It is so with Satan. Man knoweth not himself so well as Satan knows him. There are back ways and subterranean passages into man's heart which the devil doth well understand, and he who thinketh that he is safe, let him take heed lest he fall.[7]

It is dangerous for a servant of God is to become arrogant and apathetic about his own heart. Spurgeon probes, "Is there the vitality about your profession that there used to be? There are some in this house this morning, who, if they could speak, would tell you that, when to their great sorrow they fell into sin, it was because by little and little their piety began to lose its force and power of life."[8] Count on it, when piety declines, power departs! This does not always happen immediately. Many times it is a gradual drift in piety that precipitates a progressive power loss in ministry. Spurgeon describes the beginning of this drift to demise:

> Let us for a little time enjoy the full assurance of faith; self-conceit whispers, "You will retain the savor of that all your days;" and there is not quite a whisper, but something even fainter than that—"You

---

7. Spurgeon, *New Park Street Pulpit*, 4:364.
8. Spurgeon, *Metropolitan Tabernacle Pulpit*, 15:22.

> have no need to depend upon the influence of the Holy Spirit now. See what a great man you have grown. You have become one of the Lord's most valued people; you are a Samson; you may pull down the very gates of hell and fear not. You have no need to cry, 'Lord, have mercy upon me.'"[9]

How could someone who knows the Scripture so well begin to ignore the very truth which he proclaims? It seems almost unthinkable that even ministry in the local church can become a dangerous diversion from a pure and passionate heart toward God. Spurgeon had a healthy fear of falling prey to this tragedy:

> For my own self, I dread lest I should come to this pulpit, merely to preach to you, because the time has come, and I must get through an hour, or an hour-and-a-half of worship. I dread getting to be a mere preaching machine, without my heart and soul being exercised in this solemn duty . . . We must have vital godliness, and the vitality of it must be maintained, and the force and energy of our religion, must go on to increase day by day, or else, though our ways may seem to be very clean, the Lord will soon weigh our spirits to our eternal confusion.[10]

You can begin to think that what you do for Christ can compensate for the absence of a vital walk with him. No eloquence in sermonizing is sufficient to atone for hidden sin in the heart.

Another dangerous temptation for the preacher is that of living off the false perceptions his hearers have of him. You should never exchange reality for reputation. Who people *think* you are has no effect on whom God *knows* you are. He has full view of your heart. No sin is hidden from his gaze. You are not an exception to his commands. Spurgeon admonishes, "There never was a saint yet that grew proud of his fine feathers but what the Lord plucked them out by-and-bye . . . and there shall never be a saint who indulges self-conceit, and pride, and self-confidence, but the Lord will spoil his glories and trample his honors in the mire, and make him cry out yet again 'Lord have mercy upon me, less than the least of all saints, and the very chief of sinners.'"[11] Remember, "The Lord your God is a consuming fire, a jealous God" (Deut 4:24). He will even bring down your ministry should it become nothing more than an idol that has replaced him in your heart!

---

9. Spurgeon, *New Park Street Pulpit*, 3:456.
10. Spurgeon, *Metropolitan Tabernacle Pulpit*, 15:23.
11. Spurgeon, *New Park Street Pulpit*, 3:456.

## Self-Examining the Soul

The biblical preacher is in a war zone in enemy territory. When God calls a man to preach, the devil declares war on his soul. Spurgeon warns, "How many dangers surround the Christian minister! As the officers in an army are the chosen targets of the sharpshooters, so are the ministers of Christ... From the first moment of his call to the work, the preacher of the Word will be familiar with temptation."[12] Upon surviving an early onslaught from Satan, the young preacher should never anticipate the retreat of the armies of hell. When they become silent, they are simply planning the next ambush on the preacher's soul. Two realities are certain in the life of the preacher: (1) the faithful love of God, and (2) the fierce hatred of Satan. Spurgeon clarifies, "If Satan cannot destroy a Christian, how often has he spoilt his usefulness?"[13] If Satan cannot take you out of the ministry, he will attempt to take the ministry out of you. If the pastor drifts, the people backslide. When the pastor falls the people falter. The longer a man faithfully proclaims the gospel, the greater target of hell he becomes. Satan knows that to sink a minister is to shake and scatter members. Spurgeon states, with sober caution:

> When the minister of Christ turns traitor, it is as if the pillars of the house did tremble, every stone in the structure feels the shock. If Satan can succeed in overturning the preachers of the Word, it is as if yon broad-spreading tree should suddenly fall beneath the axe... All who were comforted by the preacher's words, strengthened by his example, and edified by his teaching are filled with humiliation and grief, crying, "Alas! my brother."[14]

However, divine disappointment should weigh heaviest on the preacher's soul:

> There is not a man in battle so much in danger from the shot, as thou art from thine own sin. Thou carriest in thy soul an infamous traitor, even when he speaks thee fair he is not to be trusted; thou hast in thy heart a slumbering volcano, but a volcano of such terrific force that it may shake thy whole nature yet; and unless thou art circumspect, and art kept by the power of God, thou hast a heart which may lead thee into sins the most diabolical, and crimes the most infamous... If there were no devil to tempt you,

---

12. Spurgeon, *Metropolitan Tabernacle Pulpit*, 10:85.
13. Spurgeon, *Metropolitan Tabernacle Pulpit*, 11:198.
14. Spurgeon, *Metropolitan Tabernacle Pulpit*, 10:85–86.

and no world to lead you astray, you would have need to take care of your own hearts.[15]

Spurgeon further laments, "We can recall with grief some men once eminent in the ranks of the Church, who did run well, but on a sudden, through stress of temptation, they fell into sin, and their names were never mentioned in the Church again, except with bated breath."[16] O fellow servant, pay attention to your heart and soul! However devastating the fall of a preacher may be to his flock, no matter how colossal his moral failure, the church may shake with trimmers, but God's throne and glory remain secure. "Despond not when you hear that one minister has ceased to preach the gospel, or that another is fighting against the viral truth of God. Their apostasy shall be to their own loss rather than to the hurt of Jesus and his church; and, sad though it be to see the lamps of the sanctuary put out, yet God is not dependent upon human lights, he is the Shekinah light of his own holy place ... His counsel shall stand, and he will do all his pleasure. Hallelujah!"[17] Oh, dear brother, do everything in your power to keep yourself from bringing shame to his name. Be honest with yourself! Harbor no hidden besetting sin in your heart! Take heed, lest you fall!

## Practice Soul-Searching Self-Examination and Encourage Your Hearers to Do the Same

> Let us search out and examine our ways, and
> turn back to the Lord (Lam 3:40).

> God save us from hiding from ourselves our secret faults. Let us be willing to be spoken to by the rough preacher's stern voice! Let us be greedy to read those passages of Scripture which try us most. Let it be our prayer, "Search me, O God, and try my heart." Daily and hourly let us desire to feel the refining fire go through our soul. Come with the fan in thy hand, O Savior, and thoroughly purge my floor, and let my chaff be driven away, and let nothing but the pure wheat remain![18]

---

15. Spurgeon, *New Park Street Pulpit*, 2:237.
16. Spurgeon, *New Park Street Pulpit*, 11:198.
17. Spurgeon, *Metropolitan Tabernacle Pulpit*, 29:3.
18. Spurgeon, *Metropolitan Tabernacle Pulpit*, 14:508.

## Self-Examining the Soul

Consistent self-examination solidifies personal accountability and promotes personal integrity. All self-examination should result in Scripture-application. Without faithfully checking one's heart, genuinely repenting of sin, and persistently applying truth, godliness becomes a distant memory. Spurgeon asserts, "It is a terribly easy matter to be a minister of the gospel and a vile hypocrite at the same time. My brethren in the ministry, I feel this to be only too true, and I often regret that I am not able to sit in one of those pews yonder, to listen to some faithful brother-minister, who would help me to see myself as I really am in the sight of God, and cause me to tremble before him, lest I should be either self-deceived or a deceiver of others."[19] Spurgeon viewed fallen comrades in ministry as a warning sign and heart check. "I, as a minister, am bound to examine myself, because there have been eminent preachers of the gospel who, nevertheless, have lived unhallowed lives. No preacher may dare to say, 'My office screens me from this test.'"[20] Placing confidence in labels and titles jeopardizes your trust in the Lord.

Spurgeon consistently challenged his hearers to join him in the practice of self-examination. He did not advocate sinless perfection as an absolute, nor did he promote a grace-denying legalism. Rather, Spurgeon practiced and proclaimed a biblical heart-searching dependence upon the Holy Spirit's conviction. This was marked by heart-cleansing repentance under the blood of Jesus Christ. He very clearly defined the nature of self-examination to his hearers:

> Another schoolmaster is self-examination. A very sour, crabbed schoolmaster is this one. Very few like him; especially if you take a lesson every night before you go to sleep, and look through the actions of the day. It is not a very pleasant exercise; there are so many faults to find, so many mistakes made, so many good things omitted. But, if you cannot have self-examination every day, at any rate have it sometimes. You will learn better by your mistakes than if you had never made a blunder. Sometimes even a grave fault may save you from ten grave faults, if it be well observed, and avoided in the future, and God teaches you thereby. You learn nothing by self-examination unless the Lord be your Master; but, if he be with you, then your acquaintance with yourself will help you to an acquaintance with him. There are two prayers always worth praying,

---

19. Spurgeon, *Metropolitan Tabernacle Pulpit*, 52:483.
20. Spurgeon, *Metropolitan Tabernacle Pulpit*, 50:17.

"Lord, show me myself," and "Lord, show me Thyself." May both be heard, and you will be well taught of God![21]

An indispensable quality for a life of self-examination is a tender teachable heart toward to the work of the Holy Spirit. He works through self-examination to promote Christlikeness.

Spurgeon called upon his congregation to practice self-examination on a churchwide scale. He was horrified by the thought of the Metropolitan Tabernacle losing its witness and influence. A local church easily becomes complacently conceited about its gifted leadership, denominational prominence, and/or community impact. If there was ever a church that had reason to be tempted in this manner, it was the church pastored by Charles Spurgeon. He passionately warned his congregants to guard themselves from this terrible trap:

> We are apt to grow rusty, to lean upon our weapons instead of using them, and to withdraw from the Lord's host instead of rushing on to battle with the shout of men who mean to win the victory. Ah! give us back again all the noise, and the confusion, and the strife; let us have once more the coldness, and the harshness, and evil speaking of the entire Church of God, if we may but have our early enthusiasm and earnestness for Christ. Dear friends, let me say solemnly, there are many tendencies to make this Church sleep. We come frequently into contact with professed believers who will throw cold water upon every effort—who think doing anything for Christ a work of supererogation excess, and there is a tendency in us to go with them, and to say, "Let it be so; let us be quiet"... and unless God the Holy Ghost come in with irresistible might, we shall as a Church succumb to general lethargy, and yield ourselves to apathy.[22]

Complacency toward God quickly becomes independence from him. Churches that never examine the heart of their congregation are usually led by men who have personally traveled this unexamined dead end. Drifting churches are most likely pastored by drifting men. When a church falls into the depths of pride and the pastor does not sound an alarm from the pulpit, total recovery is virtually impossible. Spurgeon warned his congregation of slipping into spiritual coma:

---

21. Spurgeon, *Metropolitan Tabernacle Pulpit*, 8:285.
22. Spurgeon, *Metropolitan Tabernacle Pulpit*, 8:285.

## Self-Examining the Soul

> We stand in a position in which God has made us eminent by his blessing; but let us take heed lest, by exalting ourselves, we become like Capernaum, once lifted to heaven, but afterwards brought down to hell. There have been many churches, which God has left because of their sin . . . They fell into sin, and God left them, and there is "Ichabod" written on every piece of mortar in the walls . . . Pastor and people alike have been weighed in the balances, and they have been found wanting. Shall it be so with us as a church? Shall we be found wanting in the time of testing?[23]

The practice of serious self-examination is not something that comes naturally to the local church, unless it involves a surface glance at the effectiveness of function, funds, and facilities. However, if a local church is led by a pastor who lives in the atmosphere of self-examination and proclaims the biblical warrant for this practice, God can turn the heart of the church back to him.

## Spend Extensive Focused Time in Heart-Searching Prayer

> Oh, what solemn heart-searchings what strict self-examinations the preacher should have! How he should lay bare his breast before the all-searching eye of God, implore the inspection of the Infallible, ask to be weighed in the balances of the sanctuary, which cannot err, and seek to be judged by almighty wisdom lest, as Paul said, after having preached to others, he himself should be a castaway![24]

Schedule and guard extended time for a heart-searching season of prayer. Use an obscure room in your church building or go on a personal prayer retreat. Welcome God's searching of your heart. Spurgeon suggests:

> Make this a special season of humbling and heart-searching. Now let every besetting sin be driven out. When God sweeps, do you search. When you are under the rod, it is yours to make a full confession of past offenses, and pray to be delivered from their power in the future. Or, have you no trial to-day, my brother? Then see if there be not something which may provoke God to send one,

---

23. Spurgeon, *Metropolitan Tabernacle Pulpit*, 48:148–49.
24. Spurgeon, *Metropolitan Tabernacle Pulpit*, 52:483.

and begin now to purge yourself from all filthiness of the flesh and of the spirit by the Holy Ghost. Prevention is better than a cure; and sometimes a timely heart-searching may save us many a heart-smarting.[25]

Spurgeon warns about the fallout from failing to search one's heart: "When we neglect prayer and self-examination we grow mighty vain fellows, but when we live near to God in private devotion and heart-searching, we put off our ornaments from us."[26] He goes on to contrast the drastic difference that is made when one properly searches the heart: "In the light of God's countenance we perceive our many flaws and imperfections, and instead of saying, 'I am clean,' we cry out, 'Woe is me, for I am a man of unclean lips... Those who think well of themselves must know little of that revealing light which humbles all who dwell in it.'"[27] It will be tempting to dwell on shallow surface symptoms rather than the depths of your heart. However, in this matter, a heedless mind results in a heartless ministry.

## Prayerfully Examine Your Heart

There is a subtle temptation to be selective in the searching of one's heart. But selective searching is no searching at all. If you are going to preach from your heart, then your heart must first be examined and cleansed. To preach from an unexamined heart is to preach an unacceptable message. Spurgeon purports:

> Go right through yourselves from the beginning to the end. Stand not only on the mountains of your public character, but go into the deep valleys of your private life. Be not content to sail on the broad river of your outward actions, but go follow back the narrow rill till you discover your secret motive. Look not only at your performance, which is but the product of the soil, but dig into your heart and examine the vital principle. "Examine yourselves."[28]

The opposite of examining yourself is deceiving yourself. Self-deception will be devastating in your life and ministry. Ask yourself these questions:

- Are you daily guarding your heart?

---

25. Spurgeon, *Metropolitan Tabernacle Pulpit*, 10:201.
26. Spurgeon, *Metropolitan Tabernacle Pulpit*, 19:305.
27. Spurgeon, *Metropolitan Tabernacle Pulpit*, 19:305.
28. Spurgeon, *New Park Street Pulpit*, 4:427.

- When was the last time that you trembled before God and his Word?
- Are you daily immersing yourself in Scripture intake apart from sermon preparation?
- Are you daily walking in the wisdom of God?
- Are you daily equipping and preparing yourself for spiritual battle?
- Are you daily tightening your grip on the sword of the Spirit?
- Are you watchful and alert to the devices of Satan in your personal life?
- Are you watchful and alert to the devices of Satan in your congregation?
- Are you studying to show yourself approved unto God by rightly dividing the Word of truth?

## Pray about Your Motives in Preaching

Every sermon must be viewed as a life-giving message from the Father to his embattled army behind enemy lines. Do not ask "What should I preach?" but "Why do I preach?" Spurgeon warns, "Pride will grow in the pulpit. It is a weed that is dreadfully rampant. It wants cutting down every week, or else we should stand up to our knees in it. This pulpit is a shocking bad soil for pride. It grows terribly; and I scarcely know whether you ever find a preacher of the gospel who will not confess that he has the greatest temptation to pride."[29] Motives can subtly and suddenly morph into something displeasing to God. Spurgeon describes how this can occur:

> Many men have been held up by the arms of men, they have been held up by the arms of praise, and not of prayer; these arms have become weak, and down they have fallen. I say there is temptation to pride in the pulpit; but there is no ground for it in the pulpit; there is no soil for pride to grow on; but it will grow without any. "I have nothing to glorify of." But, notwithstanding, there often comes in some reason why we should glory, not real, but apparent to our own selves.[30]

---

29. Spurgeon, *New Park Street Pulpit*, 1:265.
30. Spurgeon, *New Park Street Pulpit*, 1:265.

A false sense of reality should prompt a deep concern and personal heart-searching. Many men have fallen by building a personal empire rather than promoting God's kingdom. Submit yourself to Spurgeon's interrogation:

> Are you sure that you preach only for Christ's glory? Does it not sometimes happen that you are tempted to glorify yourselves and try to be fine and great when you ought to be simple, and plain, and earnest with the souls of men? Oh! when I think of some who spend all the week writing out their sermons, and touching up every line and every sentence, I fear there must be something of self there; and when I hear some preachers with such splendid diction, with words so nicely picked, I cannot help thinking that there must be a sacrificing to the genius of oratory or to the beauty of eloquence, rather than to the Master's cause. I say of every thing that is done for self—down with it, down with it . . . What have we to do with idolatrous self-worship? O Lord, deliver us from it.[31]

## Pray about Your Preaching

Spurgeon sought to preach faithfully and effectively. This focus is indispensable for everyone who consistently enters the pulpit. Spurgeon asks heart-searching, prayer-prompting questions:

> If you preached the gospel, did you preach it rightly? That is to say, did you state it affectionately, earnestly, clearly, plainly? . . . Have you preached the truth lovingly, with all your heart, throwing your very self into it, as if beyond everything you desired the conversion of those you taught? Has prayer been mixed with it? Have you gone into the pulpit without prayer? Have you come out of it without prayer? . . . If so, since you failed to ask for the blessing, you must not wonder if you do not get it.[32]

Spurgeon exemplifies what it means to pray about one's preaching. His prayers about his preaching are specific and strategic:

> "Turn us again, O Lord God of hosts." Your minister feels that he needs to be turned more thoroughly to the Lord his God. His prayer shall be, God helping him, that he may be more fearless and faithful than ever; that be may never for one moment think what any of you will say with regard to what he utters, but that he may

---

31. Spurgeon, *Metropolitan Tabernacle Pulpit*, 8:141.
32. Spurgeon, *Metropolitan Tabernacle Pulpit*, 31:176.

## Self-Examining the Soul

only think what God his Master would say concerning him . . . He desires to ask his Master that he may come here with more prayer himself than heretofore, that whatever he preaches may be so burnt into his own soul that you may all know, even if you do not think it true yourselves, that at any rate he believes it, and believes it with his inmost soul. And I will ask of God that I may so preach to you, that my words may be attended with a mighty and a divine power . . . I feel that if you have been profited by my preaching, it must have been the work of God, and God alone, and I pray to him that I may be taught to know more my own weakness . . . Will you ask such things for me, that I may be more and more turned to God, and that so your spiritual health may be promoted.[33]

Spurgeon refused to separate his preaching from his praying. He prayerfully preached and preached prayerfully. Allow these questions to guide you into prayer about your preaching:

- Can you concisely articulate how you pray concerning your pulpit ministry?
- Are you faithfully preaching the whole counsel of God?
- Does your preaching reflect sound doctrine which promotes holy living?
- Are you preaching the gospel, or are you simply preaching about the gospel?
- Are you preaching the gospel, or are you preaching about the blessings and benefits of the gospel?
- Are you preaching the gospel compassionately and clearly to keep your hands free of the blood of your hearers?

## Prayerfully Preach as a Man Accountable to God Regardless of Human Response

I come into this pulpit to please no man among you. God knoweth if I knew more of your follies you should have them pointed out yet more plainly; if I knew more of the tricks of business, I would not flinch to speak of them![34]

---

33. Spurgeon, *New Park Street Pulpit*, 5:476.
34. Spurgeon, *Metropolitan Tabernacle Pulpit*, 9:93.

Those who are called to preach Christ should be compelled to do so selflessly and unashamedly. Only a ministry that is empty of self can be full of the Savior, and only a ministry that is full of the Savior will bring him the greatest glory. You must minimize self to magnify Christ. To this you have been called by God, and to this you will be held accountable. You must proclaim the praiseworthiness of Christ. Spurgeon warns:

> Brethren, if we preach Christ with a view to get ourselves honored by it, we prostitute the sacred things of God . . . O that we would search our heart so as to be quite sure that we have no aim in all the world but Christ—"God forbid that I should glory save in the cross of our Lord Jesus Christ." You may shoot well ye brave archers, but if you aim at the wrong target you will not win the prize. If you aim at anything but your Lord's honor, you shall never hear it said, "Well done, good and faithful servant."[35]

You must be resolved to never be moved by a human "well done." Rather, you must preach with a view to the crowning "well done!" from God himself. Lesser motives have been the downfall of great men and the unraveling of their ministry.

Your role among the people of God is intimately connected to your relationship with God: "They watch out for your souls, as those who must give account" (Heb 13:17). Preaching in this atmosphere of accountability to God will be death to the carnal craving for recognition. Would you rather experience the praise of men or the power of God? Basking in the praise of people will drain your ministry of God's power. People are fickle, but God is faithful!

Active awareness of your accountability to God should fill you with urgency and boldness. No truth will be seen as uncomfortable or untimely. Spurgeon recognizes, "Sometimes God rebukes his children under the ministry. The minister of the gospel is not always to be a minister of consolation . . . The same minister who is to be as the angel of God unto our souls, uttering sweet words that are full of honey, is to be at times the rod of God, the staff in the hand of the Almighty, with which to smite us on account of our transgressions."[36] When preaching is accompanied by the conviction of the Holy Spirit it can be viewed by the carnal mind as callous condemnation.

---

35. Spurgeon, *Metropolitan Tabernacle Pulpit*, 11:389.
36. Spurgeon, *New Park Street Pulpit*, 3:454.

## Self-Examining the Soul

Your desire for the salvation of souls must override any desire for the applause of people. Faithfulness to God must be valued above the favor of man. Spurgeon professed, "I never come into this pulpit with the notion that I must not say a sharp thing, or somebody will be offended, and I must not deal with common sins, for somebody will say that I am coarse. I care not the snap of a finger what you choose to say about me, if you will but forsake sin and be reconciled to God by the death of his Son."[37] You are to say what God wants you to say, not what people want to hear. God is to be the source and subject of your sermon.

Refuse to tickle itching ears! Resolve to address depraved hearts! May these words, spoken by Spurgeon to his students, inspire you to remain faithful to the finish line:

> I shall be gone from you ere long. You will meet and say to one another, "The President has departed. What are we going to do?" I charge you, be faithful to the gospel of our Lord Jesus Christ, and the doctrine of His grace. Be ye faithful unto death, and your crowns will not be wanting. But oh! Let none of us die out like dim candles, ending a powerless ministry in everlasting blackness. The Lord Himself bless you! Amen.[38]

---

37. Spurgeon, *Metropolitan Tabernacle Pulpit*, 31:69.
38. Spurgeon, *All-Round Ministry*, 363.

# Appendix A

## Spurgeon's Sermons That Strongly Emphasize Prayer

| Title | Text | Mentions of Prayer |
|---|---|---|
| Prayer without Ceasing | 1 Thess 5:17 | 269 |
| Where True Prayer is Found | 2 Sam 7:27 | 214 |
| Why Should We Pray? | Luke 18:1 | 206 |
| Behold He Prayeth | Acts 9:11 | 205 |
| Praying in the Holy Ghost | Jude 20 | 204 |
| Brief Silent Prayer | Neh 2:4 | 195 |
| Constant, Instant, Expectant | Rom 12:12 | 190 |
| The Special Prayer Meeting | Acts 12:12 | 186 |
| Prayer—The Forerunner of Mercy | Ezek 36:37 | 175 |
| Prayer Found in the Heart | 2 Sam 7:27 | 174 |
| Golden Bowls Full of Incense | Rev 5:8 | 171 |
| Daniel: A Pattern for Pleaders | Dan 6:10 | 166 |
| Hindrances to Prayer | 1 Pet 3:7 | 164 |
| Prayer Perfumed with Praise | Phil 4:6 | 155 |
| Prayer Meetings | Acts 1:14 | 153 |

# Appendix A

| Title | Text | Mentions of Prayer |
|---|---|---|
| Unseasonable Prayer | Exod 14:15 | 148 |
| Two Guards—Praying and Watching | Neh 4:9 | 147 |
| The Touchstone of Godly Sincerity | Job 27:10 | 146 |
| Consolation for Poor Petitioners | Isa 38:14 | 145 |
| Samuel: An Example of Intercession | 1 Sam 12:23 | 145 |
| Praying and Waiting | 1 John 5:13–15 | 143 |
| True Prayer—True Power | Mark 11:24 | 139 |
| Essential Points in Prayer | 1 Kgs 9:2–3 | 138 |
| The Preparatory Prayers of Christ | Luke 3:21–22 | 136 |
| Special Protracted Prayer | Luke 6:12 | 133 |
| Prayer, the Proof of Godliness | Ps 32:6 | 131 |
| Intercessory Prayer | Ps 141:5 | 127 |
| My Personal Holdfast | Mic 7:7 | 121 |
| Restraining Prayer | Job 29:4 | 118 |
| Before Day-Break with Christ | Mark 1:35–39 | 118 |
| Inquire of the Lord | Ezek 36:37–38 | 117 |
| Preparing for the Week of Prayer | Rev 8:3–4 | 116 |
| Let Us Pray | Ps 73:28 | 116 |
| Though-Reading Extraordinary | Ps 10:17 | 114 |
| A Sermon for the Week of Prayer | Col 4:2 | 114 |
| Prayer Certified of Success | Luke 11:9–10 | 112 |
| The Holy Spirit's Intercession | Rom 8:26–27 | 108 |
| Incense and Light | Exod 30:7–8 | 104 |
| The Minister's Plea | Phil 1:9 | 102 |
| The Importunate Widow | Luke 18:1–8 | 99 |
| The Conditions and Power of Prayer | 1 John 3:22–24 | 97 |
| Ask and Have | Jas 4:2–3 | 96 |
| Spiritual Knowledge and Its Practical Results | Col 1:10 | 92 |
| Prayer, the Cure for Care | Phil 4:6–7 | 91 |
| A Prayer for the Church Militant | Ps 28:9 | 91 |
| Prayer, Its Discouragements and Encouragements | Matt 15:23 | 90 |
| Daniel Facing the Lion's Den | Dan 6:10 | 90 |
| The First Cry from the Cross | Luke 23:34 | 89 |
| Fine Pleading | Ps 106:4 | 88 |

# Spurgeon's Sermons That Strongly Emphasize Prayer

| Title | Text | Mentions of Prayer |
|---|---|---|
| The Programme Never Carried Out | Luke 15:20–21 | 85 |
| The Secret Power of Prayer | John 15:7 | 83 |
| A Call to Worship | Zech 8:21 | 83 |
| Unanswered Prayer | Ps 22:2 | 81 |
| Opening the Mouth | Ps 81:10 | 79 |
| The Throne of Grace | Heb 4:16 | 76 |
| David's Dying Prayer | Ps 72:19 | 76 |
| Jesus Interceding for Transgressors | Isa 53:12 | 75 |
| Right Replies to Right Requests | Luke 11:11–13 | 73 |
| Lead Us Not Into Temptation | Matt 6:13 | 71 |
| A Visit from the Lord | Ps 106:4 | 70 |
| The Lord with Two or Three | Matt 18:20 | 70 |
| Good News for the Destitute | Ps 102:17 | 70 |
| At School | Ps 143:10 | 67 |
| Jesus Declining the Legions | Matt 26:53–54 | 66 |
| Jesus in Gethsemane | John 18:1–2 | 65 |
| Daniel's Undaunted Courage | Dan 6:10 | 65 |
| True and Not True | John 9:31 | 63 |
| Young Man! Prayer for You | 2 Kgs 6:17 | 63 |
| A Delusion Dispelled | Ezek 14:20 | 63 |
| The Raven's Cry | Ps 147:9 | 63 |
| I Will, Yet Not As I Will | Matt 26:39 | 61 |
| Increased Faith and Strength of Peace Principles | Luke 17:5 | 60 |
| A Warning to Waverers | Jas 1:6–7 | 58 |
| The God of Peace and Our Sanctification | Heb 13:20–21 | 58 |
| My Prayer | Ps 119:37 | 58 |
| Confession and Absolution | Luke 18:13 | 58 |
| Those Who Desire | Neh 1:11 | 57 |
| The Dawn of Revival or Prayer Speedily Answered | Dan 9:23 | 57 |
| A Hasty Expression Penitently Retracted | Ps 31:22 | 56 |
| The Poor Man's Prayer | Ps 106:4–5 | 56 |
| Humility, the Friend of Prayer | Gen 32:10 | 55 |
| The Believer Sinking in the Mire | Ps 69:14 | 55 |
| Temple Glories | 2 Chr 5:13–14 | 50 |

# Appendix B

# Spurgeon: Prayer Is . . .

- Prayer is the ship which bringeth home the richest freight. "Paul's First Prayer"
- Prayer is the key that openeth the cabinets of mystery. "The Holy Ghost—The Great Teacher" Prayer is God's chosen vehicle of grace, and he is unwise who neglects it. "Comfort for the Desponding"
- Prayer is the forerunner of mercies. "Of Mercy"
- Prayer is the rustling of the wings of the angels that are on their way bringing us the boons of heaven. "Of Mercy"
- Prayer is the representative of the blessing before the blessing comes. "Of Mercy"
- Prayer is the prelude of mercy, for very often it is the cause of the blessing. "Of Mercy"
- Prayer is a sure sign of divine life within. "A Simple Sermon for Seeking Souls"
- Prayer is the certain forerunner of salvation. "A Simple Sermon for Seeking Souls"
- Prayer is the best used means of drawing near to God. "Let Us Pray"

- Prayer is the spirit, the life, the desire, the wish, the agonizing panting with God to obtain the blessing. "Grace Reviving Israel"
- Prayer is a great weapon of attack against the error and wickedness of the world. "A Sermon for the Week of Prayer"
- Prayer is a weapon which no man can effectually resist. "The Royal Pair in Their Glorious Chariot"
- Prayer is a never-failing resort; it is sure to bring a blessing with it. "Forward! Forward! Forward!"
- Prayer is a fire that needs stirring. "The Smoke of Their Torments"
- Prayer is your best means of study. "The Golden Key of Prayer"
- Prayer is the never failing resort of the Christian in any case, in every plight. "The Believer Sinking in the Mire"
- Prayer is the trading of the heart with God, and the heart never comes into spiritual commerce with the ports of heaven until God the Holy Ghost puts wind into the sails and speeds the ship into its haven. "The Raven's Cry"
- Prayer is the great cure-all for depression of spirit. "The Garden of the Soul"
- Prayer is the shadow of Omnipotence. "Praying in the Holy Ghost"
- Prayer is useful in a thousand ways. "The Dawn of Revival"
- Prayer is that great key which opens mysteries. "The Dawn of Revival"
- Prayer is like a cloud rising from the earth, sure to come back again in rain, but not always bound to return to the same spot. "Make This Valley Full of Ditches"
- Prayer is the breath of the soul, and where there is breath there must be life. "Alive or Dead—Which?"
- Prayer is an absolute necessity. "Special Protracted Prayer"
- Prayer is of the very essence of spirituality. "Daniel's Undaunted Courage"
- Prayer is a messenger that can find Jesus at any hour. "Everyday Usefulness"
- Prayer is that which links weakness with infinite strength. "The Church As She Should Be"

## Appendix B

- Prayer is always the telltale of spiritual life. "The Touchstone of Godly Sincerity"
- Prayer is our very life: ceasing prayer we cease to live. "The Touchstone of Godly Sincerity"
- Prayer is an approach of the soul by the Spirit of God to the throne of God. "The Throne of Grace"
- Prayer is in itself a blessing. "The Poor Man's Friend"
- Prayer is a method of worship. "Prayer Without Ceasing"
- Prayer is a wondrous blender of hearts and a mighty creator of love. "Intercessory Prayer"
- Prayer is the most essential thing in turning sinners from the error of their ways. "Intercessory Prayer"
- Prayer is effectual with God. "Golden Vials Full of Odors"
- Prayer is the surest and most blessed vent for the soul. "Consolation for the Despairing"
- Prayer is a divine art. "The Chariots of Ammi-Nadib"
- Prayer is the true gauge of spiritual power. "Hindrances to Prayer"
- Prayer is the intimation of God to man that he intends to bless him. It is the herald of mercy. "Solemn Pleadings for Revival"
- Prayer is an exercise in which our minds ought to be expanded, and our hearts enlarged. "Paul's Doxology"
- Prayer is the vital breath of the Christian. "A Second Word to Seekers"
- Prayer is always a joint work; the Holy Spirit within us writes acceptable desires upon our hearts and then we present them. "The Two 'Comes'"
- Prayer is the creation of the Holy Ghost. We cannot do without prayer, and we cannot pray without the Holy Spirit. "Our Urgent Need of the Holy Spirit"
- Prayer is to study what fire is to the sacrifice. "The Student's Prayer"
- Prayer is the rustling of the wings of the angels who are bringing the blessing to us "Prayer Perfumed with Praise"
- Prayer is the life-blood of duty, the secret sap of holiness, the fountain of obedience. "Constant, Instant, Expectant"

- Prayer is connected with every covenant blessing. "Constant, Instant, Expectant"
- Prayer is the channel appointed to convey to you the blessing; open the valves, and let the stream flow into your heart. "Choice Comfort for a Young Believer"
- Prayer is a great outlet for grief. "The Holy Spirit's Intercession"
- Prayer is the fiery chariot, and desires are its horses of fire. "Desires Towards God: A Sermon for the Weak"
- Prayer is the breath of the soul, and he that can do without it is dead in sin. "Holy Longings"
- Prayer is appointed to convey the blessings God ordains to give. "Without Christ—Nothing"
- Prayer is the shadow of a coming blessing. "My Hourly Prayer"
- Prayer is the breath of faith "The Best War-Cry"
- Prayer is thy vital breath, thy native air. "Jonah's Resolve," or "Look Again"
- Prayer is never out of season: it is a tree which yields its fruit every day. "God Our Continual Resort"
- Prayer is a sure evidence of spiritual quickening. "Behold, He Prayeth"
- Prayer is the autograph of the Holy Ghost upon the renewed heart. "Behold, He Prayeth"
- Prayer is an ever open door. "Jesus Declining the Legions"
- Prayer is a weapon that is usable in every position in the hour of conflict. "Jesus Declining the Legions"
- Prayer is a gift from God as well as an appeal to God. "Song for the Free, and Hope for the Bound"
- Prayer is the natural out-gushing of a soul in communion with Jesus. "The Secret Power in Prayer"
- Prayer is measured by weight, and not by length. "The Secret Power in Prayer"
- Prayer is the promise utilized. "The Secret Power in Prayer"
- Prayer is the very breath of God in man, returning whence it came. "No Fixity without Faith"

## Appendix B

- Prayer is wonderful material for building up the spiritual fabric. "Prayer, the Cure for Care"
- Prayer is real communication with God. "Prayer, the Cure for Care"
- Prayer is in itself, an education for a saint. "The Truth of God's Salvation"
- Prayer is the longing of the soul to hold communion with the Most High, the desire of the heart to obtain blessings at his hands. "Heman's Sorrowful Psalm"
- Prayer is the breath of life in the newborn believer. "Prayer, the Proof of Godliness"
- Prayer is an infallible mark of godliness. "Prayer, the Proof of Godliness"
- Prayer is the breathing in of the air of heaven, and praise is the breathing of it out again. "A Visit from the Lord"
- Prayer is always available—in every place, and in every condition of our spirit. "The High Rock"
- Prayer is an essential exercise in seeking the Lord. "Rehoboam the Unready"
- Prayer is the echo of the eternal purpose. "Pray, Always Pray"
- Prayer is a living thing; you cannot find a living prayer in a dead heart. "Prayer Found in the Heart"
- Prayer is the indispensable mark of the true child of God. "Pedigree"
- Prayer is our very life, and is essential to our health and our growth. "Lessons from the Malta Fire"
- Prayer is often the shadow of God's coming blessing. "Boldness at the Throne"
- Prayer is a mainstay of holiness. "A Gospel Promise"

# Appendix C

## Spurgeon: Preaching Is . . .

- Preaching is not child's play, it is not a thing to be done without labor and anxiety it is solemn work, it is awful work if you view it in its relation to eternity. "Paul's First Prayer"
- Preaching is the ordained means for the salvation of sinners, and by this ten times as many are brought to the Savior as by any other. "Conversion"
- Preaching is the instrument, but the Holy Spirit is the great agent. "A Mighty Savior"
- Preaching is a farce unless the minister hath fire within him, but when the fire is there, preaching is God's ordained and guaranteed way of bringing souls to himself. "Temple Glories"
- Preaching is the great weapon of God for pulling down strongholds; it will pull down the hugest blocks of stone the enemy can pile together. "Forward! Forward! Forward!"
- Preaching is he blast of the ram's horn ordained to level Jericho, and the sound of the silver trumpet appointed to usher in the jubilee. It is God's chariot of fire for bearing souls to heaven, and his two-edged sword to smite the hosts of hell. "The Restoration and Conversion of the Jews"

## Appendix C

- Preaching is a savor of death unto death, as well as of life unto life. "Messengers Wanted"
- Preaching is sowing, prayer is watering, but praise is the harvest. God aims at his own glory so should we. "The Joy of the Lord, the Strength of His People"
- Preaching is only the stalk, the real ear is the devotion which we pay to God. "Golden Vials Full of Odors"
- Preaching is the water: and while we are preaching, God will bless it, and turn the water into wine. "The Water-pots of Cana"
- Preaching is an ordinance of God, and he will be in the midst of them. "The Lord with Two or Three"
- Preaching is God's ordinance—his battle-axe and weapons of war "The Lord with Two or Three"
- Preaching is an effective means of instructing the mind, arousing the conscience, and impressing the hearts of the people. "Washed to Greater Foulness"
- Preaching is full of Jesus. Jesus is the most notable figure in Christian testimony. "Jesus Affirmed to be Alive"
- Preaching is Artesian: it wells up from the great depths of the soul. If Christ has not made a well within us, there will be no outflow from us. "The Burden of the Word of the Lord"
- Preaching is in vain unless Jesus send forth life. "The Prince of Life"
- Preaching is an exercise of faith; and when we address sinners, it ought to be as if we were about to work a miracle. "The Power of Christ's Name"
- Preaching is done in the name of Jesus, and with his authority. It is a sort of miracle-working; for we have to tell the dead to live—a most absurd thing to do, except that, God having told us to do it, we do it, and the dead live. "Disobedience to the Gospel"
- Preaching is the great battering-ram that is to shake the gates of hell. "Repentance and Remission"
- Preaching is God's chief method of winning souls unto himself: "for after that in the wisdom of God the world by wisdom knew not God, it pleased God by the foolishness of preaching to save them that believe." "Repentance and Remission"

- Preaching is the best form of church discipline. Somehow or other, carnal minds get weary of it, and they go away, and those that have not a longing and a love for the truth drop off of themselves; so they walk no more with him. "Meat Indeed, and Drink Indeed"[/BL 1–23]

# Appendix D

## Spurgeon on Ministry and Preaching in *The Sword and the Trowel*

- Acta Non Verba 1873:1, 49
- Advice Gratis, 1872:149, 197
- Advice to Young Preachers, 2:91
- Against Hastening to Remove from Our Post of Duty, 1880:325
- Alexander on Bucephalus: An Address at the College on a Friday Afternoon, 8:366
- Anarchists in Theology, 1884: 262
- Anecdotes from the Pulpit, 1883:183, 217
- Anywhere for Jesus, 1884:205
- Battlements, 1869:349
- Beaten Oil for the Light, 1892:685
- The Bible, the Church and Tradition, 1886:103
- Breaking the Long Silence, 1892:50
- Call to the Ministry, 1883:75

- Causes of Eccentricities in Ministers, 1879:321
- The Christian Minister's Private Prayer, 1868:481
- The Church at Work, 1904:153
- A Church We Know Of, 1877:145
- Clear the Road, 1878:300
- Common but Saddening, 1884:401
- Communion with Christ and His People, 1883:53
- A Continual Tooth-Drawing, 1880:259
- Crazy Ministers, 1875:360
- Dispensing the Gospel, 1882:293
- Driving the Cattle to Market, 1882:304
- Dying Ministers, 1875:357
- Earnestness in Ministers, 1877:415, 445
- An Earnest Warning Against Unbelief, 1877:371
- Earnest Work Not Extinct, 1870:546
- Eccentric but Useful, 1874:393, 441
- Ever This Our War-Cry: Victory! Victory!, 1882:49
- Faith, 1872:245, 260
- Feed My Sheep, 1877:289
- A Few Words Upon Objections to Revivals, 1874:137
- Fighting and Praying, 1889:585
- The First Baptist Minister, 1894:481, 529
- The Flock in Winter, 1889:651
- Forward, 1874:219
- From an Unexpected Source, 1881:178
- Gifts Neglected and Gifts Stirred Up, 1893:357, 421
- Gold Rims, 1872:108
- Good Cheer from Past and Future Service, 1881:201
- A Good Stayer, 1882:349

# Appendix D

- Growing on the Wall, 1889:153
- Help for Poor Ministers, 1888:60
- Hints on the Voice: For Young Preachers, 1875:207
- Holding Forth the Word of Life, 1890:4
- Holy Service on Behalf of Poor Ministers, 1880:413
- The Holy War of the Present Time, 1866:339
- How the Lambs Fee, 1876:485
- How to Attract a Congregation, 1883:417
- I Never Cared for Their Souls, 1877:353
- In My Fiftieth Year, and Getting Old, 1884:101
- Inaugural Address, 1875:193
- Inaugural Address, 1876:241
- Inaugural Address, 1877:193
- Inaugural Address, 1880:251, 317
- Inaugural Address, 1881:259, 313, 377
- Inaugural Address, 1882:401, 459
- Interruption, 1882:424
- It's Not the Harness that Makes the Horse, 1881:343
- John Ploughman Talks: On Religious Grumblers, 1867:289
- John Ploughman's Sermon on "Beware of Dogs," 1876:257
- Keeping a Cow, 1883:303
- Laid Aside? Why?, 1876:195
- Launch Out Into the Deep, 1889:15
- Less Gilding and More Carving, 1884:528
- Live Prayers, 1888:531
- London: A Plea by C. H. Spurgeon, 1875:145
- Mealtime in the Cornfields, 1882:337
- The Minister in These Times, 1889: 257
- A Minister's Equipment from the Congo, 1887:33

- The Minister's Fainting Fits, 1868:529
- The Minister's Ordinary Conversation, 1874:27
- The Minister's Three G's: Grace, Gumption, and Greek, 1904:313
- The Minister's Trumpet Blast and Church Member's Warning (Hosea 8:1–2) MTP #2772
- Ministers Sailing Under False Colours, 1870:69
- The Ministry Needed by the Churches and Measures for Providing It, 1871:215
- The Months of Spiritual Harvest, 1890:36
- More Fishers Than Fish, 1889:365
- The Need of Decision for the Truth, 1874:101
- A Neglected Duty, 1865:37
- A New Year's Letter to My Ministerial Brethren, 1870:1
- Not a Doubt of It!, 1884:49
- Odds and Ends About Preaching and Hearing, 1881:476
- Offender for a Word, 1870:569
- On Commenting, 1869:294
- Our First Sermon, 1880:3
- Our Lord's Preaching, 1877:493
- Our Treasure Trove, 1889:431
- Peril from the Pulpit: A Warning Note, 1879:176
- Points Never to Be Forgotten, 1899:491
- Poor Ministers Helped S&T, 1888:61
- Practical Effort for Truth the Best Effort Against Error, 1891:305
- Praise of Men, 1880:217
- Preach Christ in a Christly Manner, 1881:105
- The Preacher's Power, and the Conditions of Obtaining It, 1889:253; 351; 413
- Preaching the Doctrines of Grace, 1904:537
- Preaching to Sinners, 1883:546

## Appendix D

- Preaching to the Ear, or to the Heart, 1891:31
- The Preparation of Sermons, 1901:253
- Preparing the Sermon, 1883:372
- The Pulpit as a Warning Apparatus, 1880:58
- Pulpits, 1877:355
- Qualifications for Soul-Winning Godward, 1893:157
- A Questionable Ingredient of Popularity, 1884:228
- The Reality of Religion, 1896:353
- A Reminiscence and a Warning, 1891:545
- Revival of the Lord's Work, 1866:90
- A Sermon to Ministers and Other Tried Believers, 1881:454
- Sham Spirituality, 1875:549
- Slippery Places, 1867:157
- Spiritual Dredging, 1888:177
- Stand Fast, 1888:620
- Stand Fast, 1909:445; 493
- Street Preaching, 1876:551
- Sweet Fruit from a Thorny Tree, 1880:541
- Taking Stock, 1910:1; 49; 105
- Taking the Bull by the Horns, 1881:160
- This Must Be the Soldier's Battle, 1889:633
- Thoughts About Church Matters, 1890:209
- A Thump from a "Down-Easter," 1884:517
- A Word with the Obscure, 1889:201
- To Workers with a Slender Apparatus, 1873:533
- Want of Naturalness in Preaching, 1871:398, 433, 489
- What Is Eccentricity?, 1879:249
- What Is It To Win a Soul?, 1879:503, 557
- What We Aim At, 1888:569

- What We Would Be, 8:321, 355
- A Word in Season, 1888:504
- A Word to Soul-Winners, 1883:314
- Young Preachers Encouraged, 1881:4
- Young Preachers Encouraged, 1895:157, 205

# Bibliography

Bennett, Arthur, ed. *The Valley of Vision: A Collection of Puritan Prayers and Devotions.* Carlisle, PA: Banner of Truth Trust, 1975.
Bridges, Charles. *The Christian Ministry with an Inquiry into the Causes of Its Insufficiency.* New York: Robert Carter & Brothers, 1850.
Cook, Charles T., ed. *Behold the Throne of Grace: C. H. Spurgeon's Prayers and Hymns.* London: Marshall, Morgan and Scott, 1934.
Crosby, Terrence Peter. *C. H. Spurgeon's Forgotten College Addresses.* Leominster, UK: Day One, 2016.
Duesing, Jason G., Geoffrey Chang, and Phillip Ort, eds. *The Lost Sermons of C. H. Spurgeon: His Earliest Outlines and Sermons Between 1851 and 1854.* Vols. 4–7. Nashville: B & H, 2020–22.
Medhurst, Thomas William. "Important Questions: What Is the Right Kind of Preaching?" *The Christian Times*, April 12, 1867
"Mr. Spurgeon's First Student: An Interview with T. W. Medhurst." *South Wales Echo*, Feb. 3, 1892.
"Restoration of Bunyan's Tomb in Bunhill-Fields." *The Christian World*, May 30, 1862.
Spurgeon, Charles. *An All-Round Ministry.* Pasadena, TX: Pilgrim, 1983.
———. *C. H. Spurgeon's Autobiography 1–4.* London: Passmore and Alabaster, 1897.
———. "The Christian Minister's Private Prayer." *The Sword and the Trowel* 2:111–20.
———. *Commenting and Commentaries.* London: Passmore and Alabaster, 1876.
———. "Inaugural Address at the Eighteenth Annual Conference of the Pastors' College Association." *The Sword and the Trowel* 4:402–17.
———. "Inaugural Address Delivered at the Conference of the Pastors' College." *The Sword and the Trowel* 6:504–11.
———. *Lectures to My Students.* London: Passmore and Alabaster, 1875.
———. "Less Gilding and More Carving." *The Sword and the Trowel* 7:449.
———. *Metropolitan Tabernacle Pulpit/New Park Street Pulpit.* 63 vols. Pasadena, TX: Pilgrim, 1969–1995.
———. *My Sermon Notes: A Selection from Outlines and Discourses Delivered at the Metropolitan Tabernacle by C. H. Spurgeon 1.* New York: Funk and Wagnalls, 1891.

# BIBLIOGRAPHY

———. *The Pastor in Prayer: A Collection of the Sunday Morning Sermons of C. H. Spurgeon*. Carlisle: Banner of Truth, 2004.

———. *Pictures from Pilgrim's Progress*. Pasadena, TX: Pilgrim, 1992.

———. *Soul Winner*. New York: Fleming H. Revel, 1895.

———. *Speeches at Home and Abroad*. Pasadena, TX: Pilgrim, 1974.

———. "Under His Shadow." *The Sword and the Trowel* 6:42–47.

www.ingramcontent.com/pod-product-compliance
Lightning Source LLC
Chambersburg PA
CBHW051923160426
43198CB00012B/2017